Also by Anthony Kronman

Confessions of a Born-Again Pagan

Education's End

The Lost Lawyer

Max Weber

The
Assault *on*
American Excellence

Anthony Kronman

FREE PRESS

New York   London   Toronto   Sydney   New Delhi

Free Press
An Imprint of Simon & Schuster, Inc.
1230 Avenue of the Americas
New York, NY 10020

First Free Press hardcover edition August 2019

FREE PRESS and colophon are registered trademarks of Simon & Schuster, Inc.

For information about special discounts for bulk purchases, please contact Simon & Schuster Special Sales at 1-866-506-1949 or business@simonandschuster.com.

The Simon & Schuster Speakers Bureau can bring authors to your live event. For more information or to book an event, contact the Simon & Schuster Speakers Bureau at 1-866-248-3049 or visit our website at www.simonspeakers.com.

Interior design by Carly Loman

Manufactured in the United States of America

10   9   8   7   6   5   4   3   2   1

Library of Congress Cataloging-in-Publication Data

Names: Kronman, Anthony T., author.
Title: The assault on American excellence / Anthony T. Kronman.
Description: New York : Free Press, 2019. | Includes bibliographical references and index.
Identifiers: LCCN 2018044086 (print) | LCCN 2018055458 (ebook) | ISBN 9781501199516 (Ebook) | ISBN 9781501199486 (hardback)
Subjects: LCSH: Education, Higher—Aims and objectives—United States. | Education, Higher—Political aspects—United States. | Intellectual freedom—United States. | Democracy—United States. | BISAC: EDUCATION / Higher. | EDUCATION / Aims & Objectives.
Classification: LCC LA227.4 (ebook) | LCC LA227.4 .K76 2019 (print) | DDC 378.73—dc23
LC record available at https://lccn.loc.gov/2018044086

ISBN 978-1-5011-9948-6
ISBN 978-1-5011-9951-6 (ebook)

For my students

Contents

The
Assault *on*
American Excellence

Introduction

I.

IN THE LATE SUMMER OF 2015, THE *YALE DAILY NEWS* CARRIED a story that caught my attention.

Yale undergraduates live in residential units called "colleges." The story reported that the "master" of one of these had decided to change his title on account of what he judged to be its offensive connotations. Some students had complained that it reminded them of the plantation culture of the Old South. The master of Pierson College sympathized with their complaints. He said he understood why black students in particular might be sensitive to the use of the term and that he wanted them to feel equally welcome at Yale, whose traditions retained many of the cultural trappings of the almost exclusively white, Anglo, male school that it had been for nearly all of its first three hundred years. To avoid even the possibility of giving offense to those who might associate his title with the racism and hierarchy of the antebellum South, the master of Pierson announced that in the future he would refer to himself not as a master but by some more neutral term instead.

I found it hard to believe he was serious. In an academic setting, the word "master" carries none of the connotations the complaining students found offensive. Instead of mindlessly deferring to their feelings, the master of Pierson should have told them what is obvious—that in this setting the word has an altogether different meaning. More particularly, he should have pointed out that the hierarchical relation of master to student has a perfectly legitimate place in a school like Yale, which is devoted not to the promotion of equality but the recognition of excellence instead. It seemed wrong to me, in any case, that a Yale official should be allowed to change his title on his own. If the master of Pierson could do this, shouldn't others be free to modify their titles as well? I assumed he would quickly be rebuked. But Yale not only acquiesced in his decision, a few months later it announced that it would no longer use the term "master" in referring to the heads of any of the residential colleges.

At the time, the "master" debate struck me as rather silly. I thought it a tempest in a teapot—a ridiculous exaggeration of wounded feelings, anguished responses, and inflated moral concerns. What I could not know, in the fall of 2015, was that this was only the opening act in a very serious drama that played out at Yale over the next year and a half.

The drama began in earnest with the traditional welcoming address that Yale's president gave to the incoming class that August. He first reminded his audience that the summer before had been one of explosive racial tension across the country. He recalled the horrors of Charleston, SC, where in June a deranged racist had murdered nine black churchgoers at a prayer meeting at the Emanuel African Methodist Episcopal Church. He went on to tell the newly arrived students and their families that Yale too had unfinished business in America's ongoing struggle for racial reconciliation. He then drew their attention to the long-simmering controversy over the name of Calhoun College, whose namesake had, among other things, defended slavery on the grounds that it was good for slaves and masters alike.

At this point the president of Yale issued an invitation to the entire community to join him in an open-ended "conversation" about whether Calhoun should be renamed, without saying how the question would be answered, or when or by whom. It is hard to imagine a more imprudent course or a speech less appropriate to the occasion.

For the president of Yale to address a group of young people who have been on campus only a few days, not about the intellectual adventure before them, but rather their moral responsibility to help decide whether Calhoun College should be renamed—a matter about which they could have known little in advance—put the life of action before that of the mind. His speech conveyed the idea that the university to which they had come, after so much sacrifice and hard work, was first and most importantly a community of moral commitment and only secondarily one of teaching and learning. It guaranteed that the debate that followed would be seen by those on both sides in a political light. And his reckless invocation of the Charleston killings as a prelude to a university-wide soul-searching about the name of Calhoun College all but assured that those who favored keeping it would be viewed by their opponents as moral monsters, not far removed from Dylann Roof, the Charleston shooter.

The following spring, when Yale's president announced that the university had decided to keep the name, the response was predictable. Those who wanted the name changed had every reason to believe that the president did too. They understandably assumed that he had summoned the Yale community to a year of self-reflection in order to prepare the way for what was coming. In their eyes his announcement was less a disappointment than a betrayal. The reaction was intense. Hundreds of students and faculty signed letters urging him to reconsider. They protested and held marches on campus. Yale's president quickly concluded that he had no practical choice but to change course. He then did what those of an administrative temper often do: He appointed a committee to advise him. He christened it, in good Orwellian fashion, the "Committee to Establish Principles on Renaming" and charged it with producing a set of general norms to guide the university in resolving all naming disputes, including, but in theory at least not confined to, the one surrounding Calhoun College.

Everyone who was paying attention suspected that the real purpose of the committee was to give Yale's president the cover he needed to reverse his earlier decision to leave the name of the college unchanged. The committee duly reported. The president immediately appointed a second committee to address the Calhoun matter specifically. A few weeks later this second committee announced, to no one's great surprise, that in its view the principles laid down by the first committee required that Calhoun be renamed. And so it was done, and the question put to rest in a blur of administrative legerdemain that did little to conceal the absence of intellectual or moral leadership that had characterized the entire affair from the start.

While all this was happening, the Yale campus was roiled by another controversy that became an item of national news.

Shortly before Halloween 2015, Yale's Intercultural Affairs Council sent an email to Yale students emphasizing the need to avoid giving offense in their choice of Halloween costumes. The council warned against the dangers of even well-intentioned "cultural appropriations." Erika Christakis, a psychologist and scholar of early childhood development and the wife of Nicholas Christakis, the master of Silliman College, wrote an email of her own to the students in Silliman, reassuring them that they were grown-up enough to make responsible decisions about which costumes to wear. She said they did not need a set of detailed rules to instruct them and were capable of dealing, in an adult way, with any frictions that might result. Her email was moderate in tone and substance. The reaction to it was anything but. Angry students protested that Ms. Christakis's email violated Yale's spirit of inclusion. They said it made minority students feel vulnerable and less valued. They condemned Ms. Christakis for her lack of sympathy and goodwill. Her husband, Nicholas, was accosted by a mob in the courtyard of Silliman College. They screamed obscenities and told him that he and his wife were a disgrace. The incident was caught on a video seen by millions.

When, days later, the president of Yale finally came to the Christakises' defense, it was too late for their reputations to be salvaged. Worse, he spoke with such studied caution as to leave it in doubt whether he was on their side or that of the students. Yes, he reaffirmed Yale's formal commitment to free speech. But he also argued, with astonishing naïveté, that there is no real conflict between the spirit of inclusion, on the one hand, and the ideal of free expression on the other—ignoring the obvious fact that the latter is especially important precisely in those situations where speech irritates, angers, and strains the sense of inclusion in a community of shared belief. His empty words of peace and reconciliation skirted all the hard questions raised by the Halloween incident and covered the matter in an anodyne fog of pretended agreement.

Erika Christakis has since resigned from the Yale faculty and Nicholas Christakis from his position as master of Silliman College.

The Halloween episode, the Calhoun debate, and the controversy over the title of master were nominally unrelated. But they touched the same nerve, raised the same issues, and together conveyed the sense that Yale's culture was changing—or had already changed in ways these events merely confirmed.

Events on other campuses made it clear that the change was not peculiar to Yale. Everywhere, it seems, America's colleges and universities were engulfed in a similar frenzy.

At Evergreen State College in Washington, the president of the college meekly agreed not to use hand gestures when speaking because some students found them threatening. At the University of Southern California, the school's mascot was subjected to scrutiny because it had the same name as the horse Robert E. Lee rode in the Civil War. At Claremont McKenna College, Heather Mac Donald was prevented from speaking because she had suggested, in a recent book, that black-on-black crime is a bigger problem than police violence. At the University of Pennsylvania, a teacher who calls herself a "queer disabled feminist" announced that in her classes white men would be called on last to offset the privileges they already enjoy. At Oberlin, students were warned, before reading Chinua Achebe's fine novel *Things Fall Apart*, that it may "trigger readers who have experienced racism, colonialism, religious persecution, violence, suicide, and more." At Lebanon Valley College in Pennsylvania, the administration agreed to place a plaque near Lynch Memorial Hall, explaining that it was named for a former president of the college, to avoid any unwanted association with the practice of lynching. And so on, seemingly without end.

These episodes caught the country's attention. Many were ridiculed and a few lamely defended. But they are not isolated incidents that spring from local conditions. They are the representative expressions of a whole way of thinking about the aims of higher education that has captured the imagination of faculty and administrators at Yale and countless other schools across the country and done real damage to our colleges and universities.

It is a way of thinking best exemplified by the seemingly trivial but deeply revealing decision of the Pierson College master to relinquish his title.

The students who objected to his title did so, they said, because it made them think of the relation between a master and his slaves. Of course, they happily accepted other academic distinctions of rank—for example, that between students who graduate cum laude and those who do not. But rankings of this sort merely reflect the obvious and unobjectionable fact that some students do better than others in their coursework. They imply no general inequality of character or cultivation. The distinction between master and slave does. It assumes that certain human beings stand higher than others not merely with regard to their achievements in some specific field of work but in a more fundamental respect. It implies that some are more developed *as human beings*—more fully human, one might say.

This is an aristocratic idea. Every regime that accepts it is an aristocracy of some kind. The Southern slaveocracy was such a regime. In its case, this idea was joined to the racist assumption that people with white skins are more fully developed as human beings than those with black ones. This made its particular form of aristocracy odious and unjust. The Yale hierarchy of master and student had none of the features that rendered the antebellum slaveocracy so cruel and immoral. It did retain, though, a faint but detectable whiff of aristocratic distinction, and this was enough to put its legitimacy in doubt.

The Pierson master who gave up his title could not possibly have thought that he might be confused with the owner of a Mississippi plantation. What really disturbed him, and his students, was not race but rank. It was the aristocratic implication, however slight, that men and women can be distinguished according to their success not in this or that particular endeavor—the study of computer science, for example, or Greek philosophy—but in the all-inclusive work of being human. This idea has been accepted by many cultures of the most varied sorts. It has been joined with other beliefs, some pernicious and others benign. But at the most basic level, it runs against the grain of America's democratic civilization. It seems—it *is*—antidemocratic. Any institution that embraces the idea of aristocracy, even in the most modest and qualified terms, therefore puts itself at odds with our civilization as a whole.

Yet even—indeed *especially*—in our democracy it is essential to preserve a few islands of aristocratic spirit, both for their own sake, because of the rarity and beauty of what they protect, and for the good of the larger democratic culture as well. That is because a democracy is strengthened by the habit of independent-mindedness that, at their very best, these institutions value and promote. None play a more important role in this regard than our colleges and universities. An attack on the idea of aristocracy within them harms not only the few who live and work in the privileged space they afford, but all who, in Edward Gibbon's phrase, "enjoy and abuse" the democratic privileges that belong to everyone outside their walls.

II.

Alexis de Tocqueville developed this line of thought with a clarity that has never been matched. I take my point of departure from his classic account.

Tocqueville found much to admire in America's democratic civilization. He thought it the most just the world has ever known. He applauded its embrace of the idea that all human beings should have an equal say in their choice of governors and equal rights before the law. But he also believed that American democracy has a pathological side. It tends, he said, to depreciate what is noble and rare and to encourage a uniformity of opinion despite its professed devotion to the independence of the individual. Tocqueville was an aristocrat. He embraced the idea of a rank order of human greatness. He nevertheless appreciated, with a clear and steady eye, the shortcomings of the older aristocratic regimes of feudal Europe and applauded, with cautious enthusiasm, the virtues of America's young democracy and its promise of universal equality. But he thought it essential to the long-term well-being of our democracy that a few pockets of aristocratic sentiment be preserved as a bulwark against its leveling egalitarianism and its encouragement of what he called the "tyranny of the majority" in the realm of belief and opinion.

Among the institutions that Tocqueville identifies as potential counterweights of this kind, he mentions our colleges and universities. These have never been entirely aristocratic in Tocqueville's sense. They have always had a democratic side as well. And their acceptance of the aristocratic ideal of an order of moral, spiritual, and cultural excellence has at every step been contaminated by the confusion of this order with the very different one of wealth and social privilege. It has been weakened and sometimes corrupted by the exclusionary prejudices that kept women, Jews, and blacks out and the untalented children of alumni in. Yet, at their best, our colleges and universities have resisted the demand to make themselves over in the image of the democratic values of the culture as a whole. Even while striving to make the process of admission more open and fair, they have held to the idea that part of the work of our most distinguished institutions of higher learning is to preserve, transmit, and honor an aristocratic tradition of respect for human greatness.

This is important for two reasons. The first is the preservation of a cultured appreciation of excellence in human living, as distinct from vocational success. The latter produces inequalities of wealth, status, and power. But it is consistent with the democratic belief that no one's humanity is greater than anyone else's. This is true if we are talking about political and legal rights. It is false if we assume that the universal powers of enjoyment, expression, and judgment that all human beings possess are more developed in some souls than others—that in some they are particularly subtle and refined, especially when it comes to the most intellectually, aesthetically, and spiritually demanding exertions. This is an aristocratic assumption. In a democracy like ours, it is in constant danger of being derided or dismissed. But if it is, we lose something of value. Without the idea of greatness of soul, human life becomes smaller and flatter. It becomes both less noble and less tragic. Protecting this idea from democratic diminution is the first reason our colleges and universities need to nurture the aristocratic love of what is brilliant and fine.

The second is that this love itself contributes to the strength and stability of our democratic way of life.

Every adult in our country gets to vote. Each has the right to decide for him- or herself which candidates and policies are best. But the forces of conformity are great. The principle of universal equality, and its corollary the principle of individual self-rule, in fact make these forces stronger. The freedom to make up one's own mind is a large responsibility. Many ease the burden by embracing the opinions of others with little or no independent reflection. The result is a kind of groupthink, partly the result of ignorance and partly of fear. This makes it easier for would-be tyrants to manipulate the democratic masses and eventually deprive them of their freedom. Tocqueville's greatest concern for the future of America was that conformity of thought would ease the way to despotism.

There are many counterweights to this, of course. Tocqueville puts special emphasis on the role of a free press. An education in human greatness contributes to democratic life as well. To some this will seem paradoxical. How can the cultivation of a spirit of aristocratic connoisseurship make our democracy stronger? The answer is by developing the habit of judging people and events from a point of view that is less vulnerable to the moods of the moment; by increasing the self-reliance of those who, because they recognize the distinction between what is excellent and common, have less need to base their standards on what "everyone knows" or "goes without saying"; and by strengthening the ability to subject one's own opinions and feelings to higher and more durable measures of truth and justice. In all these ways, an aristocratic education promotes the independent-mindedness that is needed to combat the tyranny of majority opinion that, in Tocqueville's view, is the greatest danger our democracy confronts. It cannot by itself protect us against this danger, but it makes a real contribution. Whether as leaders or citizens, the beneficiaries of such an education are in a better position to make up their minds for themselves. Many of course fail, just like everyone else. However, in their case failure is the abuse of a special trust that their education confers on them to guard against the mob mind that our democracy is always at risk of becoming.

III.

Today, this way of thinking has hardly any place in our colleges and universities. It has been almost entirely effaced by what Oliver Wendell Holmes Jr. memorably called the "effervescence of democratic negation." Holmes used the expression in a talk he gave to the Harvard Law School Association in 1886. The subject of his talk was legal education, but in the course of it he made some striking observations about the nature of education in general.

Education, Holmes says, "lies mainly in the shaping of men's interests and aims. If you convince a man that another way of looking at things is more profound, another form of pleasure more subtile than that to which he has been accustomed—if you make him really see it—the very nature of man is such that he will desire the profounder thought or the subtiler joy." This ideal of education is threatened by a form of aggressive egalitarianism that Holmes descries. The passage is worth quoting in full.

> I think we should all agree that the passion for equality has passed far beyond the political or even the social sphere. We are not only unwilling to admit that any class or society is better than that in which we move, but our customary attitude towards every one in authority of any kind is that he is only the lucky recipient of honor or salary above the

average, which any average man might as well receive as he. When the effervescence of democratic negation extends its workings beyond the abolition of external distinctions of rank to spiritual things—when the passion for equality is not content with founding social intercourse upon universal human sympathy, and a community of interests in which all men share, but attacks the lines of Nature which establish orders and degrees among the souls of men—they are not only wrong, but ignobly wrong. Modesty and reverence are no less virtues of freemen than the democratic feeling which will submit neither to arrogance nor to servility.

Holmes hardly offers a full-throated defense of equality even in the sphere of social and political life. But here, at least, the "passion for equality" is not out of place. Indeed, in the case of politics, it is essential to the very idea of democratic self-rule. And while the social relations that exist among the citizens of a democracy like ours plainly exhibit a much higher degree of inequality than is allowable in the political sphere, even here certain expressions of rank and distinction are incompatible with the democratic spirit of the country as a whole—for example, those associated with formal titles of nobility.

Holmes concedes that in these domains the principle of equality has considerable, even decisive weight. But that is because they treat only "external" things. Where it is a question of the weight or worth of different "souls"—by which Holmes means, roughly speaking, the intellectual and spiritual life of human beings, insofar as it is directed toward the great questions of existence and finds expression in the works of science, philosophy, and art that constitute the realm of culture or cultivated experience—the principle of equality is not merely misplaced but destructive.

In Holmes's view, Harvard and schools like it have a special responsibility to look after the cultivation of souls in this sense. It is not all they do, but it is a vital part of their work. The "lines of Nature" dictate that in this work some will be superior to others—that the "souls of men" are ranked by "orders and degrees." For those lower down, the appropriate attitude is one of "modesty and reverence." To deny the existence of a rank order of this kind in spiritual matters is "not only wrong." It is "ignobly" wrong. No word could convey more strongly the aristocratic spirit of Holmes's conception of the proper function of our colleges and universities.

It is aristocratic because the "distinctions of rank" that Holmes has in mind pertain not to what people do but who they are. To say that one person is better than another at interpreting Chaucer, repairing automobiles, or predicting swings in the stock market implies nothing about their relative excellence as human beings. The work that people do is just their job. And while some do their jobs faster and more creatively than others, and get paid more for doing them, rankings of this sort are entirely compatible with the democratic belief that the worth and dignity of all human beings is exactly the same.

I doubt that Holmes would have disputed this so far as our political and legal relations are concerned. But to the extent our colleges and universities are devoted to the shaping of souls as distinct from the transmission of skills, and acknowledge that some souls are more developed than others, they necessarily assume an order of distinction in the all-inclusive work of being human.

Differences of expertise, wealth, and social standing can all be reconciled with the egalitarian premise of democratic rule. But the idea that some have finer souls than others assumes a hierarchy of worth where one might think it matters most, and can be allowed a place in a democratic country only on the condition that it be cabined within some separate sphere of life detached from that of politics and law.

Democrats properly insist on the importance of shielding the political process and the operation of the courts from aristocratic beliefs of this kind. From their point of view, anyone who claims that the souls of men and women can be graded by "degrees" is a corrupter of democratic values and should be quarantined at all costs. Holmes's view is in a certain sense the reverse of theirs. If our democratic institutions need to be protected against those who claim to be better than others, our colleges and universities must be insulated against the "passion for equality" that threatens the aristocratic spirit that sets them apart.

Holmes chooses his words carefully. "Democratic negation" is a program of leveling; of knocking down what is "subtile" and "profound"; of denying the greatness of exceptional souls; of making their greatness look less conclusive, comprehensive, or significant than the "lines of Nature" declare. It is a campaign of belittlement that draws its energy from the language and mentality of politics and law, where equality is the norm. But when, like the froth from a bottle of champagne, it giddily overspills its proper domain and invades the province of college and university life, it belittles what it ought to revere: the greatness of the highest and best things that attract the finest souls and afford them a "joy" that coarser ones never know. This is the "effervescence" against which Holmes warns.

Today, Holmes's words sound archaic. Many are likely to find the whole tenor of his speech insulting. To their ears, Holmes's caution against the "passion for equality" sounds like the death rattle of an old and discredited elitism that no responsible academic endorses any longer. But that is because, in the past forty years, this passion has swept over the world of higher education with unprecedented force and all but drowned the idea of "distinctions of rank . . . in spiritual things" that Holmes still took for granted. Some think this a good thing. They cheer the extension of democratic principles to the innermost recesses of academic life. They support the intensified campaign for ever more equality that has washed over the world of higher education in the last decade or so. But their democratic assault on our colleges and universities risks destroying something precious and rare: a reverence for human excellence that is valuable for its own sake and as an aid to the independent-mindedness on which the health of our democracy depends.

This anti-aristocratic spirit is exemplified, in an especially pure form, by the ridiculous decision of the master of Pierson College to call himself by a more democratic title instead. But, more generally, it is the unifying force behind the three movements I discuss in this book. Each is an expression of democratic commitment. Each is motivated by a legitimate concern with injustice in the society at large and with racial injustice in particular. But each does great harm to our colleges and universities when this commitment is extended to their interior culture in ways I shall explain.

IV.

The first of these movements focuses on campus speech. Some say, rightly, that a college or university is a special kind of community. They insist that speech that offends some members of this community, especially those belonging to historically disadvantaged or marginalized groups, may be forbidden or discouraged in order to protect their sense of inclusion, even if this means keeping certain speakers off campus and cleansing the language that teachers and students use to avoid giving offense. This has provoked howls of protest, mostly from those who view free speech as the indispensable condition of a robust "marketplace of ideas."

Both sides get it wrong.

A college or university *is* a special community, governed by expectations different from those that guide our interactions in the political sphere. The latter requires an uninhibited give-and-take of ideas. But the participants have no obligation to converse with one another. They have no duty to collaborate in a search for the truth. The students and faculty in a college or university do. They are the members of a conversational community. The exchanges among them cannot be understood on the model of a marketplace of ideas, where the truth emerges as the by-product of individuals relentlessly pursuing their own opinionated views of it, in the way an increase in social wealth is produced through the competition of self-interested buyers and sellers.

But this does not mean that campus speech should be restricted for the sake of protecting people's feelings. Quite the opposite: it means that no mere declaration of feeling can ever have an authority of its own; that every statement of this kind must be subjected to searching scrutiny; and that students and faculty should be prepared to expose themselves to one another more fully than they are ever required to do in a political debate. This is a higher and more demanding conception of speech than the political version of it, not a more cautious and circumspect one. It is the right ideal for a community devoted to the collaborative pursuit of the truth.

Some make more progress in this pursuit than others. But however far one gets, the pursuit itself rests on the assumption that truth is distinguished from error not because we happen to believe it but on account of its greater reality. This is an assumption as old as Western thought. One might call it the Socratic assumption. It has a natural affinity with the aristocratic belief in a rank order of human greatness, which for Socrates was aligned with an individual's proximity to truth and therefore to *being*. The attack on the idea of a community of conversation, devoted to the pursuit of the truth, in the name of a community of inclusion where no one's feelings will be wounded or judgment challenged is thus also an attack on the Socratic ideal of an aristocracy of truth-seekers that our colleges and universities ought to uphold.

The second movement rests on the belief that racial, ethnic, and gender diversity is good for higher education. This may seem so obvious as to be beyond dispute. But the group-based understanding of diversity that has prevailed on our campuses for the past forty years, since the Supreme Court's decision in *Regents of the University of California v. Bakke*, has done tremendous harm to the academic culture of our colleges and universities. It has encouraged students to view themselves as victims and wrongdoers; to act as spokespersons for the racial, ethnic, and other groups to which they belong; and to believe they are fatally confined in their loyalties and judgments by characteristics beyond their power to change. It has made all forms of hierarchy suspect except innocuous ones of achievement in narrowly defined vocational pursuits.

All of this is the result of the importation into the sphere of academic life of an ideal of social justice that *Bakke* forbid our schools to seek directly but allowed them to pursue in a roundabout way, under the rubric of diversity. When this happened, a group-based way of thinking that is appropriate in the realm of law and social policy became a norm in the academy, where it conflicts with the independent-mindedness that ought to increase the further one proceeds in the enterprise of learning and that is vital to the long-term health of our democracy. It covered our colleges and universities in a pall of mendacity by compelling them, under penalty of law, to say one thing while doing another. And it put the idea of human excellence in the Tocquevillian sense under a cloud of disrepute by assigning primary importance to an ideal of fairness instead.

The third movement concerns our relation to the past.

We live in an age that prides itself on its aspiration to overcome every form of prejudice. But there is one that remains so strong we hardly notice it at all. It is the unspoken belief that, by comparison with the morally enlightened position we occupy today, those who lived before us dwelt in darkness and confusion, groping to find truths we now securely possess. Many believe that we are no more obliged to take their backward views seriously than we are to endorse the beliefs of the medieval astronomers who put the earth at the center of things. We are free, they say, to refashion the past according to our contemporary moral scruples. Indeed, they insist we have a duty to do so. Until we have scrubbed our inheritance clean and brought it into conformity with what we now know to be the truth, the world remains disfigured by emblems of unrighteousness that spoil its integrity from an ethical point of view. The passion for renaming that is sweeping America's campuses today springs from this demand.

It is a dangerous demand. It destroys our capacity for sympathy with the very large number of human beings who are no longer among the living and therefore cannot speak for themselves. It obscures the truth that we are no more able to see things in a perfect light than our ancestors were, even if we judge their morality to have been, in certain respects, backward or incomplete. It encourages a species of pride that blinds us to the greatness of what was said and done by those whose values correspond only imperfectly to ours.

Our colleges and universities have a special duty to resist this. They are, in an obvious sense, the custodians of the past. Their libraries preserve the works, and their departments the traditions of learning, on which the continued existence of civilized life depends. But beyond this they have a particular responsibility to foster the tolerance for ambiguity and dissonance that is the best antidote to the spirit of righteous conviction that confines the soul within narrow bounds by conferring a moral authority on its existing prejudices and exposes it to the danger of blindly deferring to the opinions of the group or tribe to which one belongs. Many campus monuments need supplemental commentary. But few if any ought to be torn down or erased. Whether one should, in any particular case, is a question that calls for the most careful judgment. How it is made depends on the spirit in which it is approached. To approach it with the evangelical conviction that the past must be remade to look like the present violates an educational duty of the first importance.

What I am calling a "tolerance for ambiguity and dissonance" Learned Hand described as the "spirit of liberty." It is the spirit, he said, that "is not too sure that it is right." It encourages doubt and self-reflection and breaks the tendency to go along with what "everyone is saying." It is therefore an essential condition of democratic life. It is also a condition of the refinement and growth of the individual human being. Those who succeed in acquiring it take in more of the world and of themselves. They achieve a spaciousness of outlook and feeling that others never reach. Their souls are larger, freer, more developed. They are aristocrats of the spirit, in a sense that both Freud and Whitman would have understood and approved. This is perhaps the most credible sense of aristocracy to which we can still aspire in the "democratic centuries" that Tocqueville forecast.

The campaign for renaming aims to level the distinction between the present and the past. It too is inflamed by the spirit of "democratic negation" that inspires the current understanding of diversity and the demand that campus speech be cleansed for the sake of creating a community of inclusion. This is the common ground of all three movements. It is what unifies and explains them. And it is the reason we must resist them all, for when the egalitarianism that is vital to our political well-being is extended to those islands of aristocratic sentiment that Tocqueville wisely viewed as precious in their own right, and as a needed balance to the excesses of democratic life, it does great damage not just to our colleges and universities but to our civilization as a whole.

In politics, equality prevails. Matters are decided according to the rule "one person one vote." The leading ideal is that of justice. A corollary is the principle of non-subordination. A law or practice that treats one group as inferior to another is inherently unjust.

This has special application in the case of race. But the extension of these same values to our colleges and universities, in a mindless and dogmatic way, undermines the aspiration to nobility of spirit that ought to be a part at least of what the best of these institutions are *for*. It discredits the idea of excellence when it is applied not just to skills but persons—to the whole of life itself. It casts a pall over the radiance of human greatness, which Tocqueville believed is always endangered in democratic societies and therefore in particular need of protection within them.

There is an obvious tension between this complex of ideas and our democratic values. But instead of seeing in this tension a needed and creative tonic, many on campus today seem to want to make it disappear. Led by pious levelers, they strain to give the principle of equality, which is and ought to be the touchstone of our political life, and a sacred legal value, a more rigorous application to academic relations as well. They appear incapable of living with the thought that the internal life of the academy celebrates distinction on the basis of excellence in a way we would never countenance in politics or law. To them this seems an intolerable exception to the egalitarian principles that govern these latter domains. They are determined to reduce it to an absolute minimum and, in any case, not to extol or glorify it. At best it seems in their eyes an unavoidable embarrassment, about which the less said the better. But their hostility to the idea of human excellence, and the order it implies, is in reality a moral loathing for what our colleges and universities should aim to be.

I am no stranger to student protest and campus campaigns for greater equality. I went to college in the 1960s and was a fierce activist myself. I fought for civil rights and against the Vietnam War. I left school in the middle of my sophomore year to work for Students for a Democratic Society (SDS). I am proud of what I did. I feel a little embarrassment about the excesses of some of my protests, but none about their target or goal.

These were all political. My fellow protesters and I wanted to change the law and redirect the country's foreign policy. At times we demanded that our schools' academic routines be suspended or disrupted for the sake of these political goals. And there were occasions when we shouted speakers down or prevented professors from teaching: of this I am not proud. But our objectives for the most part lay outside the academy. In the main, we did not seek to remake our schools in the image of our political ideals. I felt no contradiction then, and see none now, between my commitment to these ideals in politics and law, and the reverence for human excellence that I learned as a student at Williams College, studying Plato and Kant with my teachers, around a seminar table, away from the noise of the world.

It is the sense of a contradiction of just this kind that distinguishes today's campus unrest from that of fifty years ago. Then it seemed to me that the most important thing was to work for greater equality in the world outside the academy. Today I think it is the protection of the spirit of nobility within it.

ONE

Excellence

I.

MANY PEOPLE HAVE AN ALLERGY TO THE WORD "ARISTOC-racy." To them it implies unearned privilege and exploitative domination. In the original sense, though, the word simply means the rule of the best.

This is an idea that makes obvious sense wherever human beings are engaged in a well-defined task with a specific and limited objective. In most pursuits of this kind, those who are best at the work ought to lead and direct it, and be the judge of whether it is well or shoddily done. They are the ones who rightly enjoy the most authority. This is as true in an automobile repair shop as a radiology clinic. The same applies in a class on the history of the American Revolution, where the teacher is presumably the one best prepared to guide the students in their examination of the subject, and in an atelier, like the one I visited some years ago in New York City, where young painters were learning the art of classical portraiture under the eye of a master. In settings like these, and countless others, the participants accept without hesitation the rule of the best, so far as the work at hand is concerned. In this sense they acknowledge, on a limited scale, the validity of the aristocratic ideal. Nor do they view the rule of the best as either unearned or exploitative. They recognize that it has been earned by superior training and accomplishment and concede that it is generally for the benefit of those who are new to the work or less skilled at it. The classroom is an obvious example.

Where people balk, of course, is at the generalization of the ideal. It may be that there are those who are best at reading a CT scan or diagnosing a cranky carburetor. But who is the best at being human? When it comes to the all-embracing work of living the best life that one can, the disagreements are so large, and the differences of judgment so profound, that the aristocratic principle seems, in the eyes of many, to no longer have any application at all. While most people accept this principle in the hospital room and repair shop, they are skeptical of the idea that there is an identifiable group of men and women who are "best" at living in some comprehensive sense. Even more emphatically, they reject the notion that there is a class of superior human beings who ought to manage the affairs of their community as a whole because of their presumptive wisdom or virtue. If this is what one means by aristocracy, it has few defenders today.

The rejection of aristocratic rule as a principle of large-scale political organization is one of the most widely shared convictions of our age. Nearly everyone claims to endorse some version of democratic rule instead. Democracy comes in many different forms: presidential, parliamentary, plebiscitary, constitutional, and the like. But the fundamental difference between it and every aristocratic regime is that democracy is essentially egalitarian in nature.

Several considerations support the belief that a large and heterogeneous society like ours can only be organized on democratic-egalitarian lines. Three in particular are worth mentioning.

The first is practical in nature. The citizens of a modern state are all entitled to some say in how it is governed. Given the variety of views about the definition and meaning of a good life, it is impossible to organize the whole of society according to any one definition of it and to distribute power and authority on its basis without alienating those who hold some other view of human fulfillment and feel entitled to a share in their country's government too. It is therefore imperative to find ways of distributing power and authority that are agnostic with respect to the question of what constitutes an excellent life overall. This inevitably leads to what the political philosopher Michael Sandel calls a "procedural" form of government. It also eliminates the possibility of every type of aristocratic rule, which always assumes some basic agreement as to what makes certain lives better than others in a general sense, and one way of living the best of all.

A second consideration that weighs strongly in favor of the democratic-egalitarian ideal of government is philosophical rather than practical. It is the widespread acceptance across party lines of what might be called the "moral" point of view. The moralist insists that every human being must be treated with equal respect—that whatever a person's race, gender, age, or economic standing he or she has certain elementary rights that deserve to be honored with the same care and concern as the equal rights of everyone else. This is a principle whose strength has been growing for centuries. No other principle today commands as much authority. Its most striking contemporary expression is the human rights movement, which extends the principle of equal rights to the whole of humankind with unprecedented moral urgency.

This is a powerful and precious idea. It is one of the most valuable legacies of Western civilization. But it also puts the aristocratic principle under a shadow of doubt. That is because, in defining a person's humanity, the moral point of view puts a heavy if not exclusive weight on those attributes that all human beings share—most importantly on their equal capacity to decide for themselves how they wish to live their lives. This tends to depreciate the other dimensions of our humanity—all those qualities of wit, intelligence, imagination, and character that human beings neither possess nor develop to the same degree.

The moral point of view puts these qualities in second place at best. It draws attention away from them and reduces their importance in our judgments about who deserves respect and why. It encourages the belief that the best way of living can be defined in simple terms as the one that conforms to the moral law. But this is too thin a conception of human excellence to support the distinctions among more and less outstanding human beings that every aristocratic ideal takes for granted. Indeed, the moral point of view is profoundly hostile to this ideal. This has hastened the near-total elimination of aristocratic values from the sphere of political life and their depreciation even outside it.

A third consideration points in the same direction. Like the second, it is more philosophical than practical. It reflects the force of an idea familiar to us all—that there is no disputing about taste. This idea fits comfortably with the moralistic view of human nature. The latter insists that we are all the same when it comes to our basic rights. The moralist also acknowledges—what can hardly be disputed—that we have the most diverse preferences, interests, and tastes. But as to these, he is generally as relaxed as he is rigorous where our rights are concerned. Moral judgments, he insists, are imperative and universal. Everyone agrees that it is wrong to steal, lie, and kill. But those who maintain that judgments of this kind are binding on us all also often declare, with equal conviction, that judgments about what is beautiful, tasteful, and refined, as opposed to ugly, crude, and base, are peculiar to those making them and cannot be weighed by anything remotely like a universal standard of evaluation. As to judgments of the latter kind, they say, each individual is entitled to his or her own. This applies to judgments about food, hobbies, sexual habits, works of art, and styles of life. When it comes to the meaning of the "best" in all these cases, meaning is widely thought to be in the eye of the beholder. Many people today insist as strenuously on the absence of objective standards of judgment outside the narrow field of morality as they do on the presence of such standards within it.

Once upon a time, judgments about the relative excellence of different preferences and tastes, and the ways of living based upon them, had the same objective solidity that today only our moral judgments possess. According to Aristotle, everyone agrees that flute playing is an activity that may be performed well or badly. Can it be, he asks, that when it comes to the activity of living in general, there is not a similar standard of excellence by which to judge the performance of different human beings? Aristotle thought that the existence of such a standard is obvious. Today, many people are likely to think that its absence is equally obvious. The reasons for this shift in perspective are many and complex. Aristotle's view rested on metaphysical, psychological, and political assumptions that are no longer credible today. Perhaps the most important cause of their displacement has been the growing authority of what I call the moral point of view, which contracts the field of objective judgment to compliance with the moral law alone, leaving everything outside it to the vagaries of private preference and taste. In any case, the reduction of human achievement to simple questions of right and wrong, and the consignment of every other dimension of human excellence to a realm of subjective preference and choice, together undermine the aristocratic belief that some live better lives than others in an overall sense. Aristotle still took this belief for granted, as did every ancient thinker. And because he did, he was able to conclude—what seems absurd today—that the best political regime is obviously the one that is led and run by the best human beings.

But if the aristocratic principle has been discredited as a basis of political organization, is its application therefore permanently shrunk to the domain of specialized activities like flute playing and automobile repair? Or might it still have some bearing on the general question of how one ought to live? Could it be that there are better and worse ways of living—that there are grades of excellence in the work of being human—even if there is no single way that is demonstrably the best of all? Could it be that there is a form of education that increases a student's chances of becoming an excellent human being, just as there are educational programs for those who want to be outstanding flute players and mechanics? And could it be that those who receive an education in human excellence are, just for that reason, better equipped to play a special and needed role in our democracy despite, or rather because of, its staunch rejection of the aristocratic principle as a basis for organizing the distribution of power and authority in society at large? This book proceeds on the assumption that the answer to all these questions is yes.

What I call "an education in human excellence" is a phrase that best fits those disciplines we still collectively describe as the humanities. These put the question of the meaning of life at the center of attention. They explore the various answers that have been given to it and invite the students studying them to make the question their own. They stress the urgency of confronting with a reflective eye the very largest topics in the wide field of human concern, rather than treating them as subjects that are too personal to reward systematic study.

What is love? Does death make life meaningless or is it, in Wallace Stevens's words, "the mother of beauty"? How should the "ancient quarrel" between philosophy and poetry be settled? What is the relation between self-knowledge and freedom? To what extent can we transcend the circumstances of our birth and join the company of others, living and dead, whose social, political, and psychological situation is remote from our own? Does modern science illuminate the human condition or obscure it? And perhaps most important, among the diverse examples of lives in which these questions have been pursued with unusual courage and clarity, and the potential for human self-inspection realized to an exceptional degree, is there one or some that might serve as an inspiration for my own?

The life of a thinker, perhaps, like Socrates or Plato? Of a statesman like Lincoln or Douglass? A scientist like Galileo? A solitary poet like Emily Dickinson? A psychologist like Montaigne or Freud? A saint like Augustine? This particular list is personal. It reflects my own education and ideas about excellence in living. Others will have different lists. But any list of the sort I have in mind will be more than a casual collection of writers one happens to like. It will reflect a considered judgment regarding the best way to live, arrived at after a disciplined study of alternatives. It will be the product of an organized program of reading and reflection founded on the belief that the question of what constitutes the best life overall is neither too personal to be approached in an "academic" way nor too deeply conditioned by prior prejudices to be worth asking at all.

This belief is the premise on which the humanities rest, today as in the past. Over the years many things have changed in the way the humanities are taught. But this bedrock belief remains the same, along with its three most important corollaries. The first is that the question of the meaning of life is not like any of the more circumscribed questions one studies in school (How does economics define the condition of general equilibrium? Could the Civil War have been avoided? Can the theory of evolution explain the development of moral culture?). The second is that, despite its generality, the question of the meaning of life is a genuine one, even if the answers students give, after the most careful study, diverge and are rarely if ever perfectly stable. And the third is that, even with these qualifications, it is possible to speak of progress in the study of the question—those who get farther experiencing, and enjoying, a fuller eng. ement with what, for lack of a better phrase, we might call the human condition, thereby becoming, in a perfectly intelligible sense, more fully developed as human beings, not just more knowledgeable in a particular field.

My experience as a teacher of the humanities confirms this. The freshman who reports, with an excitement he can barely contain, that reading *War and Peace* over spring break has been the most thrilling experience of his life and that he now cannot imagine living without Pierre, Natasha, and Prince Andrei; the young woman who tells me that Aristotle's cosmos, where everything is in its proper place, is the most beautiful thing she has ever encountered and wonders, with a mixture of resignation and resolve, whether it can be brought back to life again today; the student who, on first reading Kant's *Critique of Pure Reason*, confesses that he is baffled by the transcendental deduction but announces his determination to get to the bottom of it "if it takes a lifetime"; his classmate who has become obsessed with the disjunction between personal and cosmic time in Virginia Woolf's *To the Lighthouse* and views it as the key to the riddle of human existence—these are more than book reports; they are declarations of an existential sort that suggest a basic shift in the students' orientation toward the question of the meaning of life. I hear them all the time.

These are only anecdotes, of course, but they illustrate and validate my confidence that the humanities do more than add to one's storehouse of knowledge—that they stretch and strengthen the students' human being too. They confirm that a person's humanity can grow: that there are grades and distinctions of human fulfillment in the life of a single person and between the lives of different ones as well. They justify the conviction that better and worse, if not, perhaps, the unequivocal best, is a notion that has application beyond the realm of specific tasks, like flute playing, in the all-encompassing work of being human. And they vindicate the relevance of the aristocratic principle to this wider endeavor, as Holmes rightly assumed.

Holmes also recognized that this principle has no place in our political democracy. He nevertheless believed it essential to protect the aristocratic ideal in the academic world of "spiritual things" against the leveling effects of democratic equality. Others, before and since, have stressed the importance of doing so as a corrective to the excesses of democratic life itself. Today, these beliefs have few defenders. But they have a long and honorable lineage in American thought. In later chapters we will see how the various campus movements I survey all spring from what Holmes calls "the effervescence of democratic negation." First, though, it is important to recover some sense of how others have understood and defended the role of aristocratic habits in this most democratic of all countries, especially as these manifest themselves in the world of higher education. I want the comfort of their company, of course, but some historical perspective is essential.

John Adams was the most philosophically minded of the Founding Fathers. He gives us a good place to start.

II.

When the new constitution was drafted in 1787, Adams was in London, serving as his country's first ambassador to the British royal court. Though an important participant in the early phase of the Revolution, Adams was away when it ended and had no direct hand in fashioning the system of government that emerged from the failures of the Continental Congress. But Adams was eager that his own views about the nature and purpose of the American constitution not be overlooked or underappreciated. To this end, he set his ideas down at length in writing. In 1787, two years before he was elected vice president—a role in which he served until 1796, when he was elected president—Adams completed a massive multivolume treatise titled *A Defence of the Constitutions of Government of the United States*. He supplemented it with a further series of essays written during the early days of his vice presidency (amid what he later called "the constant scenes of business and dissipation" in which he was "enveloped"). These latter essays contain the most concise statement of Adams's political philosophy. They were published under his own name in 1805 as the *Discourses on Davila*.

When the *Discourses* were written, America was seized with the question of how to view the French Revolution and whether or not to support it. On one side were those who enthusiastically endorsed its egalitarian principles and wished to see them extended to the United States in a stronger form than the new constitution allowed. Thomas Jefferson was their champion.

On the other were those opposed to the leveling demands of the French Revolution. In their view, these represented a dangerous species of lawlessness and disorder. Against it they defended the values of tradition, hierarchy, and the balanced forms of constitutional government. In Europe, their most forceful spokesman was Edmund Burke. On this side of the Atlantic it was John Adams, who has sometimes been called America's Burke.

The *Discourses on Davila* cover a great deal of ground in a wandering and distracted style. Adams's essays are punctuated by long quotations from other works, making it difficult to extract his own views in a connected fashion. But there can be no doubt regarding Adams's central message. It is that human beings are driven by what he calls "the passion for distinction"; that distinction is a fact of life with many different sources, including beauty, brains, upbringing, and wealth; that the love of distinction is not objectionable in itself but dangerous if it gets out of hand; and that a principal function of government is to ameliorate the competition for honor and recognition in a way that preserves its good effects while avoiding or suppressing its bad ones. To this end, Adams urges the advantages of a "mixed" government that contains elements of monarchy, aristocracy, and democracy over those that are devoted to one of these exclusively—an ancient idea with roots in Aristotle's *Politics* and Polybius's *Histories*.

According to Adams, human beings have a natural "affection for the good of others; but alone it is not a balance for the selfish affections." To the passion for "benevolence," nature "has kindly added . . . the desire of reputation, in order to make us good members of society." Together these two passions counterbalance the drive for "self-preservation," which left to itself results in anarchy and ruin. But that is only if the second—the longing for distinction—is suitably directed toward a productive end. At its root, this longing is the desire not to be "out of the sight of others, groping in the dark." It is the desire to be "seen." A man can escape from obscurity through bad deeds as well as good ones. Both bring notoriety. If the passion for recognition is to strengthen rather than dissolve the bonds of social life, it must therefore be welded to genuine "merit."

Wealth and a family name bring distinction. Depending on the circumstances, it may be an honorable one. The same is true of "beauty, elegance, and grace." Adams does not discount any of these as sharply as some do. But the only enduringly good reputation, he says, is one based on "intellectual and moral qualities." Following a long line of philosophers reaching back to the Greeks and Romans, Adams summarizes these qualities in the word "virtue." In contrast to the goods of "health, strength, and agility" and those of "birth" and "riches," all of which have real if conditional value, Adams calls virtue "the only rational source and eternal foundation of honor." It is the only truly reliable basis of distinction.

But this raises an obvious question. "There is a voice within us, which seems to intimate, that real merit should govern the world; and that men ought to be respected only in proportion to their talents, virtues, and services. But the question always has been, how can this arrangement be accomplished? How shall the men of merit be discovered?"

The problem is twofold.

On the one hand, "real merit is confined to a very few." The "numbers who thirst for respect, are out of all proportion to those who seek it only by merit." But the people at large cannot be trusted to make the selection. They are subject to "intrigues and manœuvres without number . . . from all the chicanery, impostures, and false-hoods imaginable, with scarce a possibility of preferring real merit." They are subject, in particular, to the most seductive "deception" of all: the argument that "real" merit is a pretense, a disguise, a device for shielding the privileges of the rich and wellborn, and that no man possesses more of it than any other.

This is the doctrine of "levelling." It is what "the self-styled phi-losophers of the French Revolution" teach. But their teaching runs counter to nature. "Every man and woman" has "equal rights." But nature assures that some possess a degree of virtue others lack, and though their rights are the same, the "weight" or "power" they enjoy "ought not" to be. For those who are less distinguished, this is a hard truth to accept. It is a source of envy and jealousy. It makes them vul-nerable to demagogues who preach the perfect equality of all human beings. And it deepens the difficulty the many always have in identi-fying the few who possess real merit.

On the other hand, if the best are defined by an identifiable marker, like wealth, title, or the possession of land, the problem of selection is solved, but there is no guarantee that those who possess these attributes will be individuals of "real merit." In the past, most aristocracies have been defined in these terms. But every regime of this kind is subject to its own form of corruption. In each case, a gap eventually appears between the outward signs of aristocratic bear-ing and the true virtue of those who exhibit them. The divergence between the two is a perennial source of democratic opposition to all fixed orders of rank and privilege. Inheritance in particular is an imperfect mark of virtue.

Adams grants that children born to privilege, with a family name to uphold, may be more likely than those in obscure circumstances to acquire a virtuous character. But their privilege is no guarantee they will. Many with wealth and titles become vicious instead. Nature itself—a "voice within"—tells us that the best men ought to "govern the world." But Adams vehemently rejects the idea that the problem of selecting them can be solved by adopting any European form of nobility. None, in any case, could grow in America's egalitarian soil. Yet, if this solution is no good, the problem still remains and must be solved in some fashion if we are not to descend to the unnatural and destructive equality proclaimed by the champions of the French Revolution.

Adams's solution is a negative one. There is no way of guaranteeing that "power," as distinct from "rights," will be concentrated in the right hands. But if power is broken up and dispersed, that can at least help to prevent its concentration in the wrong hands—in particular, those of the people at large who as a single collectivity constitute only a "mob." In Adams's view, this is the principal function of America's constitutional government, which divides one power from another and sets them against each other in a complex system of checks and balances.

"Is there a constitution upon record," he exclaims, "more complicated with balances than ours?" These have the effect of slowing down the processes of government; creating opportunities for deliberation and the adjustment of competing interests; and discouraging (though nothing can entirely prevent) the emergence of demagogues who, speaking in defense of the equal rights of man, would abolish distinctions of wealth and status and collect all power into their own hands, claiming to be the authentic voice of the people. More particularly, our cumbersome and slow-working system of constitutional rule does a better job than the leveling "democracy of France" of giving those with real merit the time and opportunities they need to demonstrate their virtue and be chosen for it. This is the essence of Adams's defense of the American version of democracy against the French alternative.

But a further question remains. Where are the men—and, today, women—of real merit that our form of government allows to come to the fore themselves to come from in the first place? They constitute a "natural" aristocracy, as Adams repeatedly says. An aristocracy of this sort differs from the artificial one constituted by lineage and title. But how is it formed and sustained? In the latter case, the answer is obvious. It is created by birth. But natural aristocrats are known by their character and works, not their names. They are distinguished by the intellectual and moral qualities their public and private actions reveal. Are these qualities just an accident that some possess and others lack? Or are they the product of deliberate cultivation and, if so, what kind?

John Adams was a vain man. His idea of how to build and support a natural aristocracy was based on his own experience and achievements. Some may carp, but America has had few models so good.

In material terms, Adams came from modest but honorable beginnings. His family, neither rich nor poor, had been in New England from the start. It was at Harvard College, though, that Adams first began to study, in a disciplined way, the classical and modern works that were to have a profound effect on his views about the nature of political life. One may also infer from what he says about the importance of higher education that the experience had an effect on his character.

An education of the sort Adams received requires leisure. This inevitably gives it an aristocratic tenor, since "leisure for study must ever be the portion of the few." It follows that "the laboring part of the people can never be learned." The great sponsors of higher learning, from Peisistratus to the Medici, have always been aristocrats. Adams concludes that "knowledge will forever be monopolized by the aristocracy." Indeed, "the moment you give knowledge to a democrat," he declares rather extravagantly, "you make him an aristocrat." That is because he now possesses something valuable and rare that only a few can ever afford the time to acquire.

Hence, Adams says, "the more you educate, without a balance in the government, the more aristocratical will the people and the government be. There can never be, in any nation, more than one fifth—no, not one tenth of the men, regularly educated to science and letters." An education of this sort gives its possessors "no peculiar rights in society." But it deepens their understanding of human nature and political strife. This justifies our giving their more learned views a special "weight." In this sense it confers a "distinction" and "privilege" upon them.

It is not, however, merely on account of their superior knowledge that the recipients of a higher education of the sort that Adams received at Harvard in the 1750s are entitled to special respect. It is because of their character too. "There is no necessary connection," Adams concedes, "between knowledge and virtue." No one could reasonably claim otherwise. There are too many unlearned men of good character and too many well-educated villains to suppose that knowledge and virtue are necessarily joined. Still, there is a strong connection between them. Adams remarks that in his "humble opinion," "knowledge, upon the whole, promotes virtue and happiness." The intellectual process of learning tends, on "the whole," to encourage those affective qualities of moderation, decency, and fairmindedness in which a virtuous character at least partly consists.

Real merit—the kind a society requires in its leaders if it is to be well governed—does not presuppose a college education. But the two are not randomly connected. The one *conduces* to the other. It tends to *promote* it. It tends to produce the kind of natural aristocracy on which a constitutional democracy like that of the United States depends, if men and women of superior character are to be elevated to positions of leadership with sufficient frequency for the regime to survive.

The idea of a natural aristocracy is one that Adams took for granted. He recognized, of course, that it sits uneasily with the norms of democratic life. He knew, from his own experience, that it is subject to the same leveling attacks as aristocracies of the artificial kind. But he thought the distinction essential; believed that natural aristocrats ought to rule, even in America; judged the connection between their character and the education they receive an important if imperfect one; and concluded that our colleges have a vital role to play in this regard. It is striking that Adams and Jefferson, though so often on opposite sides in the political battles of the early republic, saw eye to eye in all these respects. Their belief in the idea of a natural aristocracy and association of it with the work of higher learning transcended party lines.

III.

John Adams believed that even "in the deepest democracy that ever was known or imagined," the human "thirst for respect" inevitably produces an aristocratic order of rank and distinction. He thought this not only inevitable but desirable, so long as the "passion for distinction" is properly directed toward the recognition of "true merit." The question of how to do this in a country as strongly committed to the principle of equality as the United States is the main theme of his political writings. But neither Adams nor any of his fellow Founders offer the most thoughtful account of how to secure a place for aristocratic ideals in America's democratic civilization, and why doing so matters. That honor belongs to Alexis de Tocqueville.

Tocqueville was a French nobleman. In 1831 he visited the United States for nine months. After returning home, he wrote a book about his experiences. He called it *Democracy in America.*

Tocqueville's overall appraisal is remarkably balanced. American democracy is something new under the sun. There has never been anything like it. It is also a guide to the future. It gives us a picture of what, in time, the older societies of Europe are bound to become. This is a mixed blessing. America is freer and more open than any political society has ever been. It is less constrained by the social and imaginative habits of the European aristocracies that it is destined to replace. But it is also peculiarly vulnerable to two grave dangers.

One of these Tocqueville calls the "tyranny of the majority." In America, the habit of independent thinking is on the decline. Americans tend increasingly to be steered by public opinion instead.

The other is the loss of esteem for human greatness. The master principle of American democracy is that of equality. Its triumph makes the world more "just." But at the same time it makes it less exalted. It produces a leveling of values and expectations that "finally reduces each nation to being nothing more than a herd of timid and industrious animals of which the government is the shepherd." In "democratic societies," Tocqueville writes, "I dread the audacity much less than the mediocrity of desires; what seems to me most to be feared is that in the midst of the small incessant occupations of private life, ambition will lose its spark and its greatness; that human passions will be appeased and debased at the same time, so that each day the aspect of the social body becomes more tranquil and less lofty." This is the great intellectual and spiritual danger that inevitably accompanies the new democratic order that America exemplifies in its purest form.

"The spectacle of this universal uniformity saddens and chills me," Tocqueville writes, "and I am tempted to regret the society that is no longer." But he never yields to the temptation. It would be pointless in any case. The restoration of an aristocratic order in which the different ranks of human beings are separated by a distance so great that the various castes "scarcely believe themselves to be a part of the same humanity" is now utterly out of the question. Nor does Tocqueville ever suggest that this is something we should desire even if it could be attained. The advantages of democracy are too great to justify our wanting to turn the clock back.

What Tocqueville does insist on, though, is the crucial importance of looking for ways to temper the excesses of democracy so that its greatest dangers are, if not avoided altogether, at least softened and contained. This is a theme that runs through the whole of his remarkable book. It sounds a note of practicality and measured hopefulness that offsets the fatalistic tone that a reader can sometimes hear in Tocqueville's wistful observations about how much of what is beautiful and great in human life is bound to be submerged in the democratic "centuries" that lie ahead.

Some of these tempering measures are structural. They are the institutional devices that diffuse or deflect the direct expression of popular will so that majorities cannot tyrannize as quickly and completely as they otherwise might. Tocqueville finds much in our constitutional system of government to admire for this reason. He specifically mentions the federal division of powers; the indirect election of senators (since repealed by constitutional amendment); and the role of the Supreme Court, an "immense judicial power" that represents "the spirit of conservation against democratic instability." In these respects, he follows the cautionary logic of *The Federalist Papers*.

But this is the less original part of his argument. To the institutional counterweights that Madison and Hamilton propose, Tocqueville adds other, more general cultural forces that in America tend to offset the most striking pathologies of democratic life.

He describes, for example, at some length the role the American legal profession plays as a prophylactic against the dangers of democratic excess. In America, lawyers are everywhere. They dominate its public assemblies and orchestrate the commercial and personal affairs of private life. Trained in the art of interpretation and accustomed to the rule of precedent, lawyers bring with them a habitual regard for procedure and a veneration of the past. Their professional experience inclines them to proceed by deliberate steps and to be hesitant to renovate too quickly or too often. It instills in them a reverence for established forms that moderates the democratic tendency to discount the claims of tradition. In this way, the education and practice of lawyers ensures that certain elements, at least, of an aristocratic sensibility are preserved amid the continual reforms of democratic life.

Still, the culture of the legal profession has a broadly egalitarian cast. That is because lawyers are above all concerned with the protection of individual rights. Nothing in the practice of law encourages the specifically aristocratic taste for greatness—the love of fine works and noble characters whose effacement Tocqueville considers one of the great costs of a modern democratic society. Yet, even in this respect, he finds some reason for hope.

The general temper of the American people is anti-hierarchical. Americans do not read Descartes, Tocqueville says, but they are natural-born Cartesians who refuse to take anything on authority. They rely on their own observations and value judgments instead (though their independent beliefs tend to converge in a consolidated mass opinion). They are practical-minded and eschew speculative studies when these are pursued for their own sake. They appreciate utility more than beauty. They are instinctively hostile to those who "put on airs" and pretend to be superior to others. And they violently oppose every attempt to establish an order of privilege in society at large.

But the very freedom of American life permits those with a taste for excellence and beauty to form private associations devoted to their pursuit. These include museums, literary societies, and colleges and universities. Many are formed by the "opulent or well-to-do" who enjoy a measure of leisure and are less "closely confined" than others by "the preoccupations of material life." Some among them, at least, are inclined "to engage in the works and pleasures of the intellect." The associations they form for this purpose are consecrated to the exploration and celebration of what, in Tocqueville's words, "rises toward the infinite, immaterial, and beautiful." In this respect, they have an aristocratic character, though Tocqueville is careful to remind his readers that even these most aristocratic-looking institutions are not defined by birth or sealed off from the rest of society, but are open to the outside world and founded on agreement, in contrast to the hereditary castes of European society.

They are, one might say, islands of excellence in a democratic sea. Like other private associations, they are devoted to the special ends of their members. Yet, insofar as these include the cultivation of greatness in the pursuit of what Holmes calls "spiritual things," the culture of America's colleges and universities reflects a love of rank and distinction that runs against the grain of the democratic civilization whose freedoms allow them to exist. It is an aristocratic culture by virtue of its interests and values, though one that welcomes all with a taste for "the infinite" regardless of their family name. It is, in a manner of speaking, the only kind of aristocracy that a democratic society permits, though also, just for that reason, an especially important safeguard against the leveling of humankind that Tocqueville bemoans.

Something that Tocqueville says in his discussion of religion underscores the importance of America's colleges and universities in this regard. "Give democratic peoples enlightenment and freedom," he writes,

> and leave them alone. With no trouble they will succeed in taking all the goods from this world that it can offer; they

will perfect each of the useful arts and render life more comfortable, easier, milder every day . . .

But while man takes pleasure in this honest and legitimate search for well-being, it is to be feared that he will finally lose the use of his most sublime faculties, and that by wishing to improve everything around him, he will finally degrade himself.

Religion is a counterforce. It stresses spiritual rather than material values. Tocqueville calls it "the most precious inheritance from aristocratic centuries." It therefore deserves special protection in a democratic society. "When any religion whatsoever has cast deep roots within a democracy, guard against shaking it . . ."

But the same can be said about institutions of higher learning. A few sentences after the ones I have just quoted, Tocqueville invokes Plato and Socrates as guardians of the realm of spiritual values, and earlier recommends the study of Greek and Latin because "the search for ideal beauty constantly shows itself" to an exceptional degree in these ancient languages. If religion has the power to instill in large groups of people a reverence for what rises above the everyday, and to direct their minds toward a higher order of values, the study of philosophy and the classics would appear, in Tocqueville's view, to have a similar effect on those smaller groups that are gathered on our campuses for the sake of the aristocratic life their sheltered space affords. The same reasons that he offers for the preservation of religion favor the protection of these academic enclaves as an antidote to "the ills that equality can produce."

Elsewhere, Tocqueville acknowledges "that in democratic centuries the interests of individuals as well as the security of the state requires that the education of the greatest number be scientific, commercial and industrial rather than literary." For them, the study of "belles-lettres" and "ancient literature" serves no useful purpose.

But "it is important that those whose nature or whose fortune destines them to cultivate letters or predisposes them to that taste" find schools where these subjects and others like them can be pursued in a leisurely and disinterested way by students and faculty who together form an aristocracy of the spirit, shielded from the extramural bustle of the democratic world outside their small reserves of connoisseurship and reflection. "To attain this result," Tocqueville concludes, "a few excellent universities would be worth more than a multitude of bad colleges where superfluous studies that are done badly prevent necessary studies from being done well."

For Tocqueville, the importance of preserving this elitist ideal is twofold. First, shielding a reverence for human greatness from the egalitarian hostility to it is valuable for its own sake. The cultivation of a refined appreciation for the finest works of thought and art is always difficult and rare. But in a democratic society it must also contend with the moral disapproval of all hierarchies of human perfection. Here it labors under a special stigma of disrepute. Just for that reason, it is especially important to protect the love of excellence, and the aspiration toward it, against the leveling pressure of democratic belief.

Second, an acquaintance with high standards is an antidote to the tyranny of majority opinion. It is not the only one, nor is it always effective. But it helps. An education in human excellence does not, as some suppose, encourage the slavish attitude of a copyist—a blind reverence for tradition. It teaches that every tradition worthy of the name is a living project with possibilities for growth. More important, it gives the person who acquires it an independent point of view from which to judge the partisan declarations of the moment; a wider frame of reference than the constantly shifting scenes of daily life allow; and a measure by which to weigh things other than the applause of the crowd. It promotes a spirit of independent-mindedness that provides some footing against the undertow of popular opinion. In this way our colleges and universities contribute to the health of democratic life by providing a counterweight to the herd mentality that is a breeding ground for despots. Their aristocratic culture is not, as one might think and many today believe, the enemy of democracy. So long as it remains true to itself, it is an antidote to the worst disease of democratic life. It sustains the few who long to spend their time in the company of "ideal beauty." But it also serves the many by strengthening the power to resist the flattery of tyrants that an education in excellence affords. This is the Tocquevillian ideal of college life on which Holmes could still confidently rely a half century after the publication of *Democracy in America*.

IV.

Since Holmes, others have warned against the dangers that a promiscuous egalitarianism poses to our colleges and universities and defended their privileges on aristocratic grounds. But their warnings have often been directed against these schools themselves. They accuse them of having lost the wisdom or nerve to protect the nobility of teaching and learning. The real problem, they say, is not the assault on our colleges and universities from without: It is the lack of confidence among educators in the aristocratic nature of their work. For Adams, it was obvious that the goal of a college education is the cultivation of superior souls possessed of the intellectual and moral virtues that define every natural aristocracy. Today the idea seems embarrassing even, perhaps especially, to those within the academy. Few teachers are prepared to defend it. But if that is true, then the gravest danger to our colleges and universities is now an intramural one. It reflects the disappearance within our most elite schools of the aristocratic self-assurance that Adams, Tocqueville, and Holmes all took for granted.

I will not attempt a survey of the many twentieth-century writers who expressed some version of this view. But there are two that are worth pausing to consider before passing on to ask why Tocqueville's account of American democracy, which on its face seems balanced and reasonable, has been abandoned in favor of an uncompromising egalitarianism of the kind he warned against, and why in recent years the assault on aristocratic ideals in higher education has become especially intense. One is H. L. Mencken. The other is Irving Babbitt. It is hard to imagine two men less alike in temperament and style—the first a hard-bitten, acidulous newspaperman with a contempt for nearly everyone, the other a genteel Harvard professor with a reverence for tradition. Yet their views on higher education are strikingly similar.

In 1919, Mencken published a long essay titled "The National Letters." It is his most comprehensive survey of the state of American literature. He judges it to be very poor indeed. Only a few escape Mencken's scathing indictment: Poe, Dreiser, Cabell, Whitman, and one or two others. For the rest, he says, our national literature is a wasteland of mediocrity, from the arid criticism of "the decaying caste of literary Brahmins" at Harvard and elsewhere, who pride themselves on their fidelity to standards of good taste, to the experimental writers "of Greenwich Village," who compete to show their boldness in ridiculing these standards themselves.

From top to bottom, Mencken says, our literature is boring and small-minded. It shows little of the adventurousness and depth of soul that distinguishes the best writers of Europe. For years we have been promised (in Whitman's words) "a great original literature" commensurate with our lofty political ideals. As of 1919, Mencken says, the promise remains almost entirely unfulfilled.

More interesting than his judgment, though, is Mencken's diagnosis of the cause of our failure to produce a literature of this kind. He attributes it to what he calls "a defect in the general culture of the country," one that is reflected "not only in the national literature" but "in all departments of thinking." The defect is "the lack of a civilized aristocracy, secure in its position, animated by an intelligent curiosity, skeptical of all facile generalizations, superior to the sentimentality of the mob, and delighting in the battle of ideas for its own sake."

But what does Mencken mean by "a civilized aristocracy"? The "word," he says, "despite the qualifying adjective, has got itself meanings" that he "by no means intend[s] to convey. Any mention of an aristocracy, to a public fed upon democratic fustian, is bound to bring up images of stockbrokers' wives lolling obscenely in opera boxes, or of haughty Englishmen slaughtering whole generations of grouse in an inordinate and incomprehensible manner, or of Junkers with tight waists elbowing American schoolmarms off the sidewalks of German beer towns, or of perfumed Italians coming over to work their abominable magic upon the daughters of breakfast-food and bathtub kings." But this is a "bugaboo aristocracy." It is as ridiculously shallow as the "mob mind" from which it springs. "What the inferior man and his wife see in the sinister revels" of this faux aristocracy is in truth only "a massive witness to their own higher rectitude—to their relative innocence of cigarette-smoking, poodle-coddling, child-farming and the more abstruse branches of adultery—in brief, to their firmer grasp upon the immutable axioms of Christian virtue, the one sound boast of the nether nine-tenths of humanity in every land under the cross."

Mencken's description of a "genuine aristocracy" is worth quoting in full:

> Its first and most salient character is its interior security, and the chief visible evidence of that security is the freedom that goes with it—not only freedom in act, the divine right of the aristocrat to do what he jolly well pleases, so long as he does not violate the primary guarantees and obligations of

his class, but also and more importantly freedom in thought, the liberty to try and err, the right to be his own man. It is the instinct of a true aristocracy, not to punish eccentricity by expulsion, but to throw a mantle of protection about it—to safeguard it from the suspicions and resentments of the lower orders. Those lower orders are inert, timid, inhospitable to ideas, hostile to changes, faithful to a few maudlin superstitions. All progress goes on on the higher levels. It is there that salient personalities, made secure by artificial immunities, may oscillate most widely from the normal track. It is within the entrenched fold, out of reach of the immemorial certainties of the mob, that extraordinary men of the lower orders may find their city of refuge, and breathe a clear air. This, indeed, is at once the hall-mark and the justification of an aristocracy—that it is beyond responsibility to the general masses of men, and hence superior to both their degraded longings and their no less degraded aversions. It is nothing if it is not autonomous, curious, venturesome, courageous, and everything if it is. It is the custodian of the qualities that make for change and experiment; it is the class that organizes danger to the service of the race; it pays for its high prerogatives by standing in the forefront of the fray.

Mencken's words are sharper than Tocqueville's or Holmes's. But they paint a recognizably similar picture.

For Mencken too real aristocracy is a spiritual condition. It is defined by an inner disposition. The true aristocrat possesses the self-confidence to withstand both the threats and blandishments of majority opinion. He treats ideas with a combination of seriousness and playfulness that is foreign to those who lack the security to judge things for themselves.

In this respect, his outlook is profoundly different from that of the plutocrat. Our American plutocracy "is badly educated, it is stupid, it is full of low-caste superstitions and indignations, it is without decent traditions or informing vision; above all, it is extraordinarily lacking in the most elemental independence and courage." Nor should one think that a true aristocracy is closed off to "extraordinary men of the lower orders." For them, the challenge of entry is greater. But if they succeed they leave behind the fears and superstitions of "the vast mass of undifferentiated human blanks" from whose ranks they emerge, and "breathe" the same "clear air" as the more fortunate ones whose path is eased by wealth, connections, and the like.

The freedom and courage they enjoy—"the capacity for independent thinking, for difficult problems, for what Nietzsche calls the joys of the labyrinth"—do not come naturally. Nor are they the automatic corollaries of money and privilege. They must be won by work and discipline. Their enjoyment depends, moreover, on what Mencken calls the "artificial immunities" that shield the few who love "the battle of ideas for its own sake" from the "society of half-wits" around them. These immunities create an "entrenched fold" whose protections allow for a playful experimentation with ideas that is as remote from the superstitions of the mob as it is from the pretensions of the plutocracy that rigidly prescribe what its members are permitted to think.

This is the only freedom, and the only nobility, worthy of the name. But it runs against the grain of our democracy, which, having obliterated the old aristocracy, "has left only a vacuum in its place; in a century and a half, it has failed either to lift up the mob to intellectual autonomy and dignity or to purge the plutocracy of its inherent stupidity and swinishness. . . . The whole drift of our law," Mencken writes, in words that echo Tocqueville's, "is toward the absolute prohibition of all ideas that diverge in the slightest from the accepted platitudes, and behind that drift of law there is a far more potent force of growing custom, and under that custom there is a national philosophy which erects conformity into the noblest of virtues and the free functioning of personality into a capital crime against society." The few institutions whose "artificial immunities" do permit a "genuine aristocracy" to flourish must therefore be protected with special vigilance against the democratic passion for conformity and the mob's hostility to every expression of genuine nobility in matters of the spirit.

How do our colleges and universities fare in this regard? Not well, in Mencken's view.

When "this small brotherhood of the superior is carefully examined," what "reveals itself . . . is a gigantic disappointment." True, Mencken says, the professoriate shows "all the marks of a caste of learned and sagacious men." But their learning is brittle and empty. It lacks "curiosity" and "courage." It is characterized by "pretentiousness" and a ponderous sense of dignity. The campus "*intelligentsia*" have "all the qualities of an aristocracy save the capital qualities that arise out of a feeling of security, of complete independence, of absolute immunity to onslaught from above and below. In brief, the old bogusness hangs about them, as about the fashionable aristocrats of the society columns."

The lack of adventurousness in intellectual matters that characterizes life "under the campus pump" is explained in part, Mencken suggests, by the long shadow of New England Puritanism and "the old democratic veneration for mere schooling" that the Puritans encouraged. But whatever the cause, the typical American professor, however great his learning, is today "the most prudent and skittish of all men . . . [H]e yields to the prevailing correctness of thought in all departments . . . and is, in fact, the chief exponent among us of the democratic doctrine that heresy is not only a mistake, but also a crime." Instead of using their freedom and privilege to think and speak with "the eager curiosity, the educated skepticism and the hospitality to ideas of a true aristocracy," most professors are "the loudest spokesmen of [the] worst imbecilities" of "the mob run wild." They are the mouthpieces of convention, devoted to the justification and reinforcement of what Mencken calls "correctness."

There are exceptions, of course, but Mencken insists that in general campus life is as he describes it. He cites as an example the shameful behavior of the professoriate during "the late lamentable war" (World War I). "What was the reaction of our learned men to the challenge of organized hysteria, mob fear, incitement to excess, downright insanity? . . . They fed it with bogus history, bogus philosophy, bogus idealism, bogus heroics," all in the name of "correctness." The energy with which college and university professors today rush to support the excesses of what we still call by the same name, suggests that things have not changed much since Mencken wrote a century ago.

It is disappointing if the faculty who live and work within the protected enclaves of higher education fail to make good use of the "artificial immunities" they enjoy. That is the loss of an opportunity. But it is a "*gigantic* disappointment" if they put their freedom to use in the service of correctness and convention, for in that case they become an active instrument for the promotion of the democratic status quo, which always reduces ideas to the mediocrity of public opinion. They cease to be a counterweight against the mob mind and became an accelerant instead. In Mencken's view, this amounts to a kind of betrayal, which he inveighs against with what, even for him, is unusual passion because, as he says, "all my instincts are on the side of the professors."

This brings me to Irving Babbitt.

Babbitt was a well-known professor of literature at Harvard in the early years of the twentieth century. Though not nearly as famous as Mencken, he had considerable influence as the champion (with Paul Elmer More of Princeton) of what was dubbed the "New

Humanism." Mencken writes disparagingly of Babbitt as a member of that "decaying caste of literary Brahmins" whose work amounts to little more than a "solemn, highly judicial, coroner's inquest" kind of criticism, without "intellectual audacity" or "aesthetic passion." "The thing is correctly done;" Mencken says, "it is never crude or gross; there is in it a faint perfume of college-town society. But when this highly refined and attenuated manner is allowed for what remains is next to nothing." Yet, though the difference between the two in style and self-presentation is about as wide as any in American letters, Babbitt's diagnosis of the failures of higher education is not far off from Mencken's.

In *Literature and the American College*, Babbitt bemoans the intrusion of "the democratic spirit" into collegiate life. At its core, he says, a college exists for the sake of promoting a "humanistic" culture. Humanism is to be distinguished from "humanitarianism." The latter is philanthropic. Its watchword is "service." It is concerned with the welfare of others—indeed, of humanity as a whole. In the eyes of the humanitarian, every man and woman on earth is a possible object of sympathy. In this respect, his attitude is perfectly undiscriminating. And while the humanitarian is motivated by certain abstract ideas—the most important being his unwavering belief in the equality of all human beings—his principal aim is the cultivation not of ideas but feelings, or what Babbitt calls "impressions." These constitute a bond of fellow feeling with others. They represent a universal common denominator, since everyone is capable of sharing them, of identifying with the suffering of others and feeling sympathy for them, whatever his level of intellectual and cultural sophistication. In this sense, humanitarianism is essentially democratic. It is a philosophy that fits well with the egalitarian ethos of American culture in general.

Humanism is something different. The humanist is concerned, first and most importantly, with the development of his own powers of perception and understanding. He is not indifferent to the suffering of others but believes that to judge the world's pain in a discerning way, and act with wisdom and prudence, he must strengthen his capacities for observation, selection, and evaluation. This is not something that comes naturally, like the humanitarian feeling of sympathy. It is the product of a long training in what Babbitt calls the "high and objective standards of human excellence."

This training is as aristocratic as the humanitarian's program of service is democratic. That is so for two reasons: first, because these standards themselves imply the recognition of a rank order of achievement; and second, because only a few have the time, talent, and commitment to master them properly. In Babbitt's view, whatever else a college does, it ought to nurture the aristocratic habits of humanistic study. These have their roots in the ancient and medieval worlds, and owe much to the Renaissance too, but today must be cultivated under irrevocably "modern" conditions, by which he means both the loss of a shared religious faith and the dominance of "the principle of equality" in whose shadow even the possibility of "a truly human hierarchy and scale of values" can no longer be taken for granted.

Like Mencken, Babbitt believes that our colleges need to preserve "the aristocratic principle" against the onslaught of democratic life. They must be the conservators of the natural aristocracy from which the leaders of our democracy are drawn, for the reasons John Adams maintains. Moreover, like both Mencken and Adams, Babbitt goes to great lengths to distinguish an aristocracy of this sort from the fake kind that is often confused with it. "We want no American equivalents," he says, "for the types that Thackeray has catalogued in his chapters on university snobs. . . . [A] snob may be defined as a man who, in his estimate of things, is drawn away from their true and intrinsic worth and dazzled by outer advantages of wealth, or power, or station." Babbitt concedes that "in a few of our Eastern colleges the snobbishness of family exists, but not to a dangerous degree." He may have underestimated the extent of it. But the important thing is that in his view, even a little bit is bad. A college "should be democratic in the sense that it should get rid of all distinctions of family and rank." Admission ought to be based on talent and commitment alone. Money skews the process, of course. But that too is bad and should be repaired to the extent it can, though the practical difficulties are immense.

What must never be done, though, is to corrupt the discipline of college life itself by adopting "the type of sentimental humanitarianism in [which] the delicate balance between sympathy and judgment has been lost"; that "is ready to lower the standard of an institution rather than inflict an apparent hardship on an individual"; and that views the college as "a means not so much for the thorough training of the few as of uplift for the many." In short, "the democratic contention that everybody should have a chance is excellent provided it means that everybody is to have a chance to live up to high standards." This is Babbitt's formula for reconciling the legitimate claims of democratic egalitarianism with the aristocratic premises of humanistic education. It expresses, in only slightly different words, the Tocquevillian adjustment between these different values. Behind it lies the thought, which Tocqueville shared, that the long-term well-being of American democracy depends on the survival within it of a few pockets of aristocratic culture, whose preservation is, or at least ought to be, the aim of college life.

Like Tocqueville, Babbitt believed that the preservation of this culture is important in its own right. He also insisted that it is essential to the development of a spirit of intellectual self-reliance, which in his view is bolstered by an appreciative acquaintance with high standards. And he further believed, as John Adams had a century and a half before, that the continued existence of a responsible leadership class in society at large depends on the presence in it of some who have received a humane education of this kind—a theme he develops at length in his 1924 book, *Democracy and Leadership*.

But as to whether the American college is still capable of doing a good job in this regard, Babbitt seems more than a little doubtful. Holmes's caution against the "effervescence of democratic negation" has become in Babbitt's case a mood of resignation in the face of forces too large to resist. The rise of the university, with its emphasis on specialized knowledge; the adoption, at the undergraduate level, of the elective system, which democratizes the students' selection of courses; the increasing emphasis on service as the goal of education—these and other developments, which have only intensified in the century since, together give Babbitt's defense of humanism an old-fashioned look and infect it with a note of despair. Even Babbitt himself seems at times to know his day is done. What had seemed obvious to Adams, Tocqueville, and Holmes is clear to Babbitt as well. But all his writings on college life are haunted by a question that none of them needed to ask. Why has the order of excellence in human works and human beings, which is plain to anyone who takes care to look, become so doubtful that even to invoke it today is not only a mistake but a crime?

V.

The answer is complex.

The rise of the university, with its division into specialized disciplines and emphasis on the accumulation of ever more recondite knowledge; the demise of a structured curriculum and loss of confidence in anything like a required canon of great works hallowed by tradition; the multiplication in the number and variety of institutions of higher learning; the increasing diversity of their students, who come with the most varied preparations and expectations; and the perennial suspicion that our best colleges and universities are bastions of undeserved privilege, where the sons and daughters of the well-to-do idle away their early adulthood while the children of less fortunate families struggle up the ladder toward success—all these have played a role in making Babbitt's idea of college as a place and time for the cultivation of an aristocratic reverence for standards seem hopelessly out-of-date if not morally blighted.

There is another factor, though, that is even more important. It is the rise of what I shall call the vocational ideal.

By "vocational ideal" I mean the belief that the principal arena of human fulfillment is that of work, as distinct from everything we do outside it in our leisure time. This belief is more than a concession to reality. It is a moral ideal. It assigns special worth to one domain of effort and achievement. It establishes a particularly close connection between what we do for a living and our sense of purposefulness in life.

The vocational ideal is at odds with the aristocratic belief that the proper use of leisure is the highest and most rewarding of all human activities. But it challenges the latter view at an even deeper level. It shifts our judgments about the relative status of human beings from who they *are*—from their character and competence in the art of living—to what they *do*—to the jobs they perform and the position they occupy in the economic division of labor. In this way, it gives a powerful boost to the democratic axiom that all men and women are essentially equal and entitled to the same degree of respect. Today our colleges and universities are in thrall to the vocational ideal. This compromises their ability to serve as a counterweight to the egalitarian morality of our democratic culture and puts them in service to this morality instead.

In a broad sense, of course, the vocational ideal has been a norm in American higher education from the start. Our colleges have never been protected islands of aestheticism and refined speculation, nurturing a high-minded nobility of spirit in the midst of an aggressively democratic society. They have sought less to create a sheltered space for noble pursuits than to train their students for the professional roles demanded by society at large—to be ministers, teachers, and lawyers, and eventually to perform many other useful functions as well. In this sense, the education they provide has always been instrumental. It has always been geared toward preparing their students for those extramural tasks on which the well-being of the larger community depends.

Still, even in this proto-vocational milieu, Harvard and the other antebellum colleges that followed its lead valued the development of a student's whole character over the acquisition of particular skills. So far as the classic professions of the law, the ministry, and teaching were concerned, the line between character and skill was indistinct. In this sense, the old-time college remained a zone of aristocratic culture and taste. By the time Babbitt offered his doleful diagnosis, the zone had sharply decreased. Today it has all but vanished. What we have instead are colleges and universities, nearly without number, that differ in almost every conceivable way except their shared commitment to a vocational ideal that sees the value of higher education in terms of the training it provides for success in the pursuit of a socially valued and remunerative job—of what we call a "career."

Careers come in countless different forms. The educational programs that prepare students for them are as diverse as the careers themselves. But even at the most elite schools, which pride themselves on their detachment from mere vocational concerns, the idea that one is going to college in order to prepare for a job today eclipses every other. Few students and their families think of higher education in any other terms or feel they can justify its expense except on vocational grounds. The presidents of liberal arts colleges who talk endlessly about the value of "critical thinking" only reinforce this attitude, for as soon as one asks them what the value of such thinking *is*, they reply that it is valuable because it is useful for *all sorts* of occupations. This way of thinking and speaking about the good of higher education is now so pervasive, and seems so obviously true, that Babbitt's idea of the college as a protected holdover from the age of aristocracy, devoted to the conservation and admiration of what is rare and fine among human works and human beings, looks like an insect preserved in amber.

The triumph of the vocational ideal is explained in part by the irresistible movement toward a knowledge-based economy. More and more of the adequately paying and humanly rewarding jobs in our economy demand higher levels of skill. These in turn require longer and more rigorous training. Once upon a time, a college education was not a prerequisite for meaningful and remunerative employment. There are still some jobs that pay well and provide fulfillment for which an education beyond high school is not needed. But their number is shrinking, and as it does, the pressure on our colleges and universities to provide the advanced training that any "good" job requires grows every year. No school is exempt from it, whatever its endowment or national ranking.

To be sure, the best schools confer a special vocational advantage on their graduates on account of the superior training they offer and, more importantly, because of their reputation. This creates a problem of distribution. The number of top schools is not growing. But as the degrees they confer become more valuable as a ticket to high-end employment, the number of those competing for admission increases. In the ever-fiercer competition for a spot in the entering class at any of our elite colleges and universities, applicants from well-to-do families enjoy a strong advantage. They have received a superior secondary school education; traveled abroad; sat through test-prep courses; and grown up in homes with better-educated adults. The advantage this gives them tends to reinforce the privilege they already possess and enables them to transmit it to their children in turn. The result is a self-perpetuating socioeconomic elite.

This has always been a problem. But in our knowledge-based economy, where an advanced education is a prerequisite for high-paying, high-status employment, the problem is more acute than it has ever been before. Many have pled—reasonably, I think—for greater equality of opportunity in the college admissions process. Their proposals are anti-elitist in the sense that they seek to break up the monopoly of privilege that certain applicants enjoy. They resemble the demands a half century ago for a more meritocratic system based on the SAT and the admission of students without regard to their financial need, at the few schools that could afford it.

Still, no one thinks that a more egalitarian admissions process means that students, once admitted, should not be ranked on the basis of their academic performance. By the time they graduate, some students stand at the top of their class, others at the bottom. They form a rank order of achievement that even grade inflation cannot hide. This is especially obvious in the so-called STEM fields but is true in other areas as well, including the humanities, where the criteria of judgment are more flexible. Even those who are most appalled by the role that privilege plays in the admissions process never suggest that grades and class rankings be abolished. Quite the reverse: the greater equality of opportunity they favor is *for the sake* of having a fair chance to show that one is really and truly *unequal* to other, less gifted and industrious students.

But rankings of this kind are untroubling, because they reflect a notion of excellence that is aligned with the democratic egalitarianism of our culture as a whole. To understand why, we need to take account of two things. The first is the ambiguous importance the vocational ideal attaches to work, which it simultaneously elevates and depreciates. The second is the distinction on which this ambiguity rests. This is the distinction between persons and skills. A person *has* skills but is not reducible to them. There is always more to a person than the skills he or she possesses. Ranking people on the basis of their skills is therefore not equivalent to ranking them as such. It is the former sort of ranking that prevails almost exclusively in our colleges and universities today. It gives the hierarchies they acknowledge a democratic cast and distinguishes them in a fundamental way from the aristocratic ranking of whole persons that Adams, Tocqueville, Holmes, Mencken, and Babbitt all accepted.

Nearly all of us must work for a living. Even the very rich often work, because that is how we define our place in society. When we meet a stranger, the first or second question we generally ask is "What kind of work do you do?" The best jobs not only pay well; they carry a high status too. They demand special skills and contribute to the welfare of others in a visible way. Lawyers and doctors are a classic example. But airline pilots, rock stars, and computer programmers fit the profile too.

This explains why getting a good job is worth years of preparation. But a job is only a way of making a living, not living itself. The principal reason that many people work is to be able to do the other things that matter to them most—to pay the bills, care for their kids, and take a vacation now and then. The less prestigious a job, the clearer this is. But even in the higher reaches of the world of work, a similar attitude often prevails. Lawyers and doctors worry about becoming workaholics and burning out before they can do or discover what really matters to them. Investment bankers dream of retiring at forty to pursue some project of lasting value.

On the one hand, therefore, we instinctively place people in a hierarchy of honor or esteem depending on what they do for a living. On the other, we tend to adopt what might be called an *instrumental* view of work. We believe that even the most prestigious and well-paying jobs are good, in part at least because they provide the means to other ends outside the sphere of employment. These are as various as the needs and interests of those who pursue them. One person works to buy rare wines; another to afford the time to sing in his church choir; a third to send her children to college.

Of course, some people find intrinsic satisfaction in their work. I assume that many artists, scientists, human rights lawyers, college professors, and newspaper columnists do, among others. For them, the line between work and the rest of life is indistinct. Even those for whom the line is sharper often take pleasure in a job well done. Only in the least skilled and most repetitive jobs is there likely to be little or no pleasure of this kind.

Still, the instrumental view of work is widely shared, to varying degrees, up and down the status order. For most people, the intrinsic satisfactions of work are incomplete. They almost always assign some value, and often a much higher one, to other things in the overall scheme of their lives. But this way of thinking takes the edge off the hierarchical judgments we make when we rank people according to the prestige of their jobs and how much they pay. We compulsively use work as a badge of distinction. Yet, insofar as we view it as a means to an end, it cannot be a full or accurate measure of anyone's worth. What people *do* for a living cannot be all, or even the most important part, of who they *are* as human beings.

This depends to an important degree on what they choose to do outside of work with the resources it affords them. Yet, here we are inclined to adopt the relaxed view that what people find worthwhile is so just because they do. We defer to their own judgments about what is satisfying and important. Who is to say that devoting a thousand hours to constructing a replica of the Taj Mahal is less important than spending the same time studying Italian or building homes for Habitat for Humanity? We feel little awkwardness ranking the jobs that people do by their difficulty, prestige, and social product. But when it comes to ranking the ways they choose to spend their time after hours, we balk. This looks more like ranking people themselves. It feels undemocratic, and we resist it for that reason. By confining our judgments of rank to a limited sphere of life, and demoting its importance relative to what takes place outside it, the instrumental view of work allows us to keep our egalitarian instincts intact.

What makes this view so plausible is the distinction between persons and skills.

This is a distinction we mostly all accept. People have skills but are not defined by them. Their worth as human beings is not a function of their expertise, no matter how long it took to acquire or useful it may be. Their worth depends on their humanity. This is the substrate to which a person's skills are attached. And while skills are obviously unequal, and may be ranked in various ways, many would insist that the humanity of one person cannot be higher or lower, better or worse, more or less advanced, than that of any other.

Some succeed and others fail in any program of vocational training, just as they do in the work for which it prepares them. But on the conventional view, this has no bearing on their humanity, whose equality is unaffected by distinctions of this sort. That is why the rise of the vocational ideal to a central place in higher education, despite its relentless ranking of student achievement, fits so easily with the democratic belief that all men and women are created equal. But it is also why this same ideal conflicts sharply with the aristocratic view of college life.

The aristocrat insists there is an art to being human; that this art is not a skill yet can be taught; and that those who succeed in acquiring it do better not in some particular endeavor but at the all-embracing work of being human. The vocational ideal at once elevates work to a position of supreme importance and degrades it to a mere occupation, distinguishable from the perfectly equal humanity of those who either succeed or fail in acquiring the skills demanded for a given task. It is the most powerful enemy of aristocratic belief that American higher education has ever known.

Adams's natural aristocrat is a man of superior virtue; Tocqueville's a person of cultivation and taste; Holmes's one who knows the "subtiler" joys of philosophy and art; Babbitt's a man who judges things by the "high and objective standards of human excellence"; and Mencken's an "autonomous, courageous, venturesome" and "curious" soul who pretty much thinks and does as it pleases. These are different formulations. They put the emphasis at different points, although there are common elements that connect them: the importance of studying the great works of the past; the belief that education is a moral enterprise; and, above all, the value of independent-mindedness, of freedom from what Tocqueville calls "the tyranny of the majority." But the most important feature of all these diverse formulations is their shared assumption that a truly excellent person is distinguished from inferior ones not in some delimited way but by the entirety of his or her character.

Character is difficult to define but hardly unintelligible. We all judge people on the basis not only of their acts but their characters as well. We praise or condemn them according to their most settled dispositions: their tendency to lean in one direction or another, to be generous or selfish, courageous or weak, open-minded or dogmatic. A person's character reflects those things that he or she cares about in the steadiest way—those elementary commitments that provide the general background for more specific judgments and choices.

To believe, first, that there is such a thing as character; that a person's character can be better or worse; that character is shaped by education; and that one of the goals of higher education is to instill in the student a love of those things for which a person of fine character should care—that is the essence of the aristocratic view of college life. It is distinguished by the confident belief that men and women can be ranked according to their success in the general work of being human. The vocational ideal attacks this belief like a corrosive acid.

It asserts that the main if not exclusive end of a college education is the acquisition of a set of skills that prepare one for productive work. It distinguishes sharply between the skills a person possesses and the human being he or she is. And while it relies upon the most rigorous ranking of students so far as their skills are concerned, it encourages an abstention from judgments of better and worse regarding their humanity. It is fiercely committed to excellence, but only in the restricted sphere of skills and jobs. Where the question is not "What do I need to learn to be a successful lawyer or computer scientist?" but "What makes a whole life honorable and fulfilling?" the vocational ideal not only falls silent; it delegates the question to each individual to answer for him- or herself, and reinforces the democratic belief that there is no common, objective, public basis for measuring the quality of the answers they give.

This brings the work of our colleges and universities into line with our democratic culture as a whole. It converts the academy from an enclave of aristocratic sensibility into something fundamentally egalitarian, which, despite the selectivity of the process by which one gains admission to it, is no longer an elitist preserve, existing in a fruitful tension, as Tocqueville supposed, with the habits of democratic life but wholly conformable to them instead.

The humanities are no exception.

I often hear the humanities touted for their vocational value. The study of literature, history, or philosophy is said to make one a better reader and writer. These anxious admonitions may be unnecessary. It is not at all clear that students in the humanities do less well in the job market than their classmates who have majored in STEM fields. But there is a special reason why teachers of the humanities feel particular pressure to justify their disciplines on vocational grounds. It is that these fields still retain, albeit only with an uneasy conscience, their link to the older system of aristocratic values that Tocqueville describes.

It is not extraordinary, even today, to hear the humanities praised for their intrinsic value, in terms similar to those that Holmes used in his speech to the Harvard Law School Association. Now and then a teacher or dean will say that those who study the humanities acquire a liberating knowledge of past treasures; gain a better sense of what is valuable and lasting in the world of human things; develop refined powers of enjoyment; and learn the use of leisure, which is more important than training for a job. But thoughts of this kind are most often shared in private, among those who are already convinced of their truth. When they are expressed in public, it is generally with a blush.

That is because they are antidemocratic. They hark back to an older and discredited way of thinking about higher education. They sound in an aristocratic register that today one is ashamed to acknowledge, let alone proclaim. However strongly one shares these beliefs, the push to put the humanities on a vocational footing is especially strong because of the need to distance them from an inheritance that is awkward and embarrassing when viewed in a democratic light.

This is why, as we shall see, the new wave of democratic negations that has swept over our colleges and universities in recent years has had the most immediate and damaging effect on the humanities. The egalitarians leading the charge understand instinctively that the humanities are an important object of attack because there still lingers about them the undemocratic scent of the worldview from which they emerged only a few decades ago. The movement for diversity, as this had come to be understood; the reinterpretation of campus speech as a means of furthering inclusion rather than as a medium for the discriminating pursuit of truth; and the campaign to rewrite the past so that it better conforms to our enlightened democratic beliefs—these have all struck their hardest blows in the humanities. One might even call the struggle over them a fight for the soul of the humanities, though this is only a localized and particularly intense battle in the larger war between Tocqueville's view of higher education and the democratic-egalitarian view that has almost entirely displaced it, supported by the growing authority of the vocational ideal.

But before we examine these three movements in detail, there is one last question to consider. Those who see college life as an aristocratic island in a democratic sea have been on the defensive for a very long time. From the perspective of those, like myself, who want to save as much of higher education as possible from the "effervescence of democratic negation," the triumph of the vocational ideal has made matters considerably worse. Yet just in the last few years, the tide of egalitarianism on America's campuses has reached unprecedented heights. The question is why. What explains this efflorescence of democratic passion? Once again, Tocqueville is our guide.

VI.

Tocqueville observes that there are three races in America—"white," "Negro," and "Indian." The country's otherwise expansive democracy is limited to the first.

Striking inequalities of course exist among whites too. But, as Tocqueville notes, these are fluid to a degree that distinctions between the races are not. The poorest white man may become a rich one and vice versa, or grow up in obscurity and be elected president. The opportunities of blacks and Native Americans are by contrast permanently circumscribed by their race. There are only certain things they may do, certain places they may live, and certain social relations into which they may enter with whites.

So long as every white man has an opportunity to make the most of his talents, and to rise as far as he can, it is possible to entertain the belief that all white men are equal, even if this is only an aspiration belied by the social and economic realities. The same is not true of blacks and Native Americans. The impermeable barriers that race puts in their way contradict the assumption of universal equality on which American democracy is based. They confine it within limits that cannot be reconciled with the universality of the assumption itself.

For the special sort of hierarchy that exists among the races, a special word is needed. "Class" is too weak because it also applies to the grades of wealth and power that distinguish some whites from others. The word that has conventionally been used is "caste." It captures three distinctive features of the racial wall that separates whites from blacks and Native Americans.

The first is its inflexibility and hereditability. The second is its totality. One white man may have less wealth than another, but in the polling booth each gets an equal vote. By contrast, racial distinctions are pervasive. Every human relation, public or private, is shaped by an expectation of deference and subordination. The third, which is closely related, is the implied judgment that blacks and Native Americans are inferior to whites not in some particular respect but globally, comprehensively, as beings whose very nature is degraded by comparison with theirs.

The existence of a caste order among the races poses a unique threat to the integrity of American egalitarianism. But Tocqueville could see no obvious solution. The Indians, he thought, would eventually be exterminated or absorbed into the white world. In their case, the problem would simply disappear. By contrast, the condition of blacks presents what Tocqueville viewed as an insoluble dilemma. At the time of his visit to America, the overwhelming majority of blacks were held in slavery. He could not conceive their being freed without a monumental struggle—in the South, an all-out war between the races. Even if they were freed, he believed, the racial barrier between whites and blacks would remain insurmountably high. Tocqueville noted that in the North, as blacks achieved legal equality, prejudice against them hardened. This was in 1831, in Andrew Jackson's first term. The history of the next fifty years proved him right, though the struggle he predicted took a different course than the one that he imagined.

The problem of caste remains an "American dilemma" today. The Native Americans have not been eliminated but merely forgotten. The injustices done to them are staggering. But their comparatively small numbers; the concentration of many in rural reservations, where they fall outside the public light; and the historically higher rate of intermarriage between whites and Native Americans than between whites and blacks have all contributed to making the problem of caste less visible in the case of Native Americans.

The situation of black Americans is different.

The Civil War freed those held in slavery. But an incomplete Reconstruction left the former slaves without economic or political power. In the words of W. E. B. Du Bois, "The slave went free; stood a brief moment in the sun; then moved back again toward slavery." A regime of legal apartheid reinforced caste relations between whites and blacks in ways unknown even in the age of slavery. A long fight for basic civil rights followed, culminating in *Brown v. Board of Education*, and a decade later the Civil Rights and Voting Rights Acts of the Johnson administration.

But this Second Reconstruction fizzled too. Blacks continued to be concentrated in inner city ghettoes. They still enjoyed dramatically fewer economic and educational opportunities than their white counterparts, even those whose economic status was roughly the same. Race remained, and remains to this day, a special barrier to advancement and success, independent of class.

It is true that things are better; the situation is improving; real advances have been made. Americans twice elected an African American to be their president. But caste is not a thing of the past, on which we can look back from a position beyond or outside it.

The belief that we need to attack it as an evil separate from the mere fact of inequality is expressed in the law by what some call the principle of "anti-subordination." This demands the elimination of all officially sanctioned practices that imply contempt for the worthiness or dignity of those belonging to a particular group. *Brown v. Board of Education* rested on an acceptance of the anti-subordination principle. So does the Black Lives Matter movement. At its heart, the movement is an attack on caste. Those who support it maintain, with justification in some cases, that none of the civil rights reforms of the past seventy-five years have succeeded in rooting race prejudice out of American life, where the influence of caste can still be felt, if less openly and pervasively than in Tocqueville's day. Among other things, they point to the renewed brazenness with which white supremacists now feel free to express their views, with the implicit permission of an ill-willed and ignorant president. They see this as a symptom of the disease that Tocqueville diagnosed and insist that we have not rid ourselves of it yet. At times, perhaps, they underestimate the progress we have made. But their basic point is sound. So far as race relations are concerned, we still have a long way to go in policing, housing, jobs, and the criminal justice system.

Beginning in the 1960s, a new set of programs was invented to attack the problem of caste at a more fundamental level. These included busing, redistricting, and affirmative action. Their premise was that formal legal equality is not enough to uproot the system of caste. Affirmative action in particular had a large effect on our colleges and universities. Its defenders saw it as an important weapon in the fight to implement the anti-subordination principle in the world of higher education.

Affirmative action was directed most immediately at the admissions process. But the egalitarian impulse that lay behind it spilled over into the internal culture of our colleges and universities. It morphed into an intensifying attack on everything that looks remotely aristocratic in their practices and values, including the belief that college is a training ground for human excellence and not just the preparation for a job. The vocational ideal had already put the aristocratic conception of higher education on the run. The exuberant egalitarianism of a social and political movement that sought to rid America, once and for all, of the scourge of caste, under the banner of the anti-subordination principle, dealt this conception a near-fatal blow when it became a dominant force in the academy.

Our elite schools have long been viewed as places of privilege and exclusion. The demand for a fairer system of admissions is hardly new. But the current assault on every vestige of the aristocratic idea of distinction in the pursuit of human excellence, as opposed to mere competence or skill, has a novelty and ferocity that is best explained, I think, by the extension of the anti-subordination principle to the inner life of the academy.

The idea of an order based on character, wisdom, and excellence, as distinct from expertise, shares at least one of the features of a caste system. It is not hereditary, of course, nor are those lower down exploited and abused for the sake of those above them—to secure their comfort and pride. But the idea of a natural aristocracy does assume that some human beings are more fully developed than others in an overall sense—that they have more of what it takes to live a rich and satisfying life, in which the basic human powers of observation, analysis, appreciation, articulation, sympathy, and self-understanding are engaged and expressed to an exceptionally high degree. In this respect, though this one alone, the idea of such an aristocracy touches the poisonous version of caste that makes the problem of race in America so distinctive and difficult.

In the eyes of some, this is enough to condemn it. From their point of view, the defense of aristocratic values in higher education can never be anything but a thinly veiled expression of white supremacy. They are suspicious of anything that appears to offend the anti-subordination principle in any form whatever. The moral power of the principle, its connection to the democratic ideal of equality and above all its value as a weapon in the fight against a subtle, pervasive, and intransigent culture of racism (which formal legal equality alone has been unable to cure), makes it more difficult to distinguish legitimate forms of elitism from illegitimate ones. It puts all caste-like rankings under a moral cloud.

Every conception of the college as an aristocratic counterweight to the pathologies of democratic life rests on elitist premises. It is therefore vulnerable to the demand that all our educational ideals be refashioned to conform to the anti-subordination principle. This gives the perennial mistrust of snobs a moral heft. It accelerates the advance of the vocational ideal whose technocratic rankings are compatible with the principle. And it puts those who resist the movement to remake the activity of teaching and learning in its higher reaches along strictly democratic lines, in a more cramped and defensive position than they have ever been in in the history of the American college.

The debate at Yale over the use of the title "master" is a case in point.

The students who complained about the use of the title said it reminded them of masters and slaves. It made them feel they were still living on a plantation. No explanation of the meaning of the title in an academic setting proved sufficient to meet their objection. That is because it was clothed with the moral prestige of the anti-subordination principle. The immense power this principle possesses in other settings flowed with an irresistible hydraulic force into the debate over whether the academic hierarchy of masters and students—with its faintly aristocratic overtones—should fall to this principle too. Once the question was posed, the answer was inevitable.

We are, perhaps, at the beginning of a Third Reconstruction in America. The Black Lives Matter movement, the fierce debate over Confederate monuments, the controversy over whether professional athletes should "take a knee" when the national anthem is played—all reflect a renewed preoccupation with race. If, more than sixty years after *Brown*, race remains the problem it is, how can we not assume that some whites, perhaps many, are still prejudiced against blacks? That they still regard them as their inferiors not in wealth or political power alone but in character, nature, or virtue? This is the essence of race prejudice. It is the foundation of the caste order that Tocqueville describes.

But the academic distinction between "master" and "student" represents a hierarchy of a very different kind. It is one that is open to all who wish to compete for a position of superiority within it. Those at the bottom are able to move up, and generally do. Most important, it is a hierarchy based on accomplishment, not color. Accomplishment is measured partly by skills in the narrow sense defined above. But in an elite college or university it is—or at least once was—also measured by advancement in the all-inclusive work of living as fully and well as one can. In the current political environment, however, *any* ranking that assumes some to be more highly developed than others *as human beings* is subject to intense moral suspicion. This assumption is so hateful where race is concerned that many thoughtful men and women find it difficult to accept an academic ideal that shares the caste-like property of ranking individuals according to the progress they have made toward the broad goal of human flourishing, as distinct from their achievements in limited vocational terms.

This is unfortunate. It reflects a confusion of political and academic values. When these are blurred or merged, it becomes impossible to maintain the Tocquevillian balance. In the case of race, caste thinking is an acid that destroys the soul of our democracy. Tocqueville saw this with prescient clarity. But he also recognized that our democracy tends to reduce everything exceptional and fine to a plain of mediocrity, and to promote a culture of intellectual conformism. To combat this, he said, aristocratic habits of mind, with their attunement to excellence and celebration of rank and distinction, must be preserved wherever they can, in our colleges and universities especially.

There is no reason I can see why one cannot be a democrat beyond the walls of the academy and an aristocrat within them. That in any case is what I am. A simple-minded conflation of the two, so blinded by the urgency of the campaign to rid America of race hatred that it cannot see that nobility and excellence still have a proper place in our most distinguished institutions of higher education, makes it impossible to maintain the balanced set of judgments that Tocqueville offers.

This requires that one acknowledge the excellence of those John Adams took to be, by temperament and training, the most outstanding human beings. Yes, it is impossible to separate what is owing to an individual's gifts and what to the circumstances into which he or she is born. And yes, there is an incurable injustice, if one is inclined to see it as such, in the disparity of gifts that are parceled out in what the philosopher John Rawls calls the "natural lottery" of birth. But the fact remains that certain human beings excel not merely in vocational terms but in the "enjoyment," as Thorstein Veblen put it, "of the true, the beautiful, and the good," the "salient feature" of which is "*otium cum dignitate* [leisure with honor]." This remains true even after an appropriate discount has been made for the inequities of endowment and upbringing. That was Adams's view and Thomas Jefferson's too.

Like Adams, Jefferson believed that leisure with honor is one of the supreme goods of human life. He thought that everyone should be given a realistic chance to enjoy it. As a democrat, he recommended educational reforms to ensure that the chance was more widely distributed. But as a natural aristocrat he believed that the good in question implies a hierarchy of intellectual and aesthetic excellence, with its caste-like distinction between superior and inferior human beings. Because he assumed that a person's position in this hierarchy would be determined by his individual traits, Jefferson saw no contradiction between his commitment to democracy, with its emphasis on equality, and his reverence for excellence—for the refinement, exercise, and enjoyment of those powers of thought and feeling that are uniquely ours as human beings. In this sense, Jefferson was a democrat and an aristocrat at once. So was Adams. So were Tocqueville and Holmes and, perhaps a bit more grudgingly, Mencken and Babbitt. And so am I.

Today the aristocratic spirit in our colleges and universities is beleaguered as never before. This is above all true in the humanities, which have taken the brunt of a new and particularly fierce attack on the very idea of distinction and rank, in any but banally vocational terms. The attack has been motivated by a renewed attention to the problem of race in America and the demand that we acknowledge the dimension of caste that makes it so agonizingly difficult. But this demand is misplaced in a setting where mastery still means something noble and hierarchy has a point. Every college student should be able to experience as much of this nobility as he or she can. The admissions process should be as fair as possible. But to insist that our democratic ideals be enforced with as much rigor on campus as off devalues the prize for which students ought to strive. It reduces the campaign for greater fairness in admissions to a concern with the distribution of vocational opportunities.

That is something. But it is not everything. What it leaves out of account is excellence in living. Those who give the anti-subordination principle a commanding authority in every area of life can make no sense of the idea. The best they can do is invite each of us to decide what excellence means according to our own lights. This is the mistake the master of Pierson College made when he renounced his title to calm the fear that the hierarchy it implies is inseparable from the evil of slavery.

If the good faith of academic elitists like me is to be trusted, and our arguments receive a hearing, we have a responsibility to be as vocal in our condemnation of racism as in our support of the perfectionist ideal of humanistic study and of the natural aristocracy it implies. The latter is a conservative ideal, the former a democratic one. But together they make something greater. They make an American ideal: that of a nation united in equality but free enough to leave room for nobility. Those who value both must take a stand against the apostles of clarity whose self-assured beliefs allow them to see only the first.

TWO

Speech

I.

FREEDOM OF SPEECH IS ONCE AGAIN A FIGHTING ISSUE ON America's campuses. At some schools, speakers have been shouted down because of their political views. Others have been disinvited for similar reasons. The speakers themselves run a gamut. At one end is Milo Yiannopoulos, a self-promoting provocateur. A few, like Richard Spencer, are outspoken racists. Many, like Charles Murray and Heather Mac Donald, are conservatives of a more academic bent. In some cases, the protests have turned violent. Nothing like it has happened since the 1960s.

But these are only the most dramatic cases. Other issues raise questions about the limits of campus speech too.

Academic speech codes are a case in point. Off campus, hate speech is legally protected. Attempts to outlaw it in our public universities have regularly been struck down as well. But nothing prevents a private school from adopting a code of this kind. Some in fact have done so. Indeed, the number appears to be growing. Even our public universities have found ways of evading the prohibition against speech codes or, have simply chosen to ignore it.

The demand that students be given "trigger warnings" to alert them to the possibility that something they are about to read or hear may be disturbing, and that certain spaces be designated "safe" to protect those in them from being exposed to upsetting words or ideas, also raise the question of whether campus speech should be trimmed or confined in ways that are not required outside an academic setting. So does the revision of traditional nomenclature to ensure a greater sense of "inclusion." Yale's official substitution of "first year" for "freshman" is an innocuous example. The growing insistence on the use of preferred gender pronouns is a more freighted one. The attention given in countless sensitivity training programs to so-called micro-aggressions is a third. These adjustments in the habits of speech are mostly, though not entirely, informal, and largely enforced by cultural sanctions. They are more diffuse than the conflicts that arise when a speaker is shouted down or told she is unwelcome on campus. But they too have an effect on the way that students and faculty view the purpose of academic speech, and shape their experience of it.

The issue of campus speech is therefore not one but many. It includes the debate over speech codes, trigger warnings, safe spaces, gender pronouns, and micro-aggressions as well as the more violent disputes that erupt when speakers are physically prevented from talking. But those who favor limiting academic speech in *any* of these ways generally adopt one view of it, and those who oppose such limitations another.

Proponents of the latter view say something like this: "The pursuit of truth is advanced by the free exchange of ideas. We accept this proposition without question in the political sphere. But a college or university is devoted above all to the pursuit of truth. That is its special mission. A commitment to free speech, no matter how bruising, ought therefore to be even stronger on campus than off."

Defenders of the former view reply: "A college or university is a special community, set apart from the wider society. Its members are bound by distinctive ties of collegiality and respect. Every school therefore has a responsibility to ensure that those who join its community are equally included in the venture—that no one feels less worthy or valued than another. Because words can have this effect, it is necessary to monitor and if necessary control campus speech for the sake of protecting a spirit of respect and inclusion."

This debate is all too familiar. But there is something fundamentally misguided about it. Those who favor restrictions on speech in the name of inclusion are right to emphasize that a college or university is a special kind of community. This is something their opponents overlook or downplay. But they are wrong to conclude that disinviting controversial speakers whose views will be insulting to some students, or adopting a speech code that forbids the expression of certain noxious ideas, or recommending the use of trigger warnings and the creation of safe spaces, will strengthen this community and make the experience of those in it more rewarding. Just the opposite is true. The remedies they propose tend on the whole to dilute the special character of a college or university, not vitalize or reinforce it. They make the good of membership in such a community more difficult to achieve.

That is because those who favor these restrictions do not understand what kind of community this is. They view it in a political light. They see the academy from the same egalitarian perspective as the advocates of racial, ethnic, and gender diversity. They fail to grasp that the distinctiveness of a college or university is a function of its devotion to a conversational ideal that has no place in political life (a mistake their civil libertarian opponents make too). They do not appreciate that the pursuit of this ideal is a calling that demands even less deference to the feelings of others than one reasonably expects in many nonacademic settings. And they fail to see that the spirit of inclusion it fosters is one that gathers teachers and students for the sake of discovering the truth—a uniquely difficult and demanding inquiry in which all are welcome but some get further than others and grow into a fuller possession of the liberating power of thought.

II.

Imagine two different settings in which ideas are being exchanged. One is a college seminar—on Victorian poetry, the history of the Cold War, or income inequality in the United States—any topic likely to arouse differences of opinion and judgment. The other let's call "Speakers' Corner"—a space in a local park that has been set aside for those who wish to express their views on any subject at all. The free exchange of ideas is important in both settings. Indeed, there is a sense in which each exists *for the sake* of such an exchange. But the settings are not the same. We can start by noting four obvious differences between them.

First, once they have joined the seminar, the participants cannot come and go as they please. They may even be required to participate in some more active way (by preparing discussion papers and the like). By contrast, those who have stopped to listen to a speaker in the park are free to walk away whenever they choose—perhaps because they have better things to do or don't like what the speaker is saying. They have an unconstrained freedom of exit. The students in the seminar are a captive audience.

Second, there is no designated authority figure at Speakers' Corner. The seminar, by contrast, assumes the presence of a figure of this kind. The teacher has the final word in deciding when a claim is unpersuasive and requires further defense; when one point of view needs to be balanced by another; when a speaker has failed to be sufficiently attentive to something someone else has said; and when it is time to move on to another topic. And of course the teacher alone enjoys the privilege of grading the participants on their performance. At many schools, students have the chance to evaluate their teachers too. But this does not change the basic fact that the words in a seminar are spoken within a hierarchical structure of authority that has no analogue in the more strictly egalitarian milieu of Speakers' Corner.

Third, those speaking in the park have no duty to address a common theme. They may or may not; that is up to them. They are at liberty to speak about whatever seems to them worthy of note. If a series of speeches is completely disjointed, that may disappoint the audience but it violates no rule or norm that anyone at Speakers' Corner is bound to respect. The participants in a seminar, on the other hand, are obliged to try to have a common conversation. This duty is reinforced by the assignment of a text (which may be a film, painting, or anything else, as well as a written document). The text anchors the seminar. It guides and constrains the conversation, however critical or even dismissive the reactions to it may be. There is no text at Speakers' Corner. Even if everyone there chooses to address the same topic, a speaker who picks an entirely different one is not guilty of violating a conversational norm.

Fourth, the crowd that gathers at Speakers' Corner includes men and women of all sorts. It is as diverse as the society from which they come. In particular, it includes both young and old in no predictable proportion. By contrast, the students in a college seminar are all generally younger than their teacher, although there are of course exceptions. This asymmetry in age is associated with the teacher's authority. The teacher knows more about the subject because he or she has been studying it for a longer period of time. The students in the class are also, as a rule, developmentally less advanced as human beings. There are always exceptions to this too, but the pattern is general and recognizable. That is why it is appropriate to say about a college seminar what it would be preposterous to say about the audience at Speakers' Corner: that one of its aims is to help the students *grow up*.

I shall return to this last distinction later on. But first we need to understand the deeper difference that underlies all four. It is that the participants in a seminar are trying to have a *conversation*. Indeed, they have a duty to try. No such obligation exists at Speakers' Corner. The phenomenon of heckling gives us a clue as to what this means.

At Speakers' Corner, members of the audience often interrupt a speaker, shout epithets, and hold up signs protesting what she says. If the heckling reaches a point where the speaker's words cannot be heard, the heckler(s) may be in violation of the law. California, for example, has a statute that forbids "willfully disturb[ing] or break[ing] up any assembly or meeting that is not unlawful in its character." Hecklers who cross this line are liable to be escorted away by the police. But heckling that does not rise to this level is generally lawful and indeed quite common at gatherings like the one at Speakers' Corner.

In a seminar, by contrast, interruptions of any kind are out of order. A student may burst out, in a moment of excitement, and start talking over someone else. But it is the teacher's responsibility to restore order; to give the student who has been drowned out an opportunity to complete his or her thought; and then to allow the intervener a chance to reply. This is even more obviously true of outbursts that amount to heckling. If a student exclaims, "Shut up, you stupid idiot!" or "Only a racist would think that!" the teacher has a duty to forcefully remind the student that exclamations of this kind are completely out of place in the classroom and will not be tolerated under any circumstances, however routine they may be at Speakers' Corner.

That is because a seminar is supposed to be a conversation and heckling of any kind, however limited, is antithetical to the spirit of such an exchange. It is a conversation killer. It not only causes conversations to break down; that is its aim or purpose. Heckling is allowed at Speakers' Corner—up to a point at least—because those gathered there are not trying to have a conversation. What they say and do therefore cannot be judged by the same ideal.

Even if we cannot define its meaning with precision, we all have a pretty good sense of when we are having a conversation and when one has broken down. The key element is that of *collaboration*. The parties to a conversation may differ sharply in their judgments and beliefs. But they are at least trying to discover where they differ and why; to see if they have any common ground between them; and to build on this as much and as far as they can. This does not require that anyone give up his or her convictions or even provisionally relax them. But it does assume a commitment to the goal of trying to construct together something that no participant can build on his or her own. The effort may fail; it often does. But a conversation is a joint enterprise, not just in the thin sense that it takes two to converse, in the way that it takes two to form a queue, but in the more robust sense that those involved are at least attempting to collaborate in the production of something whose authorship they share, to some degree at least. The word we most often use to describe this common product is "agreement."

A debate, for example, is not a conversation. Even if it succeeds, it does not produce agreement among the participants. A debate is a contest in which the competitors do their best to win. Debaters proceed along parallel tracks; the judge decides which one got farther. A debate lacks the collaborative dimension that conversations possess.

But at least debaters have a common subject. They are talking about the same thing. In this sense they share a "text": the question that has been set for debate. Those at Speakers' Corner lack even this. They choose their own topics and speak about whatever they wish. In this sense, their statements do not even run parallel to one another like those of debaters on a stage. Even more obviously they also lack the spirit of collaboration that is the hallmark of a genuine conversation. They are not trying to build something together. They are attempting to express their views, with as much force as possible, so that others will adopt them. They are trying to get their ideas out into a "marketplace" where they can compete with other ideas and hopefully prevail.

The metaphor is instructive. The competitors in a market do not think of themselves as engaged in a collaborative project. Each is simply trying to increase his or her market share. Success is defined by the defeat of one's competitors, however this comes about. To the extent that one competitor in a marketplace of ideas takes the views of others into account, it is for strategic purposes only: to discover their vulnerabilities and plan the best avenue of attack. Collaborations, where they exist, are temporary expedients that dissolve the minute the parties see that their separate advantage lies elsewhere. The outlook of those competing in this market, as in any, is self-centered, predatory, and indifferent to the fate of those marketing other wares.

The strongest justification for any market, including one in ideas, is that the participants' lack of a collaborative spirit produces, despite their self-absorption—or rather precisely because of it—an indirect benefit to the community as a whole. This might, I suppose, be described as a kind of collaboration. But it is an indirect and unintended one that is best achieved by encouraging the participants not to think about collaboration at all. And that is not the ideal of a conversation, which treats collaboration as a conscious goal internal to the activity of conversing itself, and judges those involved by their willingness and ability to keep it in mind.

III.

The image of a marketplace of ideas helps to explain why the law gives those at Speakers' Corner wide latitude to say what they wish. In particular, it explains why they have no duty to be respectful to others; refrain from trashing the competition; or even take competing views into account.

Apart from a few procedural rules that circumscribe their "time, manner, and place," two other sorts of restrictions have sometimes been imposed on what may be said in such gatherings. The first pertains to content. Restrictions of this sort have repeatedly been challenged. Stumblingly at first, and then with growing confidence, the Supreme Court has held that restrictions based on the substance of a speaker's views are almost always invalid. *R.A.V. v. City of St. Paul* (1992) is illustrative.

In *R.A.V.*, the Court struck down a St. Paul ordinance that made it a misdemeanor to place "on public or private property, a symbol, object, appellation, characterization or graffiti, including, but not limited to, a burning cross or Nazi swastika, which one knows or has reasonable grounds to know arouses anger, alarm or resentment in others on the basis of race, color, creed, religion or gender . . ." The petitioner and several other teenagers had burned a cross in the yard of an African-American family living across the street. That clearly constituted an act of criminal trespass. The question in *R.A.V.* was whether the petitioner had committed *an additional* crime by violating the ordinance in question. In the Court's view, the answer depended on whether an act may be criminalized *solely on account* of the substance of the view it expresses. It concluded that it may not, even if the view is as hateful as the one expressed by the petitioner. The *R.A.V.* decision explicitly confirmed what had been strongly implied in *National Socialist Party of America v. Village of Skokie* fifteen years earlier, where the issue was whether those participating in a planned march through the predominantly Jewish village of Skokie could be enjoined from wearing Nazi uniforms and displaying the swastika. (The case was decided in the marchers' favor on the procedural ground that they had been denied the right to immediately appeal the injunction a lower court had issued, effectively frustrating their right of free expression.)

Second, speech has sometimes been punished on account of its *assaultive* character, as distinct from its content alone. The distinction is a wavering one. If words strike their intended audience with the emotional equivalent of a slap in the face, it is because of their meaning. Still, the mere effect that words have has sometimes been alleged to provide a distinct basis for prohibiting or punishing them. The most famous case is *Chaplinsky v. New Hampshire* (1942).

In *Chaplinsky*, a Jehovah's Witness was taken to police headquarters after causing a scene when he made inflammatory statements about religion on a public sidewalk in downtown Rochester. At the police station, Chaplinsky verbally abused the town marshal. He called him a "damned Fascist" and a "god-damned racketeer." He was then arrested. Chaplinsky later argued that his abuse was protected speech. The Supreme Court held that it was not, and carved out an exception for "insulting or 'fighting' words" that are of "slight social value as steps to truth" and whose "very utterance inflict injury or tend to incite an immediate breach of the peace."

In the years since, the Court's statement in *Chaplinsky* has often been invoked in defense of prohibitions against hate speech—words that disparage the members of some group on account of their racial, religious, or ethnic character, and are spoken with such venom as to trigger an immediate, physical reaction on the part of those attacked. But *Chaplinsky* has been narrowed to the point where it no longer has any meaningful application except where the words in question are addressed to a specific individual and intended as an attack on him or her in particular, in which case they come so close to a form of criminal assault or actionable slander that the utility of the notion of "fighting" words as a justification for the prohibition of hate speech has been completely lost. In *Cohen v. California* (1971), by a vote of 5 to 4, the Supreme Court overturned the conviction of a young man who had been arrested for wearing a jacket that said "Fuck the Draft" inside a Los Angeles courthouse. The relevant California statute "prohibited maliciously and willfully disturb[ing] the peace or quiet of any neighborhood or person [by] offensive conduct." Since *Cohen*, *Chaplinsky* has been more or less a dead letter.

At Speakers' Corner, therefore, no one can be prevented from saying something, or punished afterward for saying it, because his or her words express a hateful idea, or on the closely related grounds that they are likely to provoke a violent reaction on the part of some in the audience. The only other basis for limiting speech in this setting is that it poses an "immediate" threat of "grievous" harm to the public at large.

To take an extreme case, a speaker cannot justify the public disclosure of secret government documents by appealing to her right of free expression. She may have a right not to be restrained in advance (although this is sometimes controversial), but if the disclosure violates the law, she will perhaps be subject to punishment. This may deter her from speaking in the first place. A law of this kind therefore chills—and hence limits—speech. Still, our courts have always recognized that the need to protect the public from the immediate threat of grievous harm *may sometimes* justify imposing limits on what citizens are permitted to say, free of the worry that they will later be sanctioned for speaking.

Much of the Supreme Court's First Amendment jurisprudence over the past hundred years has been devoted to deciding what this little word "sometimes" means. These decisions cannot be summarized in a sentence or two. But it is fair, I think, to say that the general tendency has been for the Court to look with suspicion on appeals to public safety as a justification either for restraining speech or punishing it after the fact. Along with the rejection of limitations based on content and emotional effect, the drift has been toward an increasingly libertarian conception of speech where the kind at Speakers' Corner is concerned.

This is consistent with the notion of a marketplace of ideas.

Whether a new brand of toothpaste sells depends on the preferences of those in the store. Analogously, some say, "the best test of truth is the power of the thought to get itself accepted in the competition of the market." For this "test" to do its job, the consumers must be left free to choose. Otherwise, the "test" is skewed or incomplete. In any market, including this one, "free" means having a wide array of choices and independence in choosing among them.

In fact, the freedom of the market in ideas is even greater than that of markets for other kinds of goods, like toothpaste. In the latter case, all sorts of restrictions apply that have no counterpart in the marketplace of ideas—the rules of the Food and Drug Administration, for example. These are meant to protect the safety and welfare of consumers. When it comes to toothpaste, we happily accept that consumers need to be shielded from fraud, misrepresentation, and dangers to their health, even if protection comes only in the mild form of a legally mandated warning (like that on cigarette packages).

But regulations of this sort assume that "health" is more or less objectively determinable and is something every consumer wants; that rational consumers would never buy a product if they knew it was likely to ruin their health; and that even if there is only a risk that it will, they would want to be informed in advance. Of course, it can be argued that some ideas are unhealthy too. But it is harder to define an agreed-upon measure of intellectual health—the counterpart of longevity, lower blood pressure, and the like. In the marketplace of ideas, it is right to fear that disallowing some on the grounds of their toxic effect will tilt the balance in favor of orthodox beliefs and open the door to government censorship. What all "rational consumers want" is therefore not a standard that can be invoked to decide which ideas may be marketed and on what terms without risking a still greater danger.

The result is a rough-and-tumble free-for-all in which some are bound to find the ideas of others appalling. But this is acceptable because a free marketplace in ideas, in theory at least, tends to help us separate good ideas from bad ones. It promotes the truth, though only indirectly. It also produces a second good, also by indirection. David Hume describes this as the live-and-let-live attitude that comes from frequent, peaceful contact with those whose tastes and values differ from our own—what we more grandly call a habit of toleration. This is especially true of the market in ideas. A capacity for tolerating different ideas is essential to democratic life. It also is best encouraged by minimizing restrictions on speech. The more bruising the exchange of ideas, the better it serves as a training ground for the habit of toleration. But this is no more the conscious aim of the participants than the discovery of the truth. If truth and tolerance emerge from a marketplace of ideas, it is as an unintended by-product of the self-interested actions of those involved, each striving only to get his or her beliefs accepted in a competitive process that assumes no common or collaborative goal on their part.

The result is a form of community, and a valuable one at that. But it is not a community based on the conversational ideal of the seminar classroom. The rough-and-tumble, sometimes hurtful, and often insulting exchanges at Speakers' Corner are therefore a poor model for the kind of community the participants in a college seminar are striving to achieve.

It may seem obvious that in the latter case a less abrasive and more respectful form of speech is called for. There is a sense in which this is true. Shouting, insults, and derogatory ad hominem statements are out of place in a classroom. But there is another and more important sense in which the speech in a seminar needs to be *even less restricted* than at Speakers' Corner—even more probing and relentless in its demand that all who speak defend their views with reasoned arguments.

Those who think the libertarian norms that apply at Speakers' Corner apply in a college seminar too therefore make a serious mistake. They fail to distinguish between a market, with its invisible hand, and a conversation founded on collaboration. But those who think that the spirit of inclusion in a community of conversation requires speech codes, trigger warnings, safe spaces, and a heightened sensitivity to micro-aggressions make a mistake of an equally serious kind. They also are blind to the special character of such a community and the exceptional demands it makes on its participants. The restrictions they would impose on it are, if anything, even more damaging to its rare and liberating milieu.

IV.

This seems counterintuitive. Why should there be *fewer* restrictions on speech in a college seminar than at Speakers' Corner, where everything goes? Shouldn't the restrictions be *tighter*? Don't these include, for example, an obligation to be polite—something those in the park have no duty to be? The treatment of heckling seems to prove the point. But the matter is more complicated than it appears.

At Speakers' Corner, heckling is allowed, but only up to the point that it does not prevent the speaker from speaking. Isolated shouts in a large crowd rarely do this. Persistent and effective disruption may. When it does, it is grounds to eject the heckler, by force if necessary. In a college seminar, a student who tells another to shut up is likely to be asked to apologize or leave if he will not. He may be forcibly removed if he persists. The small size of the seminar amplifies the power of each participant to disrupt it. Removal is therefore likely to come sooner here than in a large public gathering, although the rationale for it is the same. But before the student is told to go, or ejected if he refuses, something else is likely to happen that has no counterpart at Speakers' Corner.

There, neither the speaker nor anyone else has an obligation to engage a heckler in conversation, even if some do. That is because those in the park are not having a conversation. They are advertising their beliefs. If conversing with others helps in this regard, then it has instrumental value. But it is not an end in itself. By contrast, the teacher in a seminar is obliged to remind the student who tells another to shut up that a conversation is what those in the room are trying to have; that yelling epithets is antithetical to the spirit of their endeavor; that if the student has an objection to what has been said, he must reframe it as an argument instead of an exclamation; and then, assuming he does, that others in the class must be given a chance to respond with counterarguments of their own—to meet the objection on the common ground of reason. The teacher is responsible for seeing that all the students in the room conduct themselves as best they can in accordance with the norms of a conversation. No one at Speaker's Corner has a duty of this kind.

Real heckling in a seminar is rare. In forty years of teaching, I don't think I've seen an instance of it. In any case, no one condones it. But other things are often said in this and other academic settings that undermine the ideal of a conversation in a less violent but equally egregious way that *is* condoned—encouraged, even—by the view that campus speech must be restrained with an eye to creating a community of respect and inclusion.

I have in mind statements like the following: "Your views make me feel excluded"; "You only want to protect your privilege"; "Speaking as a [woman, Jew, African American, transsexual, Hispanic], I see the world in a way you can't." These appeal, respectively, to the speaker's feelings; the motives of the person addressed; and some special insight that only the members of a particular group (usually an oppressed or marginalized one) are alleged to share. More exactly, they invoke these as *sources of authority*. They present them as *reasons why* others should either defer to the view of the speaker or discount someone else's. No one in a seminar or any other academic setting should ever be forbidden from making such a claim. But it cannot be allowed to go unchallenged. The conversational ideal demands that its authority be questioned. The idea that a college or university ought to be a community of respect and inclusion is often interpreted to mean that the authority of statements of this kind should be acknowledged. It is sometimes even interpreted to mean that their authority takes precedence over that of other claims. But this amounts to a repudiation of the conversational ideal and of the special form of community based upon it.

The contrast with Speakers' Corner is instructive. There, speakers often invoke their feelings or the unique experience of those belonging to a particular group as a reason to adopt their view of things. Just as often, they cite the motives of others as a reason to reject their views. But no one at Speaker's Corner has a duty to challenge any of these appeals. The norms of the gathering do not require it. Strong expressions of feeling; charges of corruption, venality, prejudice, and the like; and defiant claims that only the members of a historically oppressed group can really understand the issue at hand are the lifeblood of political argument. Anyone who goes into public life must expect and have the resilience to endure them.

It is different in a seminar room. A teacher should never reprimand a student for invoking his feelings as a basis of judgment or for suggesting that someone else's motives disqualify her views. But it is the teacher's responsibility to point out that "arguments" of this kind are not really arguments at all; that they must be supported by reasons that everyone in the class can evaluate on a shared basis; and that all together—the student who has spoken, the teacher, and everyone else in the room—must do their best to identify these reasons and give them an adequate hearing. This is a demanding aspiration. It is the ideal of a conversational community whose members are committed to finding or building a shared ground on which all can stand. The feelings, motives, and life experiences of the participants set them apart. These therefore cannot provide a shared ground of this sort. That can only be discovered or constructed through the exercise of the universal power of critical self-inspection that since the beginning of our philosophical tradition has gone under the name of "reason."

It doesn't kill a conversation to express a feeling, or question someone's motive, or claim that the members of a certain group experience things in a way others can't. What kills it is insisting that any of these be treated as a trump. Suppose, for example, that two people are having a heated exchange. One exclaims, in response to something the other has said, "You just don't know how angry that makes me." This can have one of two meanings. It may mean that the other person has failed to notice something that needs to be explored and explained—namely, the strength of the reaction that his or her views have provoked. Understood in this way, it is a stimulus to further conversation. Alternatively, it may mean that the one who has aroused the anger is incapable of comprehending it and should accept it as a reason for deferring to the other person's point of view. In one sense, a person's anger is always incomprehensible to everyone else. Like any feeling, it is not something that can be directly shared. But when a person who is angry insists that others treat his anger as a *justification for* the truth or weight of the experience that lies behind it, he kills the conversation by putting the ground of judgment beyond the reach of the other participants, who, however hard they try, can never share the feeling themselves.

The same is true of appeals to the authority of one's experience as the member of a particular group. Suppose two people are talking about the Black Lives Matter movement. One, an African American, says, "As a black person, I can tell you that for blacks the experience of being stopped by the police is one that white people will never understand." The other, who is white, replies, "And I can assure you that no black person will ever understand what it's like to be a white police officer in a black ghetto." Each of these statements may be the starting point for a constructive exchange. But if either is taken to mean "Not being [white or black], you *cannot* grasp what I'm talking about and *will never see* things as I do," the conversation is at an end. The very possibility of reaching common ground has been ruled out in advance. The participants are now talking (or shouting) past one another, as often happens at Speakers' Corner, and without objection, because the speakers there are hawking their wares in a marketplace of ideas and not trying to converse.

Attacking a person's motives is similarly unexceptionable, in a seminar or anywhere else. Understood in one way, it is just an invitation for the person who is attacked to be more forthright about his or her reasons. But if every reason the speaker offers meets with the same objection, no conversation can get going. If each attempt on the speaker's part to reach some common ground of argument is met with the response "You say that, but you're hiding your real beliefs," the speaker is pushed back onto the private ground of interest, which in itself is no more accessible to rational defense *or* attack than any desire, wish, fantasy, or preference. When this happens, an essential condition for conversing disappears, just as it does when the participants appeal to their feelings or special life experience as a *warrant* for taking the position they do.

All of these appeals defeat the ideal of a conversation by closing off the space of reasoned argument. It is one that none inhabits beforehand or alone. It is a space that can only be constructed and sustained in a collaborative fashion by those who seek a form of agreement that is unattainable by threats, intimidation, the emphatic demonstration of feeling, or a mere show of hands. All these are allowed in the marketplace of ideas. There, they are the equivalent of the preferences that consumers reveal when they choose one brand of toothpaste over another. But the outcome at which a conversation aims can only be reached on the common ground of reason. This is what makes a conversational community so distinctive and precious. Those gathered at Speakers' Corner do not constitute or even seek a community of this kind. But it is the goal of those in my imaginary seminar, and here every challenge to the authority of reason—or, what amounts to the same thing, every assertion of authority on behalf of what is inaccessible to reason—blights this ambition at the root.

This is what those who defend restrictions on campus speech in the name of a community of respect and inclusion do. By "respect" they mean more than "give a hearing to feelings of exclusion." They mean more than "pay attention to your prejudices." They mean more than "understand that those who have experienced discrimination may see things from a different point of view." What they mainly mean is that the feelings in question should be treated as trumps; the prejudices, as grounds for rejecting whatever those who have them say; and the experiences as a validation of the truth of the point of view they represent. "Respect" in this sense goes far beyond the norms of civility that govern most exchanges, academic ones included. It confers authority on claims that are immunized from criticism, or even inspection, because they are essentially private. It *legitimates* conversation-killing statements. That is something very different from allowing them the space to be made and considered. It amounts to the destruction of this space itself.

The conversational ideal not only permits this grant of authority to be challenged; it requires it. It demands more speech than those who would restrict it for the sake of creating a community of respect and inclusion deem appropriate. But it also requires more speech than a marketplace of ideas. In the latter, one can assign one's feelings whatever authority one likes without anyone having a *duty* to object. The same is true of allegations of prejudice and appeals to the privileged experience of those who have suffered some form of discrimination. In the classroom, though, these cannot be allowed to stand.

They *must* be probed and proven. There is *an obligation to say more.* It is an obligation that falls equally on everyone in the room. Those at Speaker's Corner are under no duty of this kind. In this sense, their speech is more confined than that of the participants in a conversation. Despite its freewheeling appearance, their free market in ideas is more, not less, restricted.

V.

A conversation has an ethic of its own. It is something other than politeness. Indeed, it is consistent with quite a bit of rudeness. It certainly does not forbid exclamations of feeling, accusations of prejudice, appeals to personal experience, and the like. What it does rule out is treating any of these as an argument in its own right, whose validity is established by virtue of the feeling or experience alone, to which the speaker has an access others don't.

In this sense, it might be called an "ethic of depersonalization." It rests on the duty to convert one's private feelings and experiences into public justifications, where they can be evaluated in the common light of day. The duty is reciprocal. It falls with equal weight on those who say that a speaker's feelings are irrelevant to the issue at hand. They may be. But that too must be established by an argument based on facts and reasoning accessible to all.

The only way to tell whether the participants in a conversation are making progress toward their goal is by considering the degree of reasoned agreement among them. This is rarely if ever complete. Nor is perfect agreement even desirable. It is too often a sign of conformity or exhaustion to be made a measure of success. But when, for example, the members of a seminar agree that a view they have been debating rests on previously unnoticed assumptions; that there are identifiable arguments for and against each; and that to resolve their disagreements all these arguments must be further weighed, they have made the kind of progress that characterizes a conversational exchange.

Those at Speaker's Corner seek agreement too. But it does not matter whether it is reasoned or not. Some may agree with a speaker because they find his ideas rationally persuasive, others because he is handsome or eloquent. Agreement of the first sort is perhaps more stable and therefore preferable from the speaker's point of view. But this is only an instrumental judgment. What matters at Speaker's Corner is the external coincidence of belief, not its source or ground. Like the convergence of choice in any market, this one too is brought about by an invisible hand whose operation is indifferent to the reasons the parties have for doing what they do. By contrast, in a seminar the agreement the participants seek is a reasoned one that cannot be achieved unless their judgments coincide internally as well as externally. Whatever agreement they reach is therefore a collaborative and not merely collective achievement.

It would be a huge mistake, though, to think that the ethic of a conversation, which demands depersonalization and collaboration, is unconnected to the participants' development as *individuals*. Just the opposite is true. The purpose of a seminar is to deepen and enrich the individuality of those involved, not to obliterate it, as happens in some collaborative activities, like a quilting bee, where the individuality of the participants is lost in the final work.

Whatever agreement the participants in a seminar reach is not a work apart, like the quilt, into which their separate personalities have vanished. It is a living medium in which the individuality of each is tested, sharpened, and refined, with the result that it becomes more distinctive in the process. Indeed, this is not only the result of their conversation—it is its goal. That a heightened appreciation of one's distinctness as an individual should be the aim of an exchange governed by an ethic of depersonalization may seem a kind of paradox.

Understanding why it is not, brings us closer to the heart of the conversational ideal.

Imagine a student alone, reading a book, in a library late at night. Although she reads without saying a word, she is engaged in a conversation as real and important as any that ever takes place in a classroom.

Assume the book expresses views the student agrees with in part and disagrees with in part. As she reads, she thinks to herself "That's right" or "That's wrong." But the point of her reading is not merely to note her agreements and disagreements with the author. She is reading to learn, to become better educated, and that means discovering *why* she agrees and disagrees where she does. To do this, she must keep an open mind. She must read the book as if she were a third person, neither the author nor herself, but one as yet uncaptured by the commitments of either, able to judge the views advanced by both from a position of dispassionate neutrality, like a judge listening to the litigants in a courtroom—except that in this case she is one of the litigants too.

Few intellectual exercises are as challenging as this. But the reward is immense, for when she closes the book and reaches her verdict—as she must, like the judge at the end of a trial—it is one she can embrace with greater confidence that it is *her own* considered view and not someone else's opinion that she has swallowed in a stupor, or a conventional piety that "goes without saying." By keeping an open mind, she has grown surer of her own mind. She is better able to stand on her own. Her individuality is more secure.

One goal of education is to teach students the things that everyone should know. Another is to free them to become more forceful versions of themselves. This is part of the truth captured by the commonplace that education sets one free. It is a crucial part of the conversational ideal. The depersonalization that a conversation requires is not meant to turn the participants into the proponents of a single idea or to dissolve their identities in a collective product like a quilt. It would be more accurate to say that the purpose of a conversation is to help those involved come closer to knowing, and therefore being, the distinctive individuals they are, through the cultivation, on the part of each, of the liberating habit of open-mindedness.

This purpose directs the silent conversation of my student with the author of her book. Even more obviously, it guides the vocal conversation of those gathered around a seminar table. The latter is more than a collection of individuals sitting side by side. It is a *community* held together by its shared commitment to a specific and demanding ideal. A good definition of this community would be "a group committed to extending the common space of reason that exists among them by refusing to assert the authority of any private feeling or experience that others cannot share, *in order that* each may, through honest self-reflection, come to a better understanding of what he or she really cares about and why." The ideal of such a community implies no tension between the commonality of reason and the separateness of personality. The impersonality of the first is a medium for discovering the distinctiveness of the second. They are the two sides of a coin.

VI.

The conversations in which Socrates engaged with his fellow Athenians remain the best example we have of what a community of this kind looks like in practice.

"Engaged" is not entirely accurate. Socrates often dragooned his partners into conversation, generally on topics they believed they knew more about than he. That, of course, is what he sought to disprove. Socrates drew his interlocutors out of the private world of their experiences and beliefs into the light of reason where their prejudices could be examined in an impersonal way. Many came kicking and screaming. But he forced those with whom he conversed to subject their private convictions to a public standard of justification. He refused to let them state their beliefs and then run away. He demanded they stay and join in a collaborative venture whose goal was to discover whether these beliefs stood up to rational scrutiny.

This often made them angry and eventually got him killed. But Socrates never wavered in his belief that it is only through the rigors of a depersonalizing conversation of this kind that anyone can ever know what he *really* thinks—can "know himself," as he explained at his trial. His student Plato later came to see the conversational ideal in a different and less individualist light. But for Socrates the link between a community of conversation on the one hand and individual self-discovery on the other remained so strong that when his life was on the line, he felt he could defend the one only by invoking the other.

In one respect, this community is perfectly democratic. No one is excluded from it. Socrates drew his partners from all walks of life. He seems, though, to have taken special pleasure in deflating the pretensions of the high and mighty by showing them that their beliefs had no rationally defensible foundation. His behavior had, to this extent, a leveling effect. This is what many of his highborn contemporaries found so annoying. But, in another respect, the conversational community that Socrates sought to create was an aristocratic one too. As Nietzsche shrewdly observed, Socrates did not so much seek to destroy the older aristocratic order he inherited as to replace it with a new aristocracy based upon a different principle of rank or distinction.

The old order was an aristocracy of wealth and status. It was already decaying by the time Socrates arrived on the scene. His new aristocracy was one of knowledge or wisdom instead. It rested on the distinction between those who know and those who don't—even if the superiority of the first is only that, like Socrates, they know what they do not know, unlike those who confuse their unexamined beliefs with true knowledge. The first group is small, the second far more numerous. This is one way in which Socrates's aristocracy of philosophical souls resembles its older counterpart. But another and far more important one is that it too distinguishes among human beings on the basis of their greater or less *reality*. Every aristocracy rests on such a judgment. It affirms, or more often simply assumes, that some human beings are more *real* than others—that they possess not merely superior skills but a greater quantum of *being*. The basis of the judgment differs from one aristocracy to another. It is one thing in Homer, another in Periclean Athens, and a third in the conversational community that Socrates offers as a successor to both. But even in the last it remains aristocratic insofar as it presumes a rank order of prestige based on the relative reality of those involved.

For Socrates, the position one occupies in this hierarchy is a function of how close he is to the truth. The closer one is, the more real he becomes. Socrates conceived the truth not in conceptual terms but as a way of life—as the practice of philosophy. Those who live this way are more fully alert or alive than those who don't. The latter are like dreamers whiling their lives away. Even to see that one has been dreaming is a form of wakefulness—the first and most important kind. To be awakened in this sense is to become more real, to become an aristocrat of the spirit. Plato reinterpreted this teaching in metaphysical and cosmological terms. But for him too, movement toward the truth represents a growth in being. There is no more aristocratic idea than that of Plato's philosopher-king.

The conversational ideal exemplified by my imaginary college seminar is that of Socrates, not Plato. It has no cosmological foundation. But it reflects, as clearly as Socrates's own practice did, the conviction that our highest obligation is to know ourselves; that we do this best through the rational review of our beliefs, in collaboration with others; and that those who get further in this work live lives that are *more realized*, more fully human, than those who dream in the dark of their unexamined feelings and experiences.

The notions of respect and inclusion, as these are understood in the academy today, attack the Socratic ideal directly. They not only encourage all sorts of silly coddling, in the form of trigger warnings, safe spaces, and the like; more importantly, they assign a normative weight to private sensations and beliefs in a way that insulates them from public scrutiny and thereby destroy the possibility of Socratic inquiry.

It is hard to draw into conversation a person who feels angry or isolated. He may need to vent before the conversation can begin. After he has, his anger or isolation remains to be considered. It is transmuted into a subject of conversation. Why does he feel as he does? Are his feelings justified? If this were all the idea of a community of respect and inclusion implied, it would be entirely innocuous. But today the idea is also widely understood to mean that certain feelings of outrage and marginalization possess their own authority—that they are self-validating, that just stating them is an argument it would be disrespectful to challenge. This makes the public sphere of reason hostage to the private realm of feeling. It pushes inquiry back into the dark. It reverses the path that Socrates followed by tying the authority of what is said in the common light of day to what is felt outside it in the incommunicable recesses of personal experience. This is the death of conversation as he understood it. It kills the search for truth, destroys the possibility of collaboration, and deprives the participants of the chance for a more fully realized existence.

The idea of respect and inclusion is essentially egalitarian. It is motivated by a wish to widen the campus community to include those who have been kept out for illegitimate reasons. This is an ethical goal of high importance. It reflects the belief that everyone should have an equal chance to participate in the life of this community. It is consistent with Socrates's democratic habit of drawing everyone he met into conversation.

But some make more progress than others. They come closer to the truth and to a more real existence. This is the aristocratic hierarchy in which Socrates thought everyone should have an equal chance to find his place. By elevating feelings and experiences that others cannot share to a position of unassailable authority, the contemporary ideal of respect and inclusion collapses this aristocracy into a democracy of sentiment in which there is no up or down, because if feelings are trumps, they are distributed as equally as the feelings themselves. Under the pretense of opening the conversation up, this ideal thereby destroys the aristocratic good that makes participation in the conversation so precious in the first place—a bad egalitarianism that defeats the very purpose of the good one that welcomes everyone, without discrimination, to the strenuous and discriminating life of the mind.

VII.

The example of Socrates bears on our subject in another way.

Socrates conversed mostly with young men. As a general matter, the teacher in a college seminar is also older than her students, and while it would be insulting for a speaker in the park to treat those in the audience as children, a college teacher needs to take her students' youth into account. Some teachers are surprisingly childish and some students precociously mature. Still, as a general rule, the teacher is more of a grown-up than her students and needs to be mindful of certain developmental facts.

The most important of these is that the capacity for reasoned argument grows over time. Young people are not only less able to take a third-person view of themselves than those who are more mature, they are less able to accept critical judgments delivered from this perspective. They are more attached to their feelings and private experiences and more inclined to retreat to them when challenged in uncomfortable ways. These reactions are as natural as being human; they are part of being human. With luck and help, they become less pronounced as one matures. But this means that the students in a college seminar are likely to have a more difficult time living up to the demands of the conversational ideal just on account of their youth.

Teachers need to keep this is mind. They also obviously need to be kind. But kindness is not indulgence. Students have to be taught—gently but firmly—that although their private feelings and personal experiences may *always* be expressed and should *always* be given a hearing, they are *never* an authoritative basis for deciding any question at all. They have to be inducted into a community of conversation. This is a process of maturation, uneven and often uneasy, as much for college students today as it was for the Athenian pups who loved to argue with Socrates about everything under the sun.

The college years fall awkwardly between childhood and the world of adult responsibilities. On the one hand, students enjoy many of the protections they knew as children living at home under the watchful eye of their parents. They are physically safe. They are free, within wide limits, to fail and recover, to stumble and find their footing again. In this respect in particular, a college or university is more forgiving than most of the other institutions in which its students will live and work later in life.

On the other hand, a school is a far more permissive parent than most of the students knew before. It allows them to do all sorts of things they could not have done at home. It permits them to experiment with sex and, within limits, alcohol and drugs. It also permits them to experiment with ideas—to take courses to see if they are interested in subjects their parents have warned them against and to flirt with ideas they have been taught to view with disapproval or disgust. This is the real freedom of college life. It is meant to give students the room they need to discover who they are. But it depends on the safety of knowing they can provisionally test all sorts of crazy ideas without suffering any irremediable consequences, in a way that was hard at home and may be impossible later in life.

The security of college thus allows for a species of freedom that is greater than any the students have likely known before or are likely to know after. This special form of freedom exists *for the sake of* becoming a more open-minded and self-knowing person, and that in turn depends on the students' induction into a community of conversation—indeed, is measured by the extent to which they make its ideals their own. To do that, they have to learn that their pains and pleasures, their experiences and beliefs, are not valid simply because they are theirs. That is how children think. Students must be weaned away from this habit and helped to have the courage to subject their feelings to a cross-examination that has the power to disrupt or dislodge them because it is the students themselves who are conducting it. This is always tough. But the ideal of respect and inclusion that gives an ethical weight to so many of the restrictions on speech in our colleges and universities today, makes the process more difficult by ascribing an authority to the whole field of private experience—one that reinforces the infantile tendency that every Socratic conversation aims to reverse.

The contrast with the family is important.

Parents have educational responsibilities too. They must send their children to school or school them at home. Some parents also think it is important to introduce their children to the practice of conversation. They invite dinner table debate and force their children to defend their views with reasoned arguments. They discourage appeals to feeling.

But a child's declaration that some word or expression, spoken by a parent or sibling in a harsh or censorious tone, makes the child feel bad always carries a weight of its own. The mere fact that the child's feelings have been hurt is important in its own right, whether or not there are good grounds for it. Around the dinner table, even in the most reflective conversations, feelings play a *normative* role that is completely out of place in a college seminar. They can be, and often are, a reason for redirecting the conversation or stopping it altogether.

That is because a family is a community of love. It may have a conversational component, but it does not exist for the sake of conversation. Because it is a community of love, the feelings of its members matter in a way they do not in a college seminar. Those who, in the name of respect and inclusion, assign the feelings of students a similar kind of authority by creating safe spaces of emotional calm; warning them that something they are about to read may be disturbing; and cautioning against micro-aggressions that unwittingly hurt the feelings of others confuse these two sorts of community. They rightly insist that a college or university is not a marketplace of ideas. But they wrongly treat it as if it were a family or—what is closely related—a therapeutic institution. They fail to understand that it is neither. They lose sight of what it means to be a community of conversation with a special ethic of its own: one that is distinct both from that of the dinner table, where love rules and feelings matter, and of Speakers' Corner, where citizens compete as sellers and buyers but have no duty to converse.

The conversations that Socrates provoked are still the best example of what such a community can be. They remain a model of college life. They remind us that, in a real conversation, speech is always less restricted than it is either in the home or the park, where feelings either serve as trumps or need not be explained at all. This is the most radical freedom of speech that exists anywhere in America.

By comparison with it, the freedom of Speakers' Corner, which requires only that no one interfere, is a more limited kind. The dogma of respect and inclusion, as this is now understood and practiced on our campuses, is the enemy of the former, rarer freedom and of the aristocratic spirit it unchains.

VIII.

I have used the example of a college seminar to illustrate what I mean by the conversational ideal. But many things that happen on a college campus don't look much like a seminar at all. To what extent does this same ideal apply in other academic settings as well?

In a lecture course, students do less conversing. They mostly sit and take notes or just listen. The object of a lecture is often simply to explain certain basic concepts and techniques; survey the main works in a field; or convey some useful information. But even here the conversational ideal plays a role. If after class a student objects to the presence of a particular book on the syllabus on the grounds that it is racist or anti-feminist and makes her feel excluded; questions the teacher's approach for similar reasons; or insists that she knows more about inequality in America because she grew up in poverty, all of these challenges must be taken seriously. Each deserves a thoughtful response. But at the same time the teacher has an obligation to insist that they be supported by arguments that are open to public scrutiny, and to remind the student that his or her views cannot be *justified* by an appeal to private feelings, regardless of their strength, or to experiences others have not shared.

The ideal is at work even when students are reading and writing on their own. Many homework assignments invite a critical response of some kind. A textbook in economics may; an essay on the causes of the Civil War will. But here there is no teacher looking over the students' shoulders to remind them to read and write in a conversational spirit. The temptation to fall back on private feeling and personal experience as a standard of judgment is especially strong in these solitary moments. Students have only themselves to combat it. But that is why it is particularly important that they do so.

The habit of conversing is most deliberately cultivated in the classroom. Those in authority there have a responsibility to see that it takes root. If it does, students are more likely to take it with them when they walk out the door and to be able to converse with themselves even when there is no one else around—to be judges in their own case, applying public standards of reason to their private sentiments and beliefs. This may be the most important application of the ideal precisely because it is so difficult. In a sense, it is the measure of a successful class. Once again, Socrates is our model. Plato often portrays him lost in thought, testing his beliefs against the unrelenting requirements of his own mind.

What about non-curricular events: a debate on immigration policy sponsored by the Young Progressives or a symposium on the Israeli-Palestinian conflict organized by the Muslim Students Association? These fall outside the formal program of instruction. Students are free to come and go as they choose. There is no teacher in the room with a duty to promote the conversational ideal. Gatherings of this kind shade off into even less formal ones—the countless, sometimes heated exchanges among students in dining halls, dorm rooms, and study groups. These constitute a large part of college life. Many are social in nature. Yet they often touch on questions of intellectual and moral importance. Because there is no teacher present to steer the participants away from the isolation of their private feelings toward a community of reasoned exchange, one might think the conversational ideal is out of place here. That would be wrong.

First of all, these exchanges take place on campus. The participants are students who are there for a broadly common purpose.

Second, even the least formal ones are connected to the core function of the school insofar as they touch on intellectual, political, historical, or cultural topics. They are related to—indeed, they are a part of—the process of reflection, criticism, and sharpened self-awareness that is at the heart of the enterprise of teaching and learning. In these respects, they differ from the exchanges at Speakers' Corner. That is an extramural setting. It falls outside the dedicated space of campus life. Those present do not have to be admitted to it and are free to leave whenever they wish. They share no purpose beyond that of listening to one another and there is nothing like a diploma to mark the successful completion of their participation in the venture.

Together, these distinctions make it clear that all the extracurricular exchanges taking place on campus among students and possessing any intellectual content at all fall within the zone of the conversational ideal, even when they have no connection to the school's organized program of instruction. In this respect, they more closely resemble the exchanges that take place around a seminar table than those at Speakers' Corner. The difference is not that they belong to a marketplace of ideas as distinct from a community of conversation. It is not that they are less serious or instructive than what happens in class. It is that in these informal settings there is a duty to respect the ethic of conversation but no one with the authority to enforce it. *There is a responsibility on the part of all and authority in none.*

But this is not a reason for thinking the ethic no longer applies. To the contrary: it is a reason for students to do their best, on their own, to live up to its extraordinarily high demands. That students sometimes fail to do this when no teacher is around no more justifies surrendering the ideal here than the fact that some teachers allow students in class to take refuge in their private feelings and experiences justifies abandoning it there. The current of influence ought to run in the opposite direction. The best examples of fidelity to the conversational ideal in the formal setting of the classroom should inspire all the members of an academic community, faculty and students alike, to extend it to their informal relations. It should give them the courage to follow the ideal even when there is no one present with the *institutional* authority to insist they must. And it should invest those who do follow it with a *moral* authority that fills the gap—the student, for example, in a late-night dorm room debate about urban police practices who has the strength to point out that the question cannot be decided on the grounds of personal feelings alone.

Finally, what about the incidents that have stirred the most debate about the meaning of free speech on campus? At a number of schools, speakers with conservative or reactionary views have been shouted down and prevented from speaking. At Middlebury, Charles Murray was forced off the stage and physically assaulted as he and his faculty host left the building. Others have been disinvited or withdrawn under pressure. In 2016 the president of Williams canceled a talk by John Derbyshire, a right-wing author with arguably racist views, on the grounds that many of his opinions constituted "hate speech." These highly visible events have provoked the strongest defenses of free speech. Most often, the defense has been cast in terms of the idea of a free marketplace of ideas. They have also prompted the most vigorous arguments for limiting speech in the name of respect and inclusion.

Those who take the latter view generally make two points. The first is that certain ideas contradict some basic moral truth whose acceptance is a bedrock premise of the community of those gathered on campus for the purpose of teaching and learning. Giving a platform to those who espouse these ideas amounts, they say, to granting a small but still unacceptable degree of legitimacy to values that are at war with the community's most deeply shared norms. Second, they insist that no one be allowed to speak on campus whose views arouse feelings of physical and emotional insecurity on the part of any group of students; who challenges their claim to equal dignity; or who gives other students an excuse to express their prejudices more openly.

The first argument justifies the suppression of certain ideas on account of their content. The second, by contrast, focuses on subjective reactions. The two arguments of course overlap. If some speakers make certain students feel unwelcome or afraid, it is because of what they say. Defenders of white supremacy, like Richard Spencer, are a particularly odious example. But many other, more respectable ideas have been denied a hearing on campus because, it is said, they make some feel less worthy than others. Speakers who openly challenge the wisdom of affirmative action; question the factual and moral basis of the Black Lives Matter movement; attack gay marriage; urge that sexual harassment procedures be brought into line with the requirements of the criminal justice system; or—as a former president of Harvard did not too long ago—ask if it is worth inquiring whether there is evidence to suggest that women are less well suited than men to certain sorts of scientific research, today run the risk of being disinvited or prevented from speaking *on the grounds that allowing them to do so would cause some on campus to feel less valued, included, and welcome than others.*

Neither of these arguments for limiting what outside speakers may say on campus is persuasive.

The first is an awful confession of weakness. To say that some ideas are so inimical to a school's essential values that they cannot be uttered on campus without tearing it apart betrays a lack of confidence in the special solidarity that joins those nominally committed, at least, to the ethic of conversation. It implies that their community is more vulnerable to disruption than the one at Speakers' Corner, where even racists and other hate-mongers are allowed to have their say.

This turns things upside down. The community of faculty and students is stronger than the one made up of those assembled in the park. The latter can be disrupted by speakers who explode their verbal bombs and set passions boiling. The police are sometimes needed to maintain order or restore it. But that is because the order in question is a thin one and easily torn. It includes everyone in the entire society but joins them only for the purpose of freely expressing their views. The men and women in the park have no collaborative goal beyond that.

A college or university aims at something higher. It aspires to be a community of conversation. This confers a special dignity on those involved. The knowledge that they are engaged in a more challenging pursuit than that at Speaker's Corner ought to be a source of added pride for both faculty and students. It should inspire confidence in the strength of their community and reinforce the belief that even the most hateful words cannot cause them to abandon the ennobling ideal they share. It ought to be a source of greater resilience, not increased vulnerability. It ought to give those who condemn every drop of Richard Spencer's poisonous brew the strength to say to him and others like him, "You may be able to start a riot in the streets, but you cannot start one here. We have too much confidence in ourselves to be thrown off by what you say. You will not meet with violence on our campus. We will picket your speech, and hold a counterdemonstration; we will challenge your ideas at every turn; we will question you and do our best to make you answer. But mostly you will be met by the calm contempt of those whose ties are too deep to be torn by your shameful ideas. Say your piece and go. We don't expect you to converse with us. But we do expect that you will leave with a begrudging respect for our collaborative community of conversation, whose ideals are beyond your power to touch."

Those who invoke the need to protect a school's intellectual and moral integrity as a reason for keeping certain speakers off campus fail to appreciate the special character of a community of conversation and underestimate the strength of its ideals. But their opponents, who condemn all restrictions on campus speech on the grounds that a college is a marketplace of ideas, make a symmetrical mistake. They too miss the distinctive ethic of college life—in their case, by confusing speaking with conversing. They arrive at the right conclusion. Speakers should not be kept off campus because their views contradict a school's basic values. John Derbyshire was invited to Williams to speak in an alumni-financed and student-run program called "Uncomfortable Learning." He should have been allowed to have his say. But those who support his right to speak on libertarian grounds defend it for the wrong reasons. They obscure the meaning of the conversational ideal and ignore the special value, in a democratic society, of the aristocratic order based upon advancement in the pursuit of truth.

The second reason that is often given for denying certain speakers a platform on campus offends this ideal in an even more obvious way.

If it is feared, rightly or wrongly, that a particular speaker will make a certain group of students feel less welcome or valued, *and their feelings are treated as a sufficient reason for keeping the speaker away*, their beliefs and experiences are endowed with an authority that contradicts the most basic requirement of the conversational ideal. Around a seminar table, the force of the ideal is clear as day. That is why I chose it as an example. But if a school allows the feelings of its students to play a determining role in institution-wide decisions about which outside speakers will be given a platform and why, it validates a principle of authority that has application in every aspect of campus life. It "sets a tone from the top" that emboldens those who believe they are entitled, in other settings, to invoke their private experiences as a trump to do so with the implicit backing of their school. It even gives those in my imaginary seminar an easier way to excuse themselves from the rigors of the conversational ideal.

Again, this turns the proper order of things upside down. The ideal that is most visible in a seminar ought to be the one that shapes the whole of college life. The strenuous practice of conversing—the slow but liberating search for the common light of day; the surer sense of self that emerges from it; the growing maturity of those who make it their own—ought to be the norm in other settings too. In particular, it ought to guide those who set general policies regarding freedom of speech on campus. If it does, they will conclude that feelings of exclusion, vulnerability, and the like *are never themselves a reason for limiting speech*. They are sometimes a reason for greater security and always a reason for giving those whose feelings are at issue the opportunity to express them and to explore their meaning in public with others. But to give anyone the right to insist that the fact a speaker makes him or her feel less than fully included *is itself reason enough to bar the speaker in question*, discredits the conversational ideal up and down the line, from the largest auditorium to the smallest seminar classroom, and destroys the rare form of community founded upon it.

In endless pronouncements of tiresome sweetness, the faculty and administrators of America's colleges and universities today insist on the overriding importance of creating a culture of inclusion on campus. They stress the need to respect and honor the feelings of others, especially those belonging to traditionally disadvantaged groups, as an essential means to this end. In this way they give credence to the idea that feelings are trumps with a decisive authority of their own. That in turn emboldens their students to argue that their feelings are reason enough to keep certain speakers away. But this dissolves the community of conversation that the grown-ups on campus are charged to protect. For the high ideal of conversation, it offers as a substitute the infantilizing anti-Socratic belief that no one should be made to feel too badly about themselves or anything else because feeling is the measure of well-being and the highest authority to which anyone can appeal.

The students who invoke this idea didn't invent it themselves. They are following the lead of the faculty, who ought to know better—who turn Socrates on his head by inviting their students to defer to the power of private experience rather than working to judge it in a disinterested light. What a failure of responsibility! Missing the chance to hear others who challenge their views and to benefit from the discipline of having to articulate their criticisms of them in a clear and persuasive way—that is loss enough. But a greater loss is the depreciation of the conversational ideal that follows from the elevation of private sentiments and beliefs to the status of trumps. The only time that our college and university students are likely to experience the full force of this ideal, to have some taste of what it asks and offers, are the few fleeting years they spend on campus, in the interim between family and work. To deprive them of this experience is a pedagogical disgrace.

I end with a clown. He has something to teach us.

Milo Yiannopoulos is a thirty-four-year-old showman and political provocateur. He worked for a time at Breitbart News and has made a career of skewering liberal beliefs. Feminism and gay rights are particular targets. (Yiannopoulos himself is gay.) He works by insult and slur. His attacks are crude and cruel. Once in a while they are funny.

In 2015, Yiannopoulos began what he called the "Dangerous Faggot Tour." He spoke on a number of campuses. In each case his appearance provoked strong and sometimes violent protests. In February 2017, a crowd at Berkeley threw rocks at the police and set fire to a campus building; Yiannopoulos's talk was canceled. Ten days before, his speech at the University of Washington sparked a riot in which a man was shot. Everywhere Yiannopoulos goes, there is trouble. Trouble keeps him in the public eye. In the last few years, no one has been more consistently and deliberately at the center of the stormy debate over free speech on campus than Milo Yiannopoulos.

Yiannopoulos has cost the schools where he has appeared hundreds of thousands of dollars in extra security. That is a real problem. He has also caused many to ask why, among all the possible outside speakers in the world, he should be given a share of the limited time available to them. That is a real question.

The best answer to the latter question, I think, is that Yiannapoulos's appearances, like those of other controversial speakers, are generally sponsored by student organizations that enjoy a substantial degree of autonomy in deciding who to invite. Most schools do not decide, in a centralized way, how their scarce resources of time and space should be allocated among outside speakers, except in the case of lectures and other events that are directly sponsored by the school itself. Nor would many think it a good idea for them to do so. That would invite endless complaints of official censorship. Putting the power to make some of these decisions, at least, in the hands of students themselves ameliorates the problem but inevitably results in a distribution of speakers, topics, and perspectives that is bound to seem unbalanced from one perspective or another. (Yiannopoulos's supporters of course claim that his provocative diatribes are a welcome balance to what they perceive to be a tidal wave of progressive groupthink.)

The issue of cost is a genuine problem. It seems patently unfair that Yiannopoulos should be able to force schools to spend a hundred times what they spend on other speakers to provide security at his talks when he comes to campus for the sake of causing a ruckus. But if we ask why the cost is so great, we come to the heart of the matter.

Who is responsible for the extra police and other precautions that a Yiannopoulos appearance requires? Yiannopoulos himself, of course, at least in part. He chooses his words to give offense and can hardly claim to be surprised when they do. The same goes for the students who invite him. But neither Yiannopoulos nor his supporters can cause a riot by themselves. Those who come to his talks with the intention of disrupting them share the responsibility for creating a security risk.

But this last group—the ones with masks and rocks and shields— is relatively small. Were it not for the much larger group that reacts to Yiannopoulos with outrage and anger but don't come armed for battle, the violent disrupters would be easier to identify and control. They could not draw on the passion of a crowd. That is the fuel that sustains them; it is the medium in which they thrive. And why do those in the crowd believe their anger is so righteous? Part of the answer, of course, is that they find Yiannopoulos's ideas hateful. But part is that they live in an academic environment that elevates feelings, wounds, grievances, and the group solidarities based upon them to the status of supreme (or at least superior) values and makes their expression a good in itself—a belief antithetical to the conversational ideal.

Of course, Yiannopoulos knows this. He sees that the conversational ideal is failing in our colleges and universities. He understands that on campus feelings have become trumps. And he comes to inflame these feelings. He comes to make people mad. He wants to drive his listeners back into their feelings, not draw them out, as Socrates tried to do. Yiannopoulos is a kind of anti-Socrates. A conversation is the furthest thing from his mind.

But in his preoccupation with feelings and his determination to keep his listeners in a state of angry arousal from which they cannot be drawn into anything that looks remotely like a conversation, Yiannopoulos and the students he insults are peas in a pod. He is, in a way, a mirror of their attitudes and habits. Together they are joined in a conspiracy of sorts. One side says, "You cannot come here and attack our community by hurting the feelings of our brothers and sisters." The other replies, "You pathetic weaklings. I'm going to give you a taste of what hurt feelings are like." In this echo chamber, feeling is the touchstone on both sides. The capacity to arouse and express it is the shared measure of success. The only real casualty in this battle of look-alikes is the ideal of conversation that is nowhere to be found.

How much better it would be if Yiannopoulos were met at the campus gate by a student who spoke to him as follows:

"Mr. Yiannopoulos, you have come here to test our commitment to the ideal of conversation. You want to draw us back into our private worlds of feeling and experience. You want us to join you in putting feeling before thought. That we will not do. It would be beneath us to refuse to allow you to speak. What harm can your words do us? But for us your provocations will be an occasion to remember and to celebrate why we are here together on campus. Other conservative speakers have come here before you. Some have had open minds, others closed ones. But they did not come to attack the conditions of conversation itself. That is why you are here. But you will not succeed. Our shared devotion to the idea of a community of conversation is deeper than any of the other beliefs that set us apart. You are a welcome reminder of what we really care about and why. Come and spend a little time with us. Perhaps you will learn to care about it too."

What a noble speech that would be. If its sentiment were widely shared, there might be less need for police and pepper spray. It might also be a starting point to recall why speech on campus is not like that anywhere else—neither in the loving precincts of a family, nor in the democratic marketplace of ideas, which the extravagant freedom of campus speech does not so much exemplify as counterbalance, with its unbending devotion to truth and ranking of souls according to their ability to live in its light.

THREE

Diversity

I.

"Diversity" is the most powerful word in higher education today. No other has so much authority. Older words, like "excellence" and "originality," remain in circulation, but even they have been redefined in terms of diversity. The guidelines for faculty hiring at Boston University are typical. Faculty are told always to pick the "best" candidate but then reminded that the "best" ones are often those who "offer all students valuable lessons about the increasingly diverse world in which we live, and lessons about society, cultural differences, values systems, etc." These are dogmas that are repeated with uniform piety in the official pronouncements of almost every college and university in the country.

"Diversity," as it is understood on campus today, has a narrower meaning than its dictionary definition suggests. First and most importantly, it means diversity of race, ethnicity, gender, and sexual orientation. Other sorts of diversity are sometimes mentioned but only in a secondary way. Most schools, moreover, not only endorse this narrower meaning, they actively subsidize and enforce it.

At Yale, where I teach, there is an Office of Diversity and Inclusion, a deputy dean for Faculty Development and Diversity, an Office of Gender and Campus Culture, and an Office of LGBTQ Resources. Yale's professional schools have a dizzying array of similar programs. There are more than 60 full-time staff serving in some pro-diversity role. (If you include students, the number grows to 150.) Yale also provides financial support for racially and ethnically defined "culture houses" overseen by the Yale College dean for Student Engagement. In 2015, Yale's president announced a $50 million initiative for Faculty Excellence and Diversity.

Other schools do as much or more. Columbia recently announced that it would commit $100 million over the next five years to the diversification of its faculty. Brown has pledged $165 million of its endowment to a plan called Pathways to Diversity and Inclusion.

Many schools have revised their curricula to bring them into line with the demand for greater diversity. Hamilton College now requires that "each concentration" include at least "one course to address diversity issues, ideally as they pertain to the relevant discipline" to "help students gain an understanding of structural and institutional hierarchies based on one or more of the social categories of race, class, gender, ethnicity, nationality, religion, sexuality, age, and abilities/disabilities." At UCLA, all students must "earn at least a C in a course that substantially addresses racial, ethnic, gender, socioeconomic, sexual orientation, religious or other types of diversity." Georgetown, Cornell, the University of Pennsylvania, and Hunter College have similar requirements. At many schools with dorms, students are given the option of living in a building intended principally for those with a specific racial, ethnic, or other identity, including sexual orientation.

A large number of colleges and universities have also adopted some form of mandatory diversity training for faculty and students. Applicants for faculty positions are routinely required to affirm their commitment to diversity and to explain how they intend to promote it. There are even professional guides to help them frame a convincing reply. The details vary from school to school but the pattern is universal.

However soft their touch, all of these programs and procedures tend, moreover, to be self-perpetuating if not self-expanding. They are run by career administrators whose job is to promote the cause of diversity, not to ask why it is a value or whether it poses a threat to other academic norms. Those who hold these positions have a natural incentive to find that more diversity is always better.

The few faculty who challenge the prevailing conception of diversity thus not only find themselves opposed by a much larger group who enthusiastically embrace it, they also face an entrenched bureaucracy armed with the power to impose its vision on others. In our colleges and universities, the question of whether diversity, defined in terms of race, ethnicity, and gender, is good or bad for higher education is one that for the most part has ceased to be debatable at all.

I can put the point more strongly. In an environment in which diversity of this sort is almost universally assumed to be an educational good, diversity of opinion as to whether the assumption is justified now barely exists. No one is forbidden, of course, from challenging it. But the culture of disapproval for dissenting views, backed by an administrative regime whose role is to enforce the regnant ideal, ensures that those who question the value of diversity, defined along these now-orthodox lines, keep their mouths shut for fear of being condemned as bigots.

Today's colleges and universities thus present a paradoxical scene. On the one hand, differences of race, ethnicity, gender, and sexual orientation are celebrated with a kind of manic gusto. Faculty and students are constantly told to be respectful of these differences and to make sure that those defined by them are warmly included in their school's community. On the other hand, as to whether and why *these* sorts of differences are the *right* ones for a college or university to emphasize and extol, a uniformity of opinion prevails: an orthodoxy that represents a near-total absence of diversity in intellectual and moral conviction.

II.

That the word "diversity" possesses as much authority as it does may at first seem unsurprising. Who wants to live in a world without it? The diversity of nature is a source of pleasure and instruction. So is that of human beings. How boring it would be if all people were the same! We each prefer the company of some to others. But that everyone should be identical to those we like—no one wishes *that*. Diversity is first of all an aesthetic value. The link between diversity and beauty, in both the natural and human worlds, is so strong that to many it seems an obvious good on these grounds alone.

But if that were the only or even the main ground on which the defenders of diversity rest their case, it would be hard to understand why they advance their cause with such passion—or why a small minority oppose it with equal fervor. "Diversity" is today a fighting word in our colleges and universities because it represents a moral and political ideal. It stands for more than variety. It stands for respect and inclusion, especially as applied to racial, ethnic, and other groups that in the past have been denied their rights or viewed as less worthy than others. It is an expression of the anti-subordination principle.

This is a powerful legal and political ideal. To some, its extension from the realm of politics and law to that of higher education seems not only natural but necessary. They see the campaign for academic diversity as a means to attack the prejudices that lie at the root of discrimination within our colleges and universities as well as society at large. They contend that these same prejudices, which have produced so much social injustice, have corrupted the work of teaching and learning too. They claim that academic life will be improved if faculty and students are diversified along racial and ethnic lines.

Over the past forty years, the principal rationale for diversity in our colleges and universities has shifted from that of promoting social justice to the enrichment of instruction and study instead. But this is the result of a terrible confusion. It represents the intrusion into the academy of an egalitarian ideal of fairness that has an unimpeachable authority outside the walls of our colleges and universities but less or none within them. It confers authority on a conception of diversity that is defensible in political and legal terms but hostile to the pursuit of truth and destructive of the aristocratic ideal of becoming a more complete human being, as distinct from a well-trained professional. It does not improve the work of teaching and learning but corrupts it instead.

How did this confusion come about? A bit of history is required.

In the early 1970s, the medical school at the University of California at Davis instituted a special admissions program to increase the number of students from historically disadvantaged groups. "Blacks," "Chicanos," "Asians," and "American Indians" were singled out for preferential treatment. Students from these groups could apply and be admitted under the school's general admissions program. But they—and they alone—were also eligible for admission under a separate program for which a set number of spots in the entering class had been reserved.

Allan Bakke, a white man, applied to the medical school and was twice denied admission. He challenged the school's special admissions program on the grounds that it discriminated on the basis of race, in violation of the Equal Protection Clause of the Fourteenth Amendment and Title VI of the Civil Rights Act of 1964. The California

Supreme Court held that the program in question was not "the least intrusive means" of achieving the otherwise legitimate goal of integrating the medical profession and thus could not pass muster under a so-called strict-scrutiny standard. It ordered the Davis medical school to admit the plaintiff on the grounds that the school had the burden of proving that Bakke would not have been admitted even if its special admissions program did not exist—a challenge the school acknowledged it could not meet.

The Supreme Court of the United States heard the case in the fall of 1977. The following spring, it delivered its badly divided opinion in *Regents of the University of California v. Bakke.* For the past forty years, *Bakke* has been the starting point for all debate about the meaning and value of diversity in higher education.

Four justices voted to invalidate the school's special admissions program on the grounds that it violated the 1964 Civil Rights Act, whose language and statutory history they examined in detail. They declined to reach the larger constitutional question. Another four believed this question could not be avoided. They concluded that the Davis admissions program was constitutionally permissible. They held that what came to be known as "reverse discrimination" does not offend the Equal Protection Clause of the Fourteenth Amendment. If their view had prevailed, the structure of the existing program would have been allowed to stand and the school's justification for it accepted, despite its explicit reliance on race and ethnicity as a basis for determining eligibility under its special set-aside provisions.

This left the Court in a four-four split. The deciding vote was cast by Justice Lewis F. Powell Jr., who was not prepared to accept the view advanced by either group.

Powell held that the legislative history of the Civil Rights Act shows that Title VI prohibits "only those racial classifications" that are forbidden under the Fourteenth Amendment as well. This allowed and indeed compelled him to address the constitutional issue directly.

On the face of it, Powell said, the Davis program violated the Fourteenth Amendment because it distinguished between applicants "on the basis of [their] race and ethnic status." The question was whether distinctions of this kind are ever allowable. The school claimed that giving preferential treatment to applicants from certain racial and ethnic groups is an essential means "of integrating the medical profession and increasing the number of physicians willing to serve members of minority groups." Powell acknowledged the legitimacy of these goals. He further conceded that the underrepresentation of blacks and other minorities in the medical profession was in large part the result of widespread discrimination in the past—of what he called discrimination by "society at large." But he insisted that the discriminatory favoring of racial and ethnic minorities could not be employed as a remedy to cure the harm caused by past discrimination of this generalized kind.

This does not mean that "reverse" discrimination may never be used as a remedial tool. In Powell's view, though, it has to satisfy two conditions. First, the party using it must be guilty of past discrimination of an individualized sort. Participation in a larger social order whose culture, practices, and even laws are discriminatory is not enough. Second, the beneficiaries of the remedy must likewise show that they are the victims not just of racial or ethnic discrimination in a global sense but of specific discriminatory acts committed by the party who now proposes to use an equally specific system of preferences as a means to cure them.

In both respects, Powell's opinion is strikingly individualistic. He does not deny—who could?—that discrimination against blacks and other minorities has been a pervasive factor in American life. But, in Powell's view, it is constitutionally permissible to fight negative discrimination of this kind with a counterbalancing scheme of affirmative action only where both the wrong and the remedy are specific to the parties involved. Every sentence of Powell's opinion reflects his hostility to the idea that affirmative action may be used to repair "the effects of 'societal discrimination,' an amorphous concept of injury that may be ageless in its reach into the past."

Although he does not elaborate the point, Powell's concern seems to be both practical and moral. If we allow the use of affirmative action to remedy generalized effects of this kind, where can we draw a line? And what will become of the notion of ethical responsibility, which—intuitively at least—seems strongly tied to individual foresight and action? These concerns perhaps explain the fact that throughout his opinion Powell seems less sympathetic to the intended beneficiaries of the Davis program, who form an "amorphous" group, than to Allan Bakke, an "innocent" individual who should not be made to "bear the burdens of redressing grievances not of [his own] making."

But the individualism of Powell's approach is also its weakness. To begin with, the effects of past discrimination are hardly past. They linger on in our culture and economy. The Second Reconstruction began with the dismantling of the apartheid system that grew up in the South after the failure of the First Reconstruction. Its proponents had to confront the fact that racial discrimination in America has never been only a matter of law and that to dismantle it we need to attack its social and economic aspects as well. Even after the abolition of Jim Crow, these remain. But they are not freestanding wrongs that exist independently of the system of legal discrimination that for more than two centuries gave legitimacy and support to the caste system of race prejudice. They are its surviving aftereffects. In this sense, Jim Crow still haunts us from the grave.

In deciding whether the law should now allow the use of racial and ethnic preferences as a means to combat these aftereffects, two facts seem relevant. The first is that the benefits and burdens of past discrimination have been diffused so widely that it is now impossible to identify individual winners and losers—or, more precisely, that people *are* winners and losers, to some degree at least, on account of their being members of one group or another, regardless of what other individual traits they possess. The second is that the laws that once underwrote the entire system of racial and ethnic discrimination were themselves cast in general terms. The privileges and disabilities they assigned to individuals were based on their group membership and nothing more. (Justice Marshall makes this point with special force in his separate opinion in *Bakke*.)

Those who are impressed by these two facts will be less inclined to insist, to the degree that Justice Powell does, on the individualized nexus between wrong and remedy that he makes a condition of affirmative action. They will be more willing to allow an admissions program like the one at issue in *Bakke* that openly discriminates on the basis of race and ethnicity in order to help cure the lingering effects of past discrimination in society at large. Their belief that this is a permissible course will be strengthened by the observation that affirmative action is especially important in our colleges and universities because of the role they play as a gateway to social and economic opportunities of many other kinds. If I had been on the Court, I would have voted with Justices Brennan, White, Marshall, and Blackmun to uphold the Davis program as designed.

But Powell did something more than merely block the wiser course these four justices would have allowed. Having held that the University of California could not justify its affirmative action program on the grounds the school proposed, he offered an alternative. He sketched another argument that the school might have made on behalf of giving minority applicants a preference in its admissions process. This is the part of Powell's opinion that has proved the most consequential for higher education in the forty years since *Bakke* and damaged it in ways that Powell himself could not foresee.

If, Powell says, the Davis medical school had distinguished among its applicants on the basis of their race and ethnicity, not as a means to repair a systemic injustice in society at large, but as a way of achieving greater diversity in its student body for the sake of what he calls various "educational benefits," then its program might well have passed muster. Powell identifies a number of such benefits. These include the exposure of society's future leaders to a diversity of "ideas and mores." But the most important benefit of a diverse student body, according to Powell, is the contribution it makes to "that robust exchange of ideas that lies at the heart of the notion of academic freedom." This is "a special concern of the First Amendment." A justification of racial and ethnic favoritism that appeals to the idea of diversity as an educational good therefore relies on what Powell calls a "countervailing constitutional interest" that must be weighed against the demands of the Equal Protection Clause.

Powell's insistence that diversity is the engine of academic freedom, and not its enemy, will seem ironic to those who view its mature expression in today's colleges and universities as an instrument of orthodoxy instead. But that aside, anyone who reads his opinion in *Bakke* is bound to be struck by the spirit of individualism that consistently informs both its negative and positive parts. It is Powell's individualism that leads him to conclude that a school may not use racially tailored categories to achieve the extracurricular goal of greater fairness in society at large. But the same individualism also shapes his understanding of diversity as an educational good. In Powell's view, the good of diversity lies in the contribution it makes to a culture of "speculation, experiment and creation" whose goal is to support every participant in the search for, and expression of, his or her own distinctive view of life. It is a group-based means to an individual end.

Powell's individualism is reflected in the limits he places on the use of racial and ethnic distinctions as a means of promoting diversity. Such distinctions are allowable, he says, only where they are "only one element in a range of factors," "a 'plus' in a particular applicant's file." Strict quotas are impermissible. Every admissions decision must be made on an individual basis. To illustrate the sorts of preferential treatment he would allow, Powell appends to his opinion Harvard's then-current description of its admissions policy, which hits all the right notes with dissembling grace and stresses, in particular, the individual nature of each and every one of the college's admissions decisions.

The four justices who would have upheld the Davis admissions program without modification joined Powell in affirming that race and ethnicity may be used as factors in a "properly devised" program like Harvard's whose goal is the attainment of a "genuine diversity" in the student body. Because they could not get Powell to agree that reverse discrimination may be used to cure an extracurricular wrong, they had to settle for the weaker cup of tea he offers in the second part of his opinion. In the view of a majority of the justices, the pursuit of the academic good of diversity thus became the *only* grounds on which a school may give minority applicants a special advantage in admissions without running afoul of the Equal Protection Clause of the Fourteenth Amendment.

As a result, Powell's discussion of diversity became a road map of sorts for schools that want to give a preference to minority applicants but avoid constitutional trouble. In the years that followed, the key phrases in his opinion—"only one element," "single but important element," "an admissions program . . . flexible enough to consider all pertinent elements of diversity in light of the particular qualifications of each applicant"—served as a kind of mantra for schools that hope to insulate their affirmative action programs from legal attack.

Many of these, of course, have been challenged. Over the years, the Supreme Court has shown a growing impatience with Powell's position. It has given hints that the day may be coming when the promotion of diversity as an educational good will no longer be viewed as an acceptable justification for giving any explicit weight to race and ethnicity in college and university admissions. But that day has not yet come. The only modifications of Powell's view that the Court has so far made are of a modest kind—finding that a school's admissions program gives too much weight to race, or does so too explicitly, or comes too close to a quota system like the one outlawed in *Bakke*. At the same time the Court has repeatedly affirmed the basic premises of Powell's analysis: that diversity is an educational good; that choosing the best means to achieve it is for schools themselves to decide; and that, in doing so, they may take race and ethnicity into account, though they should be careful to make sure their judgments have a suitably individualized character and do not resemble a quota too nakedly.

These have remained the starting point for the Court's analysis of affirmative action in higher education in every case since *Bakke*. They have also pervasively transformed the culture of our colleges and universities. Powell's statement on diversity takes up only a few pages in the *United States Reports*. But it has reshaped every aspect of educational policy and experience. It has bred bureaucracies and changed the mood on campus in ways that undermine the ideas of academic freedom and individual self-discovery that Powell himself puts at the center of his defense of diversity as an academic good. Perhaps this would not have happened, or happened to the same degree, if the Court had adopted Justice Marshall's sensible view that schools may openly use race in admissions as their distinctive way of contributing to the achievement of a vital social good. But such speculation is pointless. Powell's view of diversity has controlled the discussion of race and ethnicity in higher education for four decades, with consequences of a far-reaching and destructive kind.

III.

Three are worth noting. I list them in ascending order of importance. None, though, touch the heart of the matter, which concerns the relation between group membership and individual identity. I shall return to this in the following section.

First, Powell's view converts the use of racial and ethnic categories in admissions from an urgent but temporary expedient into a permanent fixture of academic life.

No thoughtful person can doubt that African Americans and other minorities have been the victims of grievous discrimination in the past. It is also reasonable to think—*I* find it so, at least—that the victims of these historical injustices have not yet been compensated in full. There may be wrongs so great that no remedy can ever fully compensate for them. Perhaps the crimes of American slavery and Indian genocide are of this kind. But our longing to be one people, joined in affection and united in our commitment to the ideals of Jefferson's "empire of liberty," weighs in favor of closing the balance sheet of suffering and compensation. The fact that whites today, although they benefit from past discrimination, did not themselves create it points in the same direction. This implies that we ought to assign a temporal limit to the process of reparation itself. The extent of the limit is a matter of debate. But considerations of individual responsibility and political solidarity both strongly suggest that the process must come to an end at some point.

Had the Supreme Court allowed the University of California to use racial and ethnic preferences as part of a broader program of reparation, a different set of questions would have moved to the fore. Is the percentage of blacks and other minorities in the medical profession growing or shrinking? Is their overall socioeconomic condition relative to whites improving, declining, or remaining the same?

Are the academic qualifications of minority applicants improving? What do those admitted under the program do after they graduate? In each case, it would be important to distinguish between different minority groups—between blacks and Asians, for example. It would also be important to continue asking these questions at regular intervals.

But they all become moot once the rationale for affirmative action is put on the ground of diversity. The use of racial and ethnic distinctions to achieve the extracurricular goal of social justice employs the lexicon of wrong and remedy. This is the language of the law. For a wrong of a given magnitude, the law imposes a remedy sufficiently large to offset it. Enough is always enough. But if these same distinctions are justified on the grounds that they are needed to achieve a desired degree of diversity in the student body, and this in turn is characterized as an academic good "essential to the quality of higher education," it is difficult to see why race and ethnicity should *ever* cease to play a role in a school's admissions decisions, even if every past injustice has been paid in full. When it is defended in these terms, affirmative action has no built-in time limit. It becomes a permanent fixture of educational practice instead. Powell's fear that the use of reverse discrimination to cure the effects of past discrimination might become, as he says, "ageless" has thus been vindicated more fully than he could have imagined by the adoption of the diversity rationale that he himself proposed for the use of racial and ethnic distinctions in college and university admissions.

In recent years, the Supreme Court has hinted that perhaps some time limit ought to be placed on the use of such distinctions even for diversity purposes. But it is hard to see how a limit of this kind could be effective even if it were imposed. A vast academic bureaucracy has grown up to implement the ideal of diversity, defined along racial and ethnic lines. More importantly, our colleges and universities have learned to adopt strategies for the promotion of diversity that carefully blur the use of racial and ethnic categories and cover them with a reassuring appeal to individualized judgments. Even if the Supreme Court were to outlaw all programs except those that consider every facet of a candidate's personality, which of course includes his or her racial and ethnic identity, the subtlety of the schemes that today give special weight to race and ethnicity in the admissions process would make it difficult if not impossible to root them out.

This brings me to the *second* consequence of Powell's opinion in *Bakke*. The road map that Powell provides is an invitation to bad faith.

That a college or university should think of itself as having responsibilities to society at large is not only reasonable, it is unavoidable. Our earliest colleges were founded to ensure that their communities had a sufficient number of well-trained professionals to care for the bodies and souls of their members. The public universities of the nineteenth century were similarly devoted to the good of their communities. They were established to produce better farmers, scientists, and government administrators; to increase prosperity; and to spread the blessings of education among the people at large.

Consistent with this tradition of public service, an American college or university in the twenty-first century ought to assume that part of its work is to promote the core values of liberty and equality in the society as a whole. It should also assume that today this includes playing a more vigorous part than it has before in helping to achieve the goal of racial justice. These assumptions are entirely in line with the oldest traditions of American higher education.

Powell's opinion in *Bakke* puts a roadblock in the way of a school's meeting this responsibility directly. This creates a moral pressure to do so in some other way. Powell tells schools how to do this. All they have to do is convert the straightforward language of public service into the different vocabulary of diversity as an educational enrichment. But this conversion comes at a cost. It forces schools to say they are doing one thing while doing another. It breeds dishonesty in an environment where honesty should be at a premium. And it discourages reflection on whether the promotion of racial and ethnic diversity can in fact be defended on educational grounds as opposed to those of social justice.

The Harvard statement that Powell cites as a model of how a school should go about the business of composing a diverse student body offers a telling example.

Harvard states that an applicant's race and ethnicity is a factor to be considered in assembling a properly diverse group of students, though only one factor among many. In this respect, it is no different than a student's geographical home or musical and athletic talents. But in the case of black applicants, at least, one must be mindful of the fact that admitting them in "small numbers might also create a sense of isolation among the black students themselves and thus make it more difficult for them to develop and achieve their potential"—also, presumably, to contribute effectively to other students' experience of racial diversity. But when combined with this "small numbers" proviso, treating the race of black applicants as a "plus" yields a de facto quota. The end result is little different from the explicit quota system employed by the medical school at Davis, except that its reality is denied by all involved, students and administrators alike. That the percentage of black students and other minorities admitted to the nation's top colleges and graduate schools remains so steady year after year strongly suggests that something like a quota system is still at work, although it is disguised by a myriad of individual judgments and officially disclaimed by deans and college presidents.

One might respond, I suppose, that in cases like this a bit of dishonesty is a good thing. Isn't it better that black and other minority students admitted under a de facto quota be told they are there to add to the school's diversity? This puts them on a par with their

white classmates. Everyone adds diversity, no more or less than anyone else. And that erases the stigma of having been admitted, in part
at least, on the strength of one's group membership in addition to,
but also as distinct from, individual promise alone.

I have heard these arguments a thousand times. I am not per-
suaded by them. I believe it is educationally destructive to be dishonest with students about the reasons for a school's implicit racial
and ethnic quotas—to tell them these exist for the sake of academic
diversity rather than acknowledging that they serve a larger social
purpose. Students who are lied to in this way won't be charmed out
of any stigma they feel. Their feelings will go underground and fes-
ter. And when they resurface, they are likely to take the form of an
intensified demand that the diversity minority students contribute
to their school be more than merely recognized—that it be honored
and celebrated so that every doubt they or anyone else might have as
to whether they really *belong* there can be quashed by noisy demon-
strations of admiration for the cultural and other values they bring
to the table.

This process moves in familiar steps: from a demand that the
community *acknowledge* that minority students contribute an element of needed diversity; to an insistence that others *empathize* with
their experience; to the belief that even empathy falls short, and only
active *celebration* will do.

Indeed, even this isn't the end of the line. Minority students who
insist that their diversity be celebrated in a festival of multicultural-
ism may begin to worry that the veneration is a show—which, in
the climate of mendacity encouraged by the need to hide a straightforward program of social justice under the cover of an educational
ideal, is an understandable conclusion. When this happens, some
will perhaps be moved to take the final step and insist that their racial or ethnic identity—the source of their diversity—is a valuable
possession that no one but them is entitled to enjoy, and that others

who pretend to do so, by celebrating its qualities, are stealing what does not belong to them and are guilty of what has come to be called a "cultural appropriation." This is such a far-fetched and illiberal idea that it is difficult to understand how it could have gathered even the modest support it now enjoys on America's campuses. But when viewed as the last stage in a process of intensifying demands, driven by an anxiety that is the product of the culture of dishonesty that Justice Powell's opinion invites, it is perhaps easier to fathom.

It would be better, I think, to tell students the truth, if the law allowed it. It would be better to admit that minority students are given favorable treatment in a school's admissions process as its way of contributing to a nationwide program of reparative justice; while underscoring that every student, once admitted, will receive the same enthusiastic support and be held to the same high standards as all the others. Instead of lauding students for the diversity they *bring to* the school, it would be better to remind them that they are there for the sake of the common good the school *affords* them.

Most students understand this already, and telling them something else only creates an anxious dissonance that is a breeding ground for all sorts of exaggerated claims about the value of diversity. These may reassure students that none is the beneficiary of affirmative action and that minority students make an essential contribution to the educational work of their school *merely on account of their racial or ethnic identities,* so that their success is guaranteed simply by being who they are. But the psychological relief this brings is fragile. It papers over an underlying anxiety that only the truth can dispel. It drives students into their separate corners and undermines the spirit of common engagement. It encourages students to think first about what they contribute, not what they stand to gain. And it promotes a culture of dishonesty in institutions devoted to the pursuit of truth, which more than any other demands the greatest measure of honesty that human beings can summon. When Powell forbade schools from openly embracing affirmative action as a means of attacking a general social ill, and invited them to recast their programs in the language of diversity instead, he drove the truth underground and made it illegal for our colleges and universities to address their students with the honesty that the search for truth requires.

Powell's forced conversion of a moral and political ideal into an educational one has had a *third* harmful effect.

There is no more controversial topic in American politics than racial justice. Accusations of prejudice and bigotry are common and not always misplaced. The temperature is often high enough to melt goodwill and decorum. The controversy sparked by the three words, "Black Lives Matter," is a reminder of how volatile the subject remains.

There is no requirement that those on one side of a heated political debate credit the open-mindedness of those on the other. It is permissible to view them as ignoramuses who must be beaten into submission by voting, shaming, or the invocation of the law where it is available as an instrument of coercion. This is not always the best strategy but it is never an unacceptable one.

Academic disagreements are different. Important ones are often inflamed by passion too. But the goal of those involved is to persuade their adversaries with better facts and arguments—not to bludgeon them into submission by belittling their motives or shaming them with accusations of bigotry. This principle is not always honored. Yet even in the breach it remains an ideal of academic exchange. Once arguments on campus assume a political tone, shaming and the other tools of politics not only become more commonplace, they acquire a legitimacy that puts the conversational ideal itself in doubt.

Moreover, shaming need not take an explicit form. It may be more subtly expressed by the widely shared belief that only a bigot would hold a particular view. On many campuses today, anyone who responds to the claim that black lives matter by insisting that *all* lives do is likely to provoke such a reaction. The reaction cannot be forbidden. But the more it is legitimated by the belief that academic disagreements are merely the continuation of political ones by other means, the more self-confident it becomes.

Powell tells us not to think of racial and ethnic preferences as a cure for a political disease. We are to think of them as the means to an "educational benefit" instead. But when we do, the political passion that inspires the first is inevitably transposed, in a disguised form, to the second—to the educational process itself. Powell says that promoting diversity is a legitimate way of securing the values of the First Amendment. But can anyone doubt that it is a roundabout way of securing those of the Fourteenth as well? The achievement of social and legal equality may not be the stated aim of creating a diversified student body. But when this educational goal is bent to serve a political purpose, in a surreptitious way, it takes on a political character of its own. The academy is politicized. Debates within it acquire a combative edge and shaming becomes a legitimate tool of engagement.

The special form of freedom that we call "academic" depends upon a measure of disengagement from the political realities that are the subject of many academic disputes. Students and faculty can be free to express their views in a wide-open and experimental fashion only in case their arguments are without immediate political effect, unlike the act of casting a vote or giving money to a political party. Powell defends racial and ethnic diversity as a means of enhancing academic freedom. But when the line between politics and education is blurred in the way his own opinion invites, the freedom of the academy loses its special character and devolves into the general freedom that all citizens enjoy to declare their views and do everything they lawfully may to advance them, including shaming their adversaries into silence.

It is worth pausing to note how different the politicization of our campuses today is from that of the 1960s.

Student activists then (I was one) mobilized in pursuit of two main political goals: One was securing the civil rights of African Americans. The other was ending the war in Vietnam. Students disrupted speeches and occupied faculty offices. In a few cases, the violence was more extreme. But for the most part, the students who did these things did them in the belief, whether mistaken or not, that academic life could not continue as usual in the existing political environment. They insisted that the ordinary business of teaching and learning be suspended, or redirected, to meet a political emergency.

By contrast, those students who today insist that speech be sanitized to avoid giving offense, find "micro-aggressions" at every turn, and call cultural appropriation a crime are not calling for the suspension of teaching and learning in order to address an urgent political need. They are demanding that the work of the academy itself be refashioned in light of a political ideal repackaged as one of diversity. The result is a corruption of higher education from within. Their campaign is kinder and gentler in tone. Its watchword is "Include and respect!" But in the end it does more harm to the spirit of the academy than the sometimes rough-elbowed protests of the 1960s whose student leaders generally (though not always, of course) recognized the distinction between politics and intellectual inquiry. Today's student vanguard, which has grown to an acquiescent majority, views the life of the mind in a way that threatens to obliterate this distinction entirely.

IV.

Justice Powell's supreme value is that of individual responsibility. This is reflected in his insistence that reverse discrimination is allowable only where the party who employs it is *individually* guilty of having discriminated in the past and its beneficiaries those who were *individually* harmed as a result. It is reflected in his sympathy for Allan Bakke, who as an *individual* did nothing to hurt those benefited by Davis's affirmative action program. It is exemplified by the Harvard statement that he quotes with approval, which concludes by declaring that "the critical criteria" for deciding whether to admit a student "are often *individual* qualities or experiences not dependent upon race but sometimes associated with it." And it underlies Powell's interpretation of the good of diversity as the free exchange of ideas in a community of *individuals* with different opinions.

Powell's emphasis on the individual is strongly aligned with a central norm of academic life. In the humanities, students begin by learning the fundamentals of their discipline. But their apprenticeship is for the sake of eventually being able to discover and express their own perspective on it. The final aim of all study and research in the humanities is the intensification of *individual* sensibility and judgment.

The same is true, in an analogous way, in the natural and social sciences. Students of physics start with Newton and go on to Einstein and Planck. But the point of their study is not to train them to be slavish copyists. It is to put them in the position of being able to make a fresh contribution to the understanding of some topic. The highest value in physics and every other science is that of *originality*. This often takes teamwork. But it is by definition unprecedented and therefore unique. It is always an *individual* achievement.

The more prestigious the institution, the more the development of individual judgments and abilities is likely to be stressed. In our most selective colleges and universities, it is a nearly sacred value. Only at lower levels, where vocational interests predominate, is the emphasis on acquiring general skills instead.

This has not always been the case. In the earliest period of American higher education, college study was wholly conformist. Students followed a prescribed curriculum with no electives. The purpose of their education was not to cultivate their individuality or promote original thinking; it was to preserve and perpetuate established forms of thought and prepare the students for specific professional roles of importance to the wider society. This remained the pattern until after the Civil War. Looking back on his years at Harvard in the 1850s, Henry Adams wrote that the college created "a type but not a will" and produced "an autobiographical blank, a mind on which only a water-mark had been stamped."

With the rise of the elective system, the center of gravity in higher education shifted in a more individualist direction. Charles Eliot pioneered the system during his long presidency at Harvard. He urged its adoption as a means of allowing students to discover their own individual passions while promoting greater rigor through increased specialization. Eliot was inspired by the model of the German universities with their modern research ideal, which emphasized the endless growth of knowledge in all branches of study. Originality became a leading value in every discipline from philology to physics. The growth of graduate programs and the eventual acceptance of the PhD as a requirement for college or university teaching were signposts along the way.

At the same time, a new philosophy of liberal education gave even the relatively nonspecialized training of undergraduates a more individualist orientation. Despite the spread of the elective system, students at most liberal arts colleges continued to read many of the same works they had before, well into the twentieth century. But the point of studying them came to be viewed in a different light. They were no longer seen as providing models for students to memorize and imitate but as material from which each might fashion his (and eventually her) own inimitable view of life. In time this became a cliché. The purpose of a liberal education, nearly everyone eventually agreed, is to "liberate" those who receive it from their inherited prejudices through an exposure to a wide array of ideas, arguments, and exemplary human types so that they might decide for themselves which of these to endorse and how to combine them in the way that best expresses their *individual* judgments about what is important and why.

This way of thinking about the goal of liberal education only became dominant in the first half of the twentieth century. But it has deep roots in the American mind—so many, in fact, that the placement of the individual at the center of the enterprise of teaching and learning is wildly overdetermined by older American values. A full list would include many more, but three in particular are worth noting.

The first is the Calvinist insistence on the individual's responsibility for his or her own salvation. The Puritan settlers brought this Protestant idea to our shores in an especially rigorous form. The radical individualism of the Puritans, divested of their theology, permeates our culture to this day.

A second is what Louis Hartz famously called the "liberal tradition" in American life. Hartz associated this tradition with the political philosophy of John Locke. Locke's insistence on the sanctity of private property; his argument that the right to private property is natural and therefore pre-political; and his conclusion that government may not interfere with this natural right all strongly reinforce the individualist tenor of American thought on a wide range of political and personal issues.

A third—which might perhaps be viewed as a fusion of these two—is the ideal of the "self-made man" (and today woman). Benjamin Franklin, Frederick Douglass, Abraham Lincoln, and Andrew Carnegie all espoused it in one version or another. Each was also an illustration of the ideal: Franklin with his strategies of self-discipline; Douglass with his exhortation to "Work! Work! Work!"; Lincoln with his ethic of free labor; and Carnegie with his gospel of wealth. Even in our regulated age, the individualist ideal of lifting oneself up through study and toil to a better life retains its power in the American imagination.

In the realm of higher culture, the ideal of self-discovery that in time became the universal premise of undergraduate liberal education was most forcefully expressed by the writers we associate with the "Transcendentalist" movement in American letters. The Transcendentalists were the descendants of an evolved Unitarianism that had either matured or declined, depending on one's point of view, into a cosmic pantheism. They tended to identify God with nature and to find the divine in the exquisite particularity of things. As a consequence, they placed an emphasis on individual self-definition that reached a level of metaphysical grandeur unmatched before or since.

Emerson's essay "Self-Reliance" is a famous example. But it was Walt Whitman who brought this way of thinking to a climax in his long prose essay "Democratic Vistas." The end of democratic life, Whitman declares, is the cultivation of an "idiocrasy" in which every individual is encouraged and enabled to discover his or her "special nativity," "soaring its own flight, following out itself." This is the spirit of "perfect individualism" that "deepest tinges and gives character to the idea of the Aggregate." It reflects the metaphysical truth that of all the individuals in the world, no two are "alike" and every one is "good." For Whitman, this was a philosophical, political, and aesthetic axiom. It is his characteristically extravagant way of expressing the individualist ideal that in a more sedate form had become the orthodox view among liberal educators everywhere by the middle of the twentieth century. It also gives us a good starting point from which to survey the harm that the contemporary understanding of diversity has done to this ideal, for Whitman was a great champion of diversity too. But the diversity he celebrates is most emphatically that of individuals, not groups. To understand why the emphasis on diversity has become such a destructive force in higher education, it is important to see what this shift in emphasis means.

Those who today insist that our colleges and universities need to be more diverse sometimes give lip service to the diversity of individual talents, values, and judgments. But they mainly think of diversity in group terms and measure its presence or absence accordingly. When a college president or dean reports on the progress that his or her school has made toward becoming a more diverse place, it is almost always in these terms.

This is a reasonable if not necessary way of thinking in politics and law. The issue of racial justice is a powerful example. Blacks and other minorities have been discriminated against as groups. The discrimination falls, in each case, on a particular individual. But it is *because* of the individual's membership in a disfavored group that he or she is denied the opportunities and respect that others receive.

Having suffered on account of such group-based discrimination, it is fitting that any remedy be framed in similar terms as well. It is difficult, in fact, to know how else a remedy might be designed. If the individual members of a group have been wrongfully harmed solely because of their membership in the group, shouldn't the compensation they are owed be tailored to their group membership as well? That not only seems just; in many cases it is likely to be the only practical solution.

The affirmative action program at issue in *Bakke* fit this pattern. It was structured along group lines. In the view of the majority, this was its fatal flaw. But when Powell recast the rationale for programs of this sort as one of academic diversity, although he himself attached the highest value to individual responsibility, he facilitated the importation into the academy of a style of group thinking that poisons the spirit of individualism and destroys the distinctively American form of diversity associated with it—the one that Walt Whitman calls an "idiocrasy."

There are four reasons why this is so. The *first* is that a group-based way of thinking encourages a culture of grievance that narrows horizons and inhibits honest reflection.

Grievance is appropriate where injustice is concerned. "Blame," "guilt," "victimization": these are the terms we naturally apply when we are thinking about the redress of past wrongs. Things become more complicated when the lines of individual responsibility blur, as in *Bakke* itself. Still, even if a whole group is made to bear the cost of repairing the harm wrongly done to another, it is impossible not to think or speak of the members of the latter group as victims. The very idea of compensation requires it. But when a compensatory political ideal is translated into the academic value of diversity, the vocabulary of perpetrators and victims carries along a host of effects that weaken the prospects for the kind of "robust" exchange that Justice Powell exalts in his opinion.

On the one side, it encourages those who believe they are entitled to think of themselves as victims to reject every challenge to any position they take in an academic exchange as a further assault upon them—as a moral outrage and not just a mistake. It gives them grounds to reject their opponents as wrongdoers whose views cannot be taken seriously until full reparations have been made.

On the other side, it encourages those who are invited, or compelled, to think of themselves as perpetrators to substitute apology for argument, since apology is the only form of compensation they can offer. Worse, it motivates them to search for ways in which they too have been victimized by the prejudices and oversights of others. When being a victim becomes a trump card in every academic debate, who won't want to have one of his or her own?

In this way, the exchange of ideas, beliefs, and judgments is converted into a universal scramble for victimhood with the predictable result that feelings of mistreatment and abuse dull the power of honest self-appraisal and discourage those who feel undervalued from listening to anyone who has the indecency to suggest their values are misplaced. Beginning with the members of those racial and ethnic groups whose claim to be the victims of injustice in the society at large is most direct and plausible, victimization spreads and becomes the universal currency in which all arguments are redeemed. A culture of complaint and apology settles in a miasma over the academy as a whole. The result is a sharp contraction of the space in which it is permitted, let alone encouraged, to try out different attitudes and judgments in a provisional way, free of the risk of condemnation as a moral cretin or a privileged egotist blind to the suffering of others.

Second, the transmutation of the legal and political ideal of racial justice into the academic value of diversity promotes a form of solidarity that corrupts the spirit of individualism our colleges and universities still claim to respect. Solidarity is indispensable in politics. Only a party can advance a program and anyone who joins one must put at least some individual scruples aside. It is also entirely understandable that the members of a group who are owed compensation for the harms they have suffered solely because of their membership in it should feel a sense of solidarity too. But when the compensatory ideal of affirmative action is reformulated in terms of diversity and reconceived as a pedagogical norm, the spirit of solidarity that has an appropriate place in the struggle for justice is transferred to the academy, where its effects are entirely bad.

It is bad for those who, as the members of a historically disadvantaged group, feel bound to hold the party line on every issue that touches the welfare of the group as a whole. It is bad for those outside the group who find it difficult to think of themselves except in group terms too (as the members of an exploitative or racist or homophobic class). It invites on all sides a species of conformism that is more dangerous than the perennial kind, because it has a moral warrant—because it is not merely a habit but a duty. It substitutes for the older, familiar sort that has always been a curse on the ideal of self-discovery, a new one that, if anything, is harder to uproot on account of the ethical support it draws from the solidaristic norms of political life.

Third, when an individual speaks in a spirit of solidarity, there is always some pressure to do so as a representative. One who speaks in this capacity acts on behalf of others. She presents and defends the interests of her constituents. A representative may share these but need not do so. Representation is a role. To play it responsibly, one must accept some separation, at least, between one's own views and those of one's constituents. It is true that a representative is often required to exercise independent judgment. But this is only for the sake of better serving the interests of those she represents, never her own. The distinction between these is a defining feature of all political action. It undergirds the special responsibilities of those who accept its demands.

By contrast, in academic life the duty to act as a representative is not only misplaced, it has a destructive effect. It encourages those who adopt it to quiet their conscience when it conflicts with their duty to promote the cause of those they represent. It invites them to suppress the search for their own individual center of gravity as a selfish indulgence that must be postponed or put aside altogether. And it invests the views they espouse with an aggressive authority that may be an aid to political success but is the enemy of the spirit of tentativeness, experimentation, and doubt on which the search for an individual view of the world depends.

There is always some danger of this. Human beings naturally seek the comforts of group membership. They find it painful to sort things out for themselves. It is often easier to be a representative, whose views are backed by those of others, than to think and judge for oneself. But this tendency must be forcefully resisted if the academic ideal of individual self-discovery is to have even a fighting chance.

The association of diversity with a program of social and political justice, and its consequent interpretation in group terms, makes this far more difficult. If the reason a student has been admitted to a college or university is that he or she belongs to a particular racial or ethnic group—and this is justified on the grounds that *as a member of the group* the student has something distinctive to contribute to the conversation on campus—the expectation will be stronger that when the student speaks, it is as a representative of the group in question. Others are likely to feel they have no standing to challenge this assumption. After all, who are they to say? Even more damagingly, minority students will be encouraged to adopt it themselves, since from their perspective it may seem an act of treason to ignore the responsibilities of representation, which the group-based understanding of diversity carries over from the political sphere to that of academic life.

There are many students on both sides of this divide who overcome these expectations. But it requires an extra effort of imagination and a special dose of courage. The intellectual and moral culture that has been bred on America's campuses by the politicized ethic of diversity puts an obstacle in their way. It makes real independence of mind harder to achieve. And it compromises the spirit of individual expression by subtly though pervasively conveying the idea that to speak in any capacity other than as a representative of one's racial, ethnic, or gender group—whether assertively or apologetically, with pride or shame—is an act of moral weakness and selfish disregard. What damage this has done!

Fourth, and finally, all the tendencies I have described—the cultivation of an ethos of victims and wrongdoers, the strengthening of a spirit of solidarity, and the reinforcement of the norms of representation—are intensified by the fact that the groups to which the contemporary understanding of diversity attaches most importance are especially fixed. Membership in them is not a matter of individual choice. They are not groups that one enters or leaves voluntarily. This is above all true of race. To be sure, even race, which stands at one extreme, is fluid to some degree. But the color of a person's skin (to state the obvious) can be changed far less easily than his or her weight or religious beliefs. It is less a choice than a fate—not a universal one, like mortality, but the local and restricted fate of those who happen to have been born white, black, or brown, and not another color.

Because the ethic of diversity starts from the case of racial injustice, race serves as a paradigm in thinking about the value of diversity in general. On this view, students who add to the diversity of their school do so because they bring to its overall mix fixed characteristics like gender, race, and ethnicity that can be changed only with difficulty, if at all. If these traits were changeable ones—like being a liberal or conservative, an atheist or devout believer—there would be no guarantee that the diversity the school hopes to achieve through its admissions process will remain stable over time. To assure that it does, the categories of diversity must themselves be (relatively) immune to adjustment according to individual preference and judgment in the way that skin color is to an impressive degree. In this way, the relation that individuals have to their race becomes a model for the relation they have to their ethnic heritage, class position, and eventually even to their beliefs. All these come to be viewed in light of the union of fate and difference that, in America at least, is the hallmark of race.

The wrong of racism consists in treating people badly on account of a morally irrelevant characteristic they have no power to control. The fight for racial justice is therefore bound to give a prominent place to fate if only to emphasize how wrong it is to equate a person's moral and legal standing with the color of his or her skin. The contemporary understanding of diversity accentuates the prominence of fate in human life by treating all group differences on the model of race. That is worrisome enough. Fate always plays a large role in our lives. But emphasizing its scope and power has a demoralizing effect. Even more disturbingly, the group-based view of diversity that prevails on campus today invests the fateful dimension of life with an added prestige by strongly identifying a student's membership in this or that group with his or her values and outlook in general, and by equating the latter with the morally praiseworthy contribution the student makes to the diversity of his or her school as a whole. This is more than an acknowledgment of fate; it is a valorization of it. And that sickens the spirit of hope, which our colleges and universities ought to enliven, by weakening the belief that students can make some meaningful progress toward living more freely, as individuals with minds of their own, though burdened by inheritances that entangle us all to some degree.

These destructive forces are the harvest of diversity as it has been understood for the past forty years, since Powell's fateful opinion in *Bakke*. Outside the classroom, where students meet in social, athletic, and other extracurricular settings, their strength is diminished. That is because these encounters are not consciously shaped with race and ethnicity in mind. Here, the impressions that students form of one another are to a significant degree conditioned by the mass of perceptions that enter into the individualized judgment that this particular person is kind, funny, and adventurous; that other one dull, mean-spirited, and self-absorbed. It is on the basis of judgments of this kind that students form the friendships they do. This is not always the case. Some friendships are born in a spirit of solidarity. Others never start because active or unconscious prejudice stands in the way. But friendship often begins at an individual level, with the unnamed and perhaps unnamable attraction that one person feels toward another, and when those who are already friends reflect on their racial and ethnic differences (if they do), it is within the framework of the relation of affection and trust that exists between them. The latter is the prism through which these differences are viewed, not the other way around. This is a good thing and produces friendships of an even richer kind. To the extent that a racially and ethnically diverse student body contributes to the enrichment of student friendships in this way, it is a good thing too.

In the classroom, though, the perspective is often reversed. Wherever race and ethnicity are even remotely relevant topics, the selection of texts, the organization of the syllabus, and the teacher's presentation of the materials are frequently shaped by the felt need to make the class more "diverse"—which in practical terms means that the racial, ethnic, or gender identity of each author is highlighted and students encouraged to evaluate what the text says from this point of view. The author's status as a member of some victimized group, for whose experience he or she is expected to speak with a representative voice, thus becomes the lens through which his or her other attributes are weighed. Students are of course not barred from looking at things the other way around, in class or out. But it is in the classroom that they are taught what their schools think they ought to think. It is here that the orthodoxy of diversity is officially proclaimed. This sends a message that spreads a pall over campus life as a whole. It infects the entire academy. The intellectual and cultural damage this has done is most visible in the classroom and especially in those where the humanities are taught. But no corner of campus life has been untouched by Justice Powell's ruinous conversion of a political value into an academic ideal.

V.

The present understanding of diversity puts the emphasis on differences among groups rather than individuals. It also reflects a view of the *relation between* individuals and groups. Or rather, it reflects two views, between which it oscillates in an inconsistent fashion.

On the one hand, those who think of diversity as an educational good often stress how deeply our identity is shaped by being a member of one group or another. They say that being black, Hispanic, female, gay, white, or heterosexual conditions one's perceptions, tastes, and treatment by others at a fundamental level, in ways that are often unnoticed and largely unchangeable. It is therefore an essential part of one's being. That is why it must be acknowledged and given prominence in our colleges and universities. The failure to do so amounts to a kind of "erasure." It is a form of "social death."

On the other hand, the defenders of diversity are in general fiercely opposed to every form of "privileging." They attack those who, in their view, enjoy special advantages because they are white, male, and hetero-normal. They consider these privileges unjust. No one has a right, they say, to look down on others or treat them less well because of their race, sex, or sexual orientation.

That is because, at bottom, every human being is "just as good" as every other. But how do we reach this "bottom"? We cannot do it with our eyes. A thought experiment is required. We have to gather in one imaginary bundle all the characteristics that distinguish each group of human beings from every other, drain these characteristics of their intrinsic moral worth, and then transfer their value to some other, invisible characteristic that every human being is assumed to possess to exactly the same degree, *which we now declare to be the true, exclusive, and enduring source of their entitlement to equal respect*. This amounts to a monumental act of erasure—one that denies the equation of an individual's race, sex, and other group-based characteristics with his or her identity in the only morally relevant sense. But it cannot be avoided if the hatred of "privileging" is to be put on a solid foundation.

There is precedent for this. The Christian religion demands an erasure of precisely this kind. Its philosophical reinterpretation of the Jewish teaching that man is made in the image of God becomes in its most refined version the doctrine that every human being is an autonomous member of what Kant calls "the kingdom of ends," as well as a "natural" being with all sorts of characteristics that God does not possess (including a racial, ethnic, and gender identity). Like God, we have the power to choose right over wrong, although unlike God we often make mistakes. The capacity for freedom is our passport to membership in the kingdom of ends. If we honor rather than abuse it, it entitles us to a place by God's side. It is therefore not only of value; it is *infinitely* more valuable than every other characteristic we possess (the color of our skins, our sexual tastes and distastes, and the like). Measured against our dignity as free and equal persons created in the image of God, the latter have no value at all.

This ancient theological idea has been reframed in secular terms to bring it into line with modern democratic beliefs. John Rawls's *Theory of Justice* is a striking example. Behind Rawls's famous "veil of ignorance," we are all alike. We are all just persons with the power to plan our lives. This is the only thing about us of intrinsic value. None of our other characteristics possess any inherent moral worth at all. The purpose of Rawls's "veil" is to accomplish the erasure that morality demands. It forces us to think of ourselves and everyone else as *standing above* all our other, more limited identities and *freely assigning* them whatever value they possess.

The champions of diversity wobble back and forth between these two inconsistent views of the relation between an individual and his or her group characteristics. One is a nearly fatalistic view that treats these characteristics as the ineradicable mark of who a person really is. Its proponents say, "You *are* your race or sexual orientation. I cannot see or judge you except in and through these terms." The other view is just the opposite. It is a version of the Rawlsian idea that race and characteristics like it have nothing to do with our identity, in the only sense that really matters. Its defenders say, "You *are* a moral person who just happens to possess certain characteristics that have no intrinsic value of their own." The first underlies the attack on erasure, the second the campaign against privileging.

This is important less because the two views are inconsistent than because both strike, from opposite sides, at the aristocratic ideal of education. This ideal assumes that it is possible through study and learning to make progress toward a more refined and fulfilling life as a human being. It distinguishes advancement in this enterprise from the acquisition of an expertise. And it is unafraid to say that some get further than others. Whether they grasp the identitarian horn of their dilemma or the egalitarian one, today's defenders of diversity attack the aristocratic ideal head on. That is why, beyond promoting a culture of victimization and politicizing the search for truth, the campaign for diversity undermines the spirit of higher education at a vital point that few today still seem inclined to defend.

As to the first of these views, two comments will suffice. First, telling students that their identity is tied, in a restricting way, to their race, gender, or sexual orientation is bound to have a depleting effect on the struggle—it is always a struggle—to shape the materials that one has been given in life into something more expansive and self-critical. It is a truism to say that one begins this struggle with a given set of experiences, preferences, and loyalties. But it is a doctrine of despair to claim that these finally condition all of one's subsequent judgments, as if it were impossible ever to see things except from the perspective they fix at the start. That is an extreme version of the identitarian view but one that is often in the background of more modest ones. It is the enemy of freedom in teaching and learning. The aristocratic ideal values freedom above all else, though not, as we shall see in a moment, the kind that democrats admire.

Second, the more tightly their identity is fastened to immutable characteristics like race and gender, the more students will be encouraged to think of their education as a means for acquiring a better understanding of these characteristics and of affirming their value. If they are stuck with their race and gender, shouldn't they make a special effort to discover what these mean and to find the grounds for taking pride in what cannot be avoided? Again, this is a matter of degree. African-American history is a subject of great importance. Every American should know something about it. The same is true of gender studies. But to the extent these disciplines become cheering sections for those who share these identities, they push their education back toward self-absorption and self-congratulation rather than out into a wider, scarier world of human possibilities. In this very specific sense, they have an anti-humanistic thrust. They point away from the aristocratic ideal, which cultivates pride too, but in the human condition, with its mix of hope, fear, tragedy, and splendor.

The more serious challenge to this ideal, though, comes from the other side—from the egalitarianism that underlies the attack on privileging.

Equality is a norm in political life. Everyone gets one vote, no matter how rich or smart. It is also a norm in the law. Our courts are expected to dispense equal justice to all, regardless of wealth or social standing. The principle of equality is not always honored in either domain, but it is the proper measure for judging the behavior of officials and the health of institutions in both.

The principle has a more limited application in the sphere of economic relations. Some maintain that equality means that everyone should have the same amount of wealth. Many more believe that it means equality of opportunity. If the members of a particular group have fewer opportunities because of their gender, or surname, or skin color, most would say that violates the principle of equality in a straightforward way. The best remedy may be to give them extra opportunities for a period of time. This was the idea behind affirmative action programs like the one at issue in *Bakke*. It is perfectly consistent with the egalitarianism that informs our political, legal, and—up to a point—economic thinking.

The college and university admissions process lies on the border between what goes on outside our schools and what happens within them. It straddles these domains. Insofar as it looks outward and seeks to adjust the competition for a valuable resource, considerations of fairness apply. Depending on the circumstances, it may be reasonable to think that fairness requires giving the members of certain groups a leg up in the process. Some disagree, but the debate is over the meaning of equality of opportunity. It proceeds on the shared ground of egalitarianism—which is appropriate so long as we think of the admissions process as one belonging to the realm of legal, political, and economic relations.

This way of thinking is loosely associated with phrases like "All men are created equal" and "I'm just as good as you are." When philosophers explicate the meaning of these phrases, they do so by sketching a picture of what human beings are like—a portrait of the human soul. One familiar picture depicts each human being as a complex of abilities, disabilities, inheritances, and other endowments, *and in addition* as a free agent with the power to choose which items in this mix to emphasize and develop, and which to subordinate or repress. This is the picture that John Rawls paints in *A Theory of Justice*. Egalitarians like Rawls put all the moral weight on the second of these components—on our freedom to decide who we shall become, within the limits our endowments allow. Endowments differ, but no one has more of this freedom than anyone else. It is what makes each equal to every other and, in a moral light, just as good.

Whether this picture is "true" in an ultimate sense depends on whether you believe that freedom of this kind actually exists. That is a metaphysical question as old as the idea of freedom itself. But regardless of how one answers it, the Rawlsian picture, or some version of it, does a reasonably good job of supporting the conviction that, in politics and law, everyone should have the same rights and receive the same respect. It is a useful way of explaining why we share this conviction. But when affirmative action is reconceived as a program for promoting academic diversity, the egalitarianism that properly informs our thinking about the admissions process in its outward-looking aspect is transferred to the inner world of teaching and learning, and when this happens, the picture of the human soul that underwrites the principle of equality in politics and law is transferred along with it. But here this picture clashes with the aristocratic ideal and undermines its authority. That is because this ideal rests on a picture of the soul that is incompatible with it.

There are several versions of the aristocratic picture. Aristotle offers one, Spinoza another, and Walt Whitman a third (surprisingly, perhaps, given his love of democracy). The differences among them are profound but for present purposes less important than the element they have in common. This is their reliance on the distinction between potential and fulfillment, rather than that between choice and endowment, as the key to understanding the nature and work of the human soul.

The key idea here is that of development or growth.

All human beings possess certain powers of understanding and enjoyment and the ability to express to others what they know and relish. At the start of life, these powers exist in a rudimentary form but one with the potential for further development. As we mature, our powers become stronger, suppler, freer. On an aristocratic view of the soul, this is the meaning of freedom itself: the ability to do more things in more ways.

The first view of the soul assumes a split within it. Even in its secular versions, this view betrays its theological roots in the Christian distinction between the natural and the supernatural. The second view does not. It pictures the soul as a collection of powers existing on a continuum of potency and realization. As individuals move along this continuum, they become more fully realized as human beings. Their humanity increases. That is a quaint-sounding way of describing the process. It runs against the grain of the democratic-egalitarian belief that no one's humanity can ever be greater or less than anyone else's. But it is the premise on which every aristocratic regime rests.

The idea of growth or development poses no threat to egalitarian ideals so long as it is contained within acceptable limits. No one disputes that people grow in their capacity to understand, enjoy, and do a vast range of different things. We desire this and devote enormous educational resources to it. The vocational ideal is founded on it. But when the idea of growth is generalized to the whole of a person's humanity, and progress defined as the process of becoming a more accomplished and therefore real human being, it immediately presents a threat to our democratic beliefs and challenges the picture of the soul that underlies them. This picture assumes a split within the human soul between the realms of freedom and nature. It necessarily implies that no one is more human than anyone else, whatever the level of their respective achievements. For those who embrace this view, the expressions more "real" and "accomplished" are acceptable only so long as their range is confined in some fashion—to being a "real" mathematician, dancer, doctor, or anything else. When we apply them without qualification to the whole of a person's humanity, the offense to the principle of equality is obvious and unavoidable.

The democratic assault on the aristocratic idea that some are more fully human than others employs two familiar strategies.

The first is to associate this idea with an odious regime of oppression—in America, with slavery in particular. The defenders of slavery maintained that whites exist at a higher level of human development than blacks. (Many opponents of slavery thought and said the same.) But the evil of slavery was not its reliance on the belief, which it shared with every aristocratic regime, that some human beings are more fully realized than others. It was the fusion of this belief with the absurd assumption that the distinction between higher and lower is correlated with the color of a person's skin. To reject the aristocratic distinction between more and less developed human beings just because it has often been entangled with other indefensible ideas, and used to legitimate political and social practices of a brutal and unjust kind, amounts to conviction by association. This may be politically expedient, but it is intellectually dishonest. It avoids the challenge of having to meet the aristocratic ideal on its best and most attractive terms. And it sidesteps the question of whether a democracy committed to the principle of equality for all is not better off if islands of aristocratic belief are preserved within it, rather than flattened out and made to conform to the principle too.

The second strategy starts from the observation that the philosophical defenders of aristocracy do not agree among themselves as to how we should define the meaning of human fulfillment, and that different aristocratic regimes have defined it differently at different times and places. From this, those who hate the idea of aristocracy draw the conclusion that human fulfillment has no fixed content and that we are free to choose among the various versions of it in whatever way we please. They say this proves the truth of the democratic picture of the soul and justifies the egalitarianism associated with it.

The observation, of course, is correct. For Aristotle, fulfillment meant the development and exercise of a set of political virtues plus the attainment of philosophical wisdom. For Spinoza, it meant endless progress in understanding why things happen as they do. For Whitman, it meant the expansion of one's capacity to see that all things are divine—something only a poet knows. These ideals are, by turn, political, scientific, and aesthetic. They put the emphasis on different powers and conceive them in ways that at points are inconsistent. (Aristotle, for example, believed that a state of complete fulfillment is attainable despite our limitations. Spinoza and Whitman did not.)

But what this shows is not that there is nothing to the aristocratic ideal. It proves only that there is room for disagreement about it, and variety within it—that, like every ideal, this one too is a perennial subject of interpretation and debate. The debate in question is not formless, though. It rests on the shared assumption that growth is realization; realization, freedom; and that some get further, and become freer, than others. This is enough to distinguish all these thinkers from those who claim that every soul has the same quantum of freedom as every other. It defines a commonality of outlook that, coupled with the variety of ways one may pursue it, gives the aristocratic ideal its liveliness and excitement, makes its elaboration an open-ended challenge, and allows for the recognition and enjoyment of diversity in human excellence. By defining excellence as a matter of individual choice, the egalitarian understanding of diversity eliminates it as a meaningful topic of debate.

The thinkers I have mentioned agree that there is such a thing as greatness in the work of being human and that its achievement is uncommon if not rare. This distinguishes them from those who acknowledge greatness only in particular pursuits and confine their judgments about human beings *as such* to the standards of morality, which everyone is capable of meeting. The latter view fits comfortably with the egalitarianism of our political and legal institutions and the vocational ideal in higher education.

The former fits with neither. It is a threat to both. And while those who share it disagree, in thought-provoking ways, as to what human greatness means, the differences among them are less important than the one that separates them as a group from the defenders of diversity in our colleges and universities today. The latter rely on the egalitarian principle that no one is better than anyone else and assault the idea of rank with indiscriminate vigor, except in the nonthreatening case of hierarchy based on achievement in some limited endeavor, like a test, course, major, or job. The idea that some do better than others as human beings, *however* one elaborates and defends it, is in their view a wicked belief that corrupts our democratic ideals.

The campaign for diversity began when the demand for racial justice was transmuted into an academic value. This gave the spirit of egalitarianism a heightened prominence and greater authority in our colleges and universities. In particular, it brought the principle of anti-subordination with it. This principle has special application to questions of racial justice, which are complicated by a history of caste prejudice. But in the academy it strikes at the heart of every version of the aristocratic ideal, with its scale of distinction in the work of being human.

Protecting this ideal is one of the things our colleges and universities must do. It is not the only thing. They have a responsibility to advance knowledge in all fields of learning and to prepare their students for rewarding careers as well. But cultivating a respect for human greatness is important for two reasons. It is a condition of the individual's refinement and growth as a human being, which becomes directionless and vain if students are told that greatness lies in the eye of the beholder. And it promotes a combination of sureness and modesty in judgment that is one of the best antidotes to what Tocqueville calls the tyranny of majority opinion. We need it for its own sake and because of the contribution it makes as a counterweight to the "effervescence of democratic negation."

No college or university may discriminate against any group of applicants on the basis of their race, ethnicity, or gender. Every applicant has a right not to be treated in this way. In addition, to the extent it believes it has responsibilities to society as a whole; that these include doing its part to help achieve a fair or just social order; and that affirmative action is an appropriate means to this end, a school is justified in taking a candidate's race or ethnicity into account in a positive way. Those it admits on these grounds it has a further duty to support, at additional expense, in order to ensure that they have a real chance to succeed. In all these respects, its preoccupation is with justice—with treating applicants fairly and promoting a just arrangement of opportunities in society at large.

But this is hardly the end of the matter. Indeed, it is only the beginning. A college or university admits its students not in order to ensure they are treated with equal respect or to secure a greater measure of social justice. It admits them for the sake of giving them an education. This includes instruction, training, and the development of vocational skills. In our most ambitious schools, it has also always been thought to include an education in human greatness as well. This idea has been under attack for some time. But the ever-growing demand for greater racial, ethnic, and other group-based forms of diversity—and the defense of this demand in terms that are sometimes identitarian and sometimes egalitarian—has accelerated the pace of attack. It has put the aristocratic ideal in a more embattled position. It has made it harder to affirm that some are more advanced than others not in specialized endeavors, where the idea of expertise applies, but in the comprehensive work of living well and fully as a human being—unlike the citizens of Lake Wobegon where, as Garrison Keillor said, "all the children are above average." This is the ideal that prevails in our colleges and universities today. It is unimpeachably egalitarian. But it is bad for the souls of our students and bad for democracy too.

FOUR

Memory

I.

AMERICA'S CAMPUSES ARE STREWN WITH MEMORIALS TO THE famous and not-so-famous dead. Some were slave owners or Confederate heroes. Others were segregationists or white supremacists. The buildings and statues that honor these morally compromised figures seem to many, emblems of hate. They regard their presence on campus as an insult to black and other minority students and demand that the offending memorials be removed or renamed. Those who oppose renaming observe that most people in the past, even the greatest ones, were contaminated by racist beliefs; insist that it is unfair to judge those who lived in an earlier age by the standards of our own; and argue that once we begin erasing some from our honor rolls, there is no principled place to stop.

At Princeton, for example, students campaigned (unsuccessfully) to have Woodrow Wilson's name removed from one of the university's most prestigious programs on account of the role he played in segregating the federal civil service in the early twentieth century. A Harvard committee recommended that the law school's shield be redesigned because, they said, the sheaves of wheat depicted on it subtly honored a Massachusetts landowner who had been active in the pre-Revolutionary slave trade. Amherst students protested the continued use of their school mascot, modeled on the college's eighteenth-century namesake, on the grounds that he had given smallpox-infected blankets to Native Americans during the French and Indian War. At Yale, the question of whether to rename Calhoun College convulsed the university for a year and a half. In all but the first case, the name or symbol was changed.

Some of these disputes seem rather silly. At USC, a debate broke out over whether the horse ridden at football games by a man dressed in a Trojan costume should be renamed because the first such horse, given to the school in the 1950s, had been named after the one Robert E. Lee rode in the Civil War. Others are more serious. After years of protest, Middle Tennessee State University agreed to rename Forrest Hall because Nathan Bedford Forrest, a formidable Confederate general, had been a founder of the Ku Klux Klan. Students at the University of North Carolina toppled a statue, known as "Silent Sam," that had been erected on the campus in 1913 as a memorial to the soldiers of the Confederate Army.

When the president of Yale appointed a committee to address the Calhoun question in 2016, he expressed the hope that it might produce a set of general rules that would be of help to other schools grappling with similar issues. But the "rules" contained in the committee's report are in reality no more than a checklist of potentially relevant factors that a school may wish to consider in weighing the arguments for and against renaming in a particular case. The committee itself made no effort to put these rules in an order of priority or even to specify their relative weight. Indeed, it is difficult to see how this could be done in a meaningful way. The facts in each dispute are peculiar to it. So is the history of the institution in question. Rules of any kind are able to provide nominal guidance at best. What is required in each case is an act of judgment. This may be balanced and wise, or the opposite. But its outcome cannot be settled in advance by anything that might be called a "law" of renaming. No such law exists.

Much depends, therefore, on the mood or spirit in which one approaches the task of judgment. This is bound to color the way one weighs the arguments for and against, and in many cases to determine the outcome. Today the prevailing mood on campus inclines toward removal or renaming. That is because it draws strength from the same commitment to equality that inspires the movement for greater racial and ethnic diversity, and for limiting speech in the name of inclusion. Like these, the campaign for renaming seeks to reshape campus life in the light of a political ideal. Its essential aim, like theirs, is to flatten or level—in this case, by erasing the most awkward reminders that some of our predecessors subscribed to values sharply different from our own.

Recent events off campus have given this campaign added momentum. The alt-right rally in Charlottesville in May of 2017 convinced some that preservationists are just racists in disguise. But this puts the reasonable case for preservation in an unfair light. It taints it by association. It fails to address the strongest argument that weighs in favor of preserving even those memorials that grate most annoyingly on our contemporary moral beliefs—supplemented by whatever further forms of memorialization seem appropriate—instead of tearing them down or removing them to the anesthetized precincts of a museum. Most important, it draws attention away from the *special* responsibility that our colleges and universities have to cultivate the capacity for enduring the moral ambiguities of life. This includes—indeed, it is often first aroused by—the need to acknowledge the complexities of a checkered and sometimes discreditable past. The ability to do this is moral strength. It is a species of moral imagination as valuable as it is rare, and as vital to the health of our democracy as to that of our colleges and universities themselves. Its neglect, or suppression, is an educational disgrace.

II.

The Czech writer Milan Kundera tells a story at the beginning of *The Book of Laughter and Forgetting* that bears on our subject:

> In February 1948, the Communist leader Klement Gottwald stepped out on the balcony of a Baroque palace in Prague to harangue hundreds of thousands of citizens massed in Old Town Square. That was a great turning point in the history of Bohemia. A fateful moment . . .
>
> Gottwald was flanked by his comrades, with Clementis standing close to him. It was snowing and cold, and Gottwald was bareheaded. Bursting with solicitude, Clementis took off his fur hat and set it on Gottwald's head.
>
> The propaganda section made hundreds of thousands of copies of the photograph taken on the balcony where Gottwald, in a fur hat and surrounded by his comrades, spoke to the people. On that balcony the history of Communist Bohemia began. Every child knew that photograph, from seeing it on posters and in schoolbooks and museums.
>
> Four years later, Clementis was charged with treason and hanged. The propaganda section immediately made him vanish from history and, of course, from all photographs. Ever since, Gottwald has been alone on the balcony. Where Clementis stood, there is only the balcony. Where Clementis stood, there is only the bare palace wall. Nothing remains of Clementis but the fur hat on Gottwald's head.

There is never a moment in our lives when we are not retelling the past. We are constantly reshaping its content and rephrasing its meaning. The effort to live a coherent and meaningful life does not begin where the past leaves off. Our changing understanding of what *really* happened and *why* it was important is as much a part of this effort as the plans we make for the future, where nothing has yet happened at all.

We long for things to make sense, to be all of a piece. This directs the way we look ahead, when we plan. It also shapes the way we look behind, when we remember. Remembering is always revision. We are never free to reinvent the past from whole cloth. But neither is it a strictly factual record that we can grasp with objectivity from some neutral point of view. The past is always, to some degree, a work of fiction. That is because, in our relation to it, we are interested parties.

This is true at both an individual and a political level. We are forever rewriting our personal past—turning it into stories that fit better with the people we wish or aspire to be. Sometimes we repress it so completely that we are able to insist, with complete honesty, that it never happened at all. Nietzsche describes the situation succinctly: "Memory says, 'I did that.' Pride replies, 'I could not have done that.' Eventually—memory yields." Thanks to Freud, we know more about this age-old habit than we once did.

Its political counterpart is captured by the platitude that history is written by the winners. It has always been their privilege to rewrite the record—to make their motives look better, and their objectives nobler, than they were in fact. One might even say that this is what people fight for in the first place.

But this revisionary instinct has a pathological potential. Beyond a certain point, it is as destructive of our humanity as, within some range of normalcy, it is expressive of it. Carried to an extreme, the tendency to turn the past into an anecdote, or repress it altogether, shrinks our lives and narrows their horizons. In the realm of personal experience, it corrupts our connection to others and blights the experience of love. In politics, it breeds indifference and cruelty. There is no formula to tell us at what point the all-too-human process of rewriting the past becomes a destructive pathology. But that is why we have to be continually alert to the harm that it can do. This is the subject of Kundera's novel, which interweaves a series of personal and political stories that explore the cost of forgetting at both levels.

One of the characters in the book is a man named Mirek. He is tormented by the "immense love" he once felt for an "ugly" girl named Zdena. He wants "to efface her from the photograph of his life not because he had not loved her but because he had." People may say they live for the sake of the future, but Mirek's obsession suggests otherwise. The future is "only an indifferent void no one cares about, but the past is filled with life, and its countenance is irritating, repellent, wounding, to the point that we want to destroy or repaint it. We want to be masters of the future only for the power to change the past. We fight for access to the labs where we can retouch photos and rewrite biographies and history."

Mirek's private campaign of forgetting has a public analogue.

The streets of Prague are filled, Kundera says, with "the ghosts of monuments torn down," of buildings, statues, and names erased by successive rewriters of history—the champions of the Reformation, the Counter-Reformation, the Czech Republic, the Communist Party. The last of these are not only the most recent but the most ruthless as well. In 1969, the Russians installed Gustáv Husák to restore the authority of the Party after the abortive Czech Spring. Kundera calls him the "President of Forgetting." To a group of children who are "applauding and shouting his name," Husák exclaims " 'Children, never look back!' " What this means, Kundera says, is "that we must never allow the future to be weighed down by memory. For children have no past and that is the whole secret of the magical innocence of their smiles." The novelist puts his own mature view of life in the mouth of Milan Hübl, one of the many Czech historians removed from their positions by Husák. " 'You begin to liquidate a people,' Hübl said, 'by taking away its memory. You destroy its books, its culture, its history. And then others write other books for it, give another culture to it, invent another history for it. Then the people slowly begins to forget what it is and what it was. The world at large forgets it still faster.'"

After telling the story of Clementis's hat, Kundera has Mirek say, "The struggle of man against power is the struggle of memory against forgetting." It might serve as the motto of the book. Kundera is fully aware that we cannot live without forgetting. Every step we take begins with a selective reconstruction of the past. But he also knows that "organized forgetting"—the kind that allows no exceptions and tolerates no ambiguities—ends by substituting fantasy for life (or trying to, since, as the hat on Gottwald's head suggests, the past has a resilience that can never be completely destroyed). These beliefs give Kundera's novel its humanism and humor. They also suggest a moral of sorts (these are my words, not his): "Be mindful of the fact that you are an animal that loves to forget, that needs to forget; see the humor in your stratagems of self-delusion; but be on guard lest in forgetting too easily or too much, you become an anecdote or an angel—the fleshless, humorless imitation of a human being, without the weight of a real one, and hence without the responsibility."

The "organized forgetting" that Kundera fought with humor and anger was the kind practiced by the propaganda ministries of the Soviet Union and the Nazis. The ideologies of these two systems differed fundamentally. But their administrative methods shared something in common. Each did more than engage in the time-honored forms of historical revisionism that ascendant powers have always employed. Their manipulation of the past was based on the assumption that it could be rewritten to coincide with the truth. They shared a common disdain for the stubbornness of the past. They believed that the record of what people have *actually* thought, believed, and honored in the past could be erased and reassembled so that it becomes a perfect image of what they *ought to have* thought, believed, and honored *if* the past had been nothing but a preparation for the victory of truth over error.

The propaganda machines of the Nazis and Soviets thus did more than write winners' histories. They sought to obliterate even the possibility of any friction between history and truth as they defined it. Were this possible, the result would be a radical adjustment in one of the fundamental conditions of human experience and judgment. Human life as we know it would no longer be the same. Indeed, one might without exaggeration say that human nature itself would be different. The novelty of the totalitarian regimes of the twentieth century consisted, in part, in their embrace of this ambition.

Those in power have always sought to work around human nature or to manipulate it for their advantage. Machiavelli's classic advice to princes accepts this as a given. But before the Nazis and Soviets attempted it, no ruler had ever set out to remake the very nature of human beings themselves (except, perhaps, Plato, and he attempted it only in theory, and acknowledged that his ideal city could never come into being precisely because a transformation of this sort is impossible in fact). Their campaign against memory was something new under the sun. Kundera lampoons this extravagant and inhuman ambition in *The Book of Laughter and Forgetting* as George Orwell had thirty years before in *1984*. But no one offers a more probing account of its underlying assumptions than Hannah Arendt.

The key text is Arendt's 1967 essay "Truth and Politics." In it she draws two important distinctions. The first is between rational truth and political judgment.

The former compels assent. Its hallmark is self-evidence. There is no debating the truth once it has been discovered. One does not have an "opinion" about it. In those activities in which rational truths are discoverable, the only relevant distinction is between knowledge and ignorance. Truths of this kind are therefore necessarily authoritarian. Mathematics has always been the paradigm example.

By contrast, politics calls for judgments that lack the transparency and compelling authority of mathematical and other scientific truths. The element of opinion can never be eliminated from them. The particularity of the vantage point from which they are delivered is a part of their makeup. It cannot be removed either in theory or practice—unlike the truths of science, which, ideally at least, always express what the philosopher Thomas Nagel calls the "view from nowhere." Every political judgment is made from an "opinionated" point of view, although Arendt is careful to insist that it can never be defended merely on the grounds that it expresses the opinion of the one who has proposed it, as if that were enough to validate the judgment in question.

In political debates, the authority of a particular opinion can therefore never be established *either* by reference to some nonperspectival standard of truth *or* by appealing to the brute fact that one happens to hold it. Its authority can be convincingly communicated only by taking the opinions of others into account. The uniquely human power of imagination enables us to do this. Our imaginations allow us to see and judge things from others' points of view and to respond to their concerns in terms they understand and appreciate. The exercise of imagination leads to what Arendt calls an "enlarged mentality" whose increasing breadth is the only basis on which even the provisional and incomplete authority of any political judgment can ever be founded.

Arendt's second distinction is between factual truths and rational ones.

The latter are necessary. They cannot be otherwise. It is inconceivable that the Pythagorean theorem is false. The former, on the other hand, are only contingently true. They are what philosophers call "accidental" truths. Unlike the Pythagorean theorem, it is only accidentally true that Napoleon lost the Battle of Waterloo. It is perfectly possible that he might have won it if a few things had gone otherwise.

Because mathematics is concerned with rational truths only, facts are a matter of indifference to it. A mathematician does not care whether the circle she has drawn on the board to illustrate a proposition in geometry is, as a matter of fact, a true circle or not. That is why the study of rational truths is ahistorical. History is the record of what has actually happened. Those who study the past for the sake of learning from it, cannot help but be impressed by the contingency of events as they unfold in time. The historian might, in this sense, be called a connoisseur of contingency. Those thinkers, like Hegel and Marx, who have tried to convert the study of history into a scientific discipline are guilty, Arendt says, of confusing the distinction between factual truths and rational ones or of attempting to erase it altogether.

This is where her two distinctions coincide. In Arendt's view, the erasure of the line between rational and factual truths undermines the realm of politics itself. History plays an authoritative role in political debates that has no counterpart in scientific ones. The latter too are never-ending. But scientific debates concern the proper understanding of truths that, although they can only be discovered in time, have a validity that transcends historical experience. In politics, by contrast, history is a source of authority in its own right. The mere fact that something happened in the past is often itself a reason for doing something now—either to honor the past or repair it. The authority of precedent in law is an example. In science, precedent loses all its weight whenever it conflicts with the truth.

The competing views that political actors offer of the best future for their community always rest, in part at least, on differing interpretations of its past. Only in revolutionary moments are things mostly up for grabs (and even then not completely). For the rest, politics is a work of renovation and repair in which the question of how to proceed depends on an interpretation of the meaning of the course that has been followed to that point. This matters because every political community not only exists in time but strives to be faithful to the meaning, value, and purpose of its inheritance and destiny, which are always linked and always disputable. Facts, and the histories that record them, have a normative weight in politics that they never possess in science. Scientists strive to transcend history, politicians to honor it.

Because they do, the actuality of the past acts as a special check upon what they may say and do in its name. Tethered as they are to the authority of history, politicians are less free to ignore or deny it than those who seek truths beyond the horizon of time. In the political realm, the facts that history records are in this sense peculiarly "stubborn." They curb the excesses of those who would drain them of their authority by converting history to reason. Some have tried to do this. But the attempt is always a threat to the very existence of political life—of a sphere of diverse and conflicting opinions, shared by those competing for the authority to claim that their view of the future of their community is the one that puts its past in the best light.

The stubbornness of the past is compromised at a theoretical level when the history of what actually happened is rewritten to make it appear that it had to occur in exactly the way that it did. To the extent the effort succeeds, the future becomes a blank sheet, to be inscribed by the hand of reason alone. The past no longer offers any resistance to what is necessarily true.

The same thing happens, at a material level, when the physical reminders of the past are removed or reshaped so that nothing remains of them except what conforms to the visionary ideal that directs the reshaping. In totalitarian regimes, these two strategies go hand in hand. Here the assault on the stubbornness of the past reaches a limit and the realm of politics shrinks to a minimum. This is what drew Arendt's attention to the phenomenon of totalitarianism and caused her to describe it as something unique in the annals of human society.

The erasure of the past, in theory and practice, as exemplified in an extreme form by the totalitarian regimes of the Nazis and Soviets, signified for Arendt the destruction of the special form of responsibility that politics invites and requires. This is the responsibility, as she saw it, to cultivate an "enlarged mentality" by striving to grasp, in imagination, others' points of view, and to understand why they value the things they do. The willingness to attempt this is itself a form of collegiality. It is the basis of a kind of political solidarity. For the members of a political community who disagree about their common good in profound and lasting ways, it is the most elementary form of solidarity available to them.

The only other way to achieve solidarity in the face of such disharmony is to deny or destroy it. This is what the erasure of the past seeks to do by encouraging the idea that all right-minded citizens have always been of *one* mind, and that nonconformists, living or dead, stand "on the wrong side of history." In Arendt's view, this is the special evil of totalitarianism, whose architects and administrators sought to destroy the most basic condition of political life. Following Aristotle, she describes this as the condition of "plurality": the gathering of many in a single community for the sake of a better life together, without collapsing the "space" that sets them apart. The totalitarian erasure of the past for Arendt meant the destruction of plurality. It signified the death of politics. And it entailed the destruction of the special form of responsibility that only arises in a political community where each has an obligation to imaginatively entertain the views of others, in a contest of opinions whose authority is tied to history in a way the truths of reason are not.

III.

Arendt's essay on truth and politics is a philosophical version of Kundera's story about the fate of Clementis's hat. They both illuminate the special awfulness of totalitarian rule. But what do their reflections on the worst evils of the twentieth century have to do with the question of whether to remove a statue or rename a school building because the person it honors defended slavery or fought for the South in the Civil War?

It is important to keep a sense of proportion. There is an immeasurable distance between the Soviet Politburo and Yale's Committee to Establish Principles on Renaming. But Kundera and Arendt help us understand what is at stake in these disputes and why those who favor an almost exception-less presumption against renaming believe the question touches an issue of special concern to our colleges and universities.

Consider, for example, the law school at the University of California in Berkeley. Its main building is named after John Henry Boalt, a prominent nineteenth-century lawyer and judge who gave the money to construct it. In 1877, Boalt delivered a speech in which he declared that Americans must always look upon the Chinese with an "unconquerable repulsion." Today, we find his view repulsive. No one disputes that he was wrong. The question is whether his name should be removed from the building. Doing so perhaps seems a costless way of asserting our present values and affirming the dignity of those maligned by his beliefs. The gain, in any case, is clear. What loss might weigh against it?

We can start by noting that the continuing presence of Boalt's name, and others like it, serves as a stimulus to modesty in two respects. First, it reminds us how difficult it has been to reach the more enlightened position we occupy today. It is easy to forget how much it took to get from there to here. Second, it reminds us that even we, with our more enlightened ideals, are human beings, with the same imperfections as our predecessors, bedeviled by the same tendency to overestimate ourselves and confronting the same gap between ideals and reality.

Morally serious people want to close this gap. They want to make the world more just. But changing the name on a building does little to achieve this result. It may even distract attention from more serious problems and create the self-satisfied illusion of progress where none has been made. Moreover, it has a real cost. It runs the risk of encouraging the immodest belief that we not only have better values than our forebears did but are better human beings. It makes it easier to think that we are less likely than they to be deformed by selfishness, small-mindedness, and a cowardly deference to convention, or by the all-too-human passions of jealousy and fear. That is a comforting thought. But it blinds us to our own deficiencies and puts our ancestors at a greater distance than any mere change in values can justify or explain. It promotes an evangelical confidence in the righteousness of our own beliefs, impugns the humanity of those who oppose them, and destroys the bridge of sympathy between the present and the past.

It will be objected that I am being overly dramatic. "Aren't we constantly taking old memorials down and putting up new ones, as our values change? Isn't the landscape of memory always being rebuilt? Aren't there some memorials—those to Hitler and Stalin, for example—that *must* come down? Isn't removing them a way, perhaps an essential way, of affirming our commitment to the values that define our community now? Isn't leaving these memorials up a sign of shameful irresolution about something or someone whose wickedness is beyond doubt, and a continuing insult to those who suffered from their crimes?"

To all these questions I would answer: "Yes." But I would add a qualification. I would insist that it is a mistake to take the most extreme cases as a model for how we treat less egregious ones. That betrays a lack of judgment, which depends on the ability to distinguish among individuals and crimes. It shows poor judgment to say that Amherst's mascot is the moral equivalent of a statue to Stalin or that the Woodrow Wilson School of Public and International Affairs at Princeton is as offensive as a monument to Hitler. Even the name of Calhoun College, to which I shall return, does not rise to this level. I would also point out that in all these cases there are alternatives to leaving the memorial in place, unadorned, and removing it completely. One is to add without subtracting: to leave things as they are but add another memorial, or additional commentary, that reflects the current view of things. I would insist that this is always the better course in all but the limiting case, which none of the actual renaming disputes on America's campuses presents.

Maturity means recognizing that these disputes raise questions that are more complex than those presented by a (hypothetical) statue to Hitler or Stalin. It means preferring addition to subtraction wherever it is physically possible. Most important, it means acknowledging that we do not need to erase the past in order to confirm our commitment to the values we now hold. If anything, this commitment is strengthened by the fact that those who share it are able to live with a past that does not conform to their ideals—who, in order to feel sure of themselves, do not require that their landscape be unspoiled by any awkward reminders that their community is relatively new, has been achieved only with great difficulty, and—like any community with high aspirations—is imperfectly realized still. Erasing these reminders may feel good, like pulling a thorn from one's side. But it does little to boost a real spirit of moral solidarity, which is better strengthened by facing the past than running away from it. It also invites a swaggering pride that weakens the power of moral imagination itself.

It is on account of this power that we are able, in partial ways at least, to glimpse the world from outside the circle of those values and beliefs that at any moment ground our confidence in it. We might think of it as a third eye. Acquiring it is never easy. All our inclinations are against it. But the habit of modesty helps. It makes it marginally easier to hold on to our values while probing their infirmities and questioning their reach. It affords a little bit of extra room to consider why others do not share our values and whether there is something in what they say (even if, on closer examination, we conclude there is not). It gives us a slightly better chance of achieving a reflective posture that is neither cynical nor doctrinaire.

The memorials that remain like thorns in our side, even after they have been surrounded with new ones that better express the values we cherish today, do not starve but feed the power of moral imagination. They remind us that others in the past, with human shortcomings like ours, have not always lived up to the better angels of their nature, and that we shall fail to do so as well. They remind us that our moral achievements are hard-won and never entirely secure. To insist that these memorials be erased in order to ensure that all are now welcome on campus, regardless of their heritage, gender, or race, is a counsel of weakness, not strength. It amounts to a confession that it is just too hard to be courageous and modest at once. It dissolves the union of confidence and vulnerability that is the essence of the "enlarged mentality" that Hannah Arendt describes as a prerequisite for living with others whose opinions differ from one's own. And it subverts one of the central responsibilities of our colleges and universities, which have a special duty to cultivate this quality of mind.

We hear a great deal on our campuses today about something that sounds like Arendt's "enlarged mentality." Students are constantly reminded to be respectful of others, to use their imagination to sympathize with the suffering of disadvantaged or marginalized groups, to learn to see the world from points of view distant from their own. But the similarity is an illusion. The respect and sympathy so often invoked today is underwritten by a shared morality that is enforced with crushing rigor. Few dare challenge its egalitarian assumptions. That manliness is a real trait of some possible value; that black culture is partly self-defeating; that some human beings are not only brighter than others but wiser, nobler, more advanced in the art of living—whether these beliefs are right or wrong, there are many outside the academy who are still prepared to defend them. But inside its walls, doing so is a recipe for isolation and disgrace. This is what is meant by the elastic term "political correctness." Anyone who has spent any time on an American campus knows how thick the atmosphere of political correctness has become and understands that the mantra of respect and sympathy is one of its chief supports, slyly converting what sounds like open-mindedness into an instrument of close-mindedness instead. The result is an academic environment in which the pursuit of a truly "enlarged mentality" is increasingly rare.

The uniform morality that today holds most faculty and students in its grip fills every nook and cranny of campus life. The presence of anyone or anything that challenges its dominion is an irritant and a threat. Among the most potent of these are those remnants from the past that serve as a physical reminder that not so long ago our predecessors held values at odds with those we hold today. The past is a great reservoir of political incorrectness, of views and practices that repel or shock us. To the extent that it remains alive among us, the past has the power, perhaps more than anything else, to jolt us out of the sheeplike torpor that the spirit of political correctness induces—to widen our minds to possibilities that fall outside the range of an increasingly impoverished imagination.

The most important of these possibilities is that human beings are rarely as simple as an idea; that even those who subscribe to bad ideas often hold good ones too; and that while we may not be excused from the responsibility to judge, we ought to meet it with a tolerance for ambiguity, which makes the task harder but more human. This is not the tolerance that is preached on campus today. That allows little room for ambiguity. A greater capacity to live with ambiguity—even, perhaps, an acquired taste for it—would do our academic culture good. The past, with its record of incorrigibly incorrect beliefs, is a particularly potent stimulus to the development of such a taste. So long as one remains within the conformist milieu that exists on campus today, the chances of acquiring it are slim.

IV.

There is an obvious sense in which our colleges and universities are especially concerned with the record of the past. They are depositories in which materials from the past are gathered and arranged so that they may be studied in a perspicuous and accessible fashion. Their faculties are arranged in small platoons that are devoted to the advancement of knowledge in the various fields of learning but have a duty to carry their past with them as they go. In this sense they are engaged in a work of conservation, even when the past they carry forward is a record of error and confusion. The minute a student walks onto campus, she is drafted into this work of conservation too.

But this is only the condition for something more important. It is the essential first step in acquiring a tolerance for ambiguity. The past is uniquely challenging because it confronts us with the spectacle of men and women whose values, habits, instincts, and beliefs were wildly different from our own *and yet* were human beings like us. This is a fruitful tension. One can escape it, of course, in a variety of ways: by writing our ancestors out of the respectable branch of the human family; insisting that their values, properly understood, anticipated our own; or dismissing their ideas as the product of superstition, prejudice, and the like. In the end, one or another of these conclusions may be irresistible. But the longer one lives with the tension, rather than rushing to relieve it, the more complex the whole picture becomes. The more difficult it is to say that someone was all bad—Andrew Jackson, for example, or Robert E. Lee or John Calhoun—and the easier to see why others find something inspiring in him.

Living with this tension is difficult in any case. None of us is terribly good at it. But it is made easier in an academic setting because here the need to come to a decision is relaxed. Obviously some decisions must be made quickly here too. But many need not be made at all. The students and faculty of a college or university are under no pressure, for example, to come to a judgment about the rights and wrongs of the Israeli-Palestinian conflict or the case for black reparations. They are under no requirement to act on these or any other questions of political morality. They have "all the time in the world" to consider them from every angle. This is even more obviously true with respect to the past. There is no deadline for deciding whether Andrew Jackson was a champion of democracy or a genocidal racist. More than most other settings, the campus allows for a leisurely approach to the task of judgment. It gives those on it the time for a more extended encounter with ambiguity, above all in judging the past, which demands no action at all. Indeed, this is part of what a college or university *is for*. In addition to advancing knowledge and training students for careers, it exists *for the sake* of strengthening their ability to live with more ambiguity than one generally finds comfortable, and that many other institutions do not tolerate let alone reward.

The urgency to decide increases as one comes closer to the present. It is natural to feel that something must be done about the issues of the day. Even with respect to these, the distinction between academic debate and political decision remains fundamental. But it is harder to sustain. The need to commit is bound to feel pressing. It decreases, though, as one turns from the present to the past. We cannot change the past, in the way we can change the country's foreign policy or strategy for dealing with climate change. All we can change are our judgments about it. In the view of some, this is an urgent political task too. But we should resist the assimilation of the past to the present, especially in a college or university devoted, among other things, to the cultivation of a tolerance for ambiguity.

We are freer looking backward than ahead. We are able to put off the need to draw a line under all our pros and cons and act accordingly. The more insistently our judgments about the past are treated as contemporary political acts, the narrower this freedom becomes. As it shrinks, a uniquely valuable opportunity for living with ambiguity shrinks too, and one of the distinctive aims of our colleges and universities is frustrated in the process.

This is why the debate over how to treat campus memorials to the less-than-honorable dead is so important. Because they do not merely preserve the past but honor it, the demand to remove or rename them seems to some a political task *right now*. But the demand must be resisted for the sake of ambiguity, which may appear a weak and formless thing but, viewed in a different light, is an essential resource in the effort to sustain a tolerance for the contradictions and tragedies of human life.

This does not mean leaving things as they are. The collection of memorials on a campus at any one time reflects a hodgepodge of decisions, some well-thought-out, others less considered, motivated by a range of different concerns. It has an accidental, even arbitrary composition. There is no sanctity to it. Moving memorials around or removing them altogether is not a crime against our ancestors. Architectural considerations, for example, often warrant changes of this kind. But where a particular memorial has become controversial *because* it is thought to reflect a view or value no longer shared by the faculty and students, the reasons for leaving it in place are *stronger, not weaker,* than they were before. It now serves an educational purpose that most memorials do not. It is a reminder of the stubbornness of the past. It is a provocation to reflection on the changeability of mores and motives and on the complexity of human beings. It is a text in ambiguity and ought to be especially valued for that reason—not despite but because it has become an irritant in a way most memorials, which never provoke even a passing thought, are not.

The reasons for leaving a memorial in place thus increase with its offense, up to a limit that has not yet been reached on any American campus. Whatever one thinks of Robert E. Lee and Junípero Serra, they are not Hitler or Stalin. This will seem paradoxical to those who think that the argument for removal is strongest when the offense is greatest. But that is because they insist on smoothing out the bumps that deform the past so that the life of their school will be less ambiguous—more of a piece, more uniformly consistent with prevailing ideals. They view ambiguity not as an aid to education but its enemy. They approach the question of removal or renaming from the wrong direction.

If one approaches it in the spirit I propose, the most important issue will be how to make the most of the educational opportunity an offensive memorial presents. Short of a statue to Hitler, removal or renaming is *never* justified—not even "Silent Sam" or Calhoun College. But the same concern *always* demands amplification, contextualization, or further acts of memorialization that accentuate ambiguity rather than avoiding it or leaving the viewer to discover it on his or her own. These can take many different forms. Which is best depends on circumstances unique to the history of each school.

The only meaningful generalization is that retention plus contextualization is preferable in every case to destruction, or storage in a warehouse, or even removal to a museum, where it becomes too tempting to think that we are a different species of human being than those whose remains we now view through a pane of glass or behind a velvet rope.

Living with ambiguity is better served by leaving even the most painful memorials where they sit, uneasily, in the midst of everyday life. They remind everyone who passes by that we are all, as the psalmist says, "broken vessel[s]"; that the world of human affairs is ruled by the law of unintended consequences, whose operation is easier to see looking backward than ahead, where the illusion of control is strengthened by the blankness of the future; and that humility should grow in proportion to the strength and uniformity of our ideals. This is not a recipe for resignation or indifference. It is the condition of moral maturity—that of a person whose commitments are not shaken by jarring reminders that many in the past have fallen short of their ideals and that no one will ever fulfill them completely. It is the attitude of a grown-up man or woman who knows that his or her ideals cannot be achieved simply by changing the name of a building or treating important parts of the past as a gallery of horrors that ought to be closed for good. It is what Hannah Arendt means by "an enlarged mentality."

This is not an expertise. It is a trait of character, a disposition, a quality of temperament as much as mind. Those who possess it are distinguished from those who lack it not by what they know but by who they are. In this respect, it resembles other virtues, like courage, temperance, and generosity. It is an excellence of soul, a better way of being human. Like these other traits, it is difficult to acquire. It runs against the grain of a basic instinct—in this case, the impulse to relieve the psychological and practical discomfort of ambiguity by ignoring or suppressing it. Some succeed to a greater degree than others. Their "mentality" is more "enlarged." The most successful ones are relatively few. Their achievement is a rarity. The same is true of the expert. Her knowledge or skill is rare too. But her superiority is limited to something she has or does. It is not an aristocratic excellence—a mark of who she is as a human being, regardless of her field or occupation. The capacity to live with ambiguity, without either erasing it or using it as an excuse to avoid the responsibility of decision, is an excellence of the latter kind. It is an aristocratic strength and one our colleges and universities have a duty to foster, among other ways by summoning the will to live with their morally mixed past instead of painting it over or putting it in a museum where it no longer offends the eye.

To this it will be objected that all my talk about excellence and aristocracy is fine for those who already feel at home on campus but fails to take account of the sense of exclusion that many minority students experience in the presence of memorials that honor those, like John Henry Boalt, who were outspoken racists or bigots. The education a school offers is for all its students, on equal terms. How can this commitment be met when some students are made to feel unwelcome the minute they arrive on a campus littered with reminders of its racist past? What kind of answer is it to say that they are there for the sake of cultivating the aristocratic virtue of an "enlarged mentality"? To many, I know, the answer seems insulting—a symptom of the problem, not a compassionate or even comprehending response to it. But it is the right answer nonetheless.

To tell anyone seeking admission to one of our colleges and universities that they are not welcome because of their color or ethnicity or sexual orientation is against the law. It is immoral. It violates the spirit of education itself. Nor should a school turn a blind eye to the fact that some applicants are disadvantaged in the competition for one of its scarce spots on account of the subtle and not-so-subtle forms of racism that still deform American life, to our collective shame. Some affirmative action in the admissions process is morally justified, even required, although whether the law will permit it under one pretense or another remains an open question today. All of this is to say that the principle of equality applies with special force at the threshold of college life, in the admissions decisions that determine who among those in the larger society will be invited to participate in its selective and privileged milieu.

Within this milieu, however, the principle of equality plays a different and diminished role. Just as no student may be denied admission to a school on the basis of race or gender, none may be denied admission to a particular class, or any other educational opportunity, for the same reason. But for the sake of what are students admitted in the first place? Partly, of course, to acquire an expertise—the knowledge and skills that will equip them for a career once they graduate. That is obvious and uncontroversial. But also partly, at least, for the sake of becoming more complete human beings.

The demand that our campuses be cleansed of offending memorials to those who held openly anti-egalitarian views is another expression of the "effervescence of democratic negation" that fails to see, and refuses to accept, the aristocratic goals of college life that exist alongside the more widely embraced professional and meritocratic ones. It confuses an "enlarged mentality" with the egalitarian commitment to show a vigilant sympathy for the victims of racism and other forms of injustice. It condemns every remnant of the past that casts the least doubt over the steadfastness of this commitment. It substitutes fidelity to an easily recognized and universally accepted political value for the more difficult task of acquiring the strength to live with ambiguity—to meet one's responsibilities as a moral and political agent without simplifying the challenge by turning away from the complexities and contradictions and tragic failings of other human beings and therefore from one's own. In the process, it sacrifices the aristocratic good for whose sake, in part at least, a school extends an equal welcome to all its students, regardless of their race, ethnicity, or gender. This amounts to throwing away one of the prizes, and not the least valuable, for which the competition to be admitted exists in the first place.

A school should recognize that the offense felt by a memorial often falls most heavily on minority students who also, for perfectly understandable reasons, may feel like recent arrivals in an institution that has historically been all white and all or mostly male. Their concerns should be taken with special seriousness. This means devoting extra resources to contextualizing the offending memorial in one or another of the many ways this can be done: by placing an explanatory plaque nearby; adding another memorial that recognizes the contribution the school has made to the cause of civil rights or the achievements of a distinguished black or Hispanic or female graduate; requiring campus tour guides to address the matter directly by pointing out the circumstances under which the memorial was erected, and the subsequent history of the school; and so on.

These are all techniques that can be and have been used at colleges and universities around the country. Every one of them is costly. The demand to adopt one or another, or perhaps several, is therefore a call on the school's resources. Minority students have a special standing to make this call and their schools have a special duty to respond. But both the demand and the response are in the service of a fuller engagement with ambiguity. Both advance an educational good of importance to all students, whatever their color or gender. Minority students who insist on contextualization therefore do so for the sake of a common educational value in which they too of course share.

Following Hannah Arendt, I call this good that of an "expanded mentality." I associate it with a tolerance for ambiguity and distinguish it from the absence of prejudice and sympathy for the victims of injustice that today is most often thought to be the essence of toleration. These are important qualities. They are indispensable on campus and off. But they are not the same as a capacity for living with ambiguity. Indeed, often enough today they encourage a leveling of judgment with respect to the past that *weakens* this capacity.

As it declines, something is lost that is even rarer than a tolerant regard for the values of others and compassion for the suffering of the marginalized and mistreated. The latter is something we should expect of everyone. The former is an exceptional power. It goes beyond the baseline of toleration. The relation between them is like that between good citizenship, on the one hand, and great statesmanship on the other. Our colleges and universities have an obligation to teach the first. We might call this their democratic function. But they also have a duty to encourage the second, however rare it may be. The traditional way of putting this is to say that our colleges and universities must produce leaders. John Adams expressed the idea in exactly these terms. So did Irving Babbitt 130 years later. We might call this their aristocratic function. The flattening of memory to produce an unambiguous landscape of uniform and self-congratulatory objects, names, emblems, and signs attacks this function at its root.

This is bad for our colleges and universities. It is also bad for our democracy. American democracy depends on the spirit of its citizens. Without a good measure of toleration and mutual respect, the divisions that exist among us are hard to contain. But it also depends on statesmen whose largeness of soul sets them apart as the members of a natural aristocracy. If anything, their leadership becomes more important the more thoroughly democratic the society becomes. Tocqueville understood this, and before him James Madison too, although Madison was realistic enough to know that "statesmen will not always be at the helm" and saw the need to design a form of government that would work well enough without them. But even those who share Madison's realism (as I do) have every reason to want to conserve all the resources our democracy allows for the cultivation of the enlarged mentality that sets the statesman apart. Among these resources, our colleges and universities figure prominently, and among the ways they cultivate this strength is by supporting the habit of living with the ambiguities of the past—although it is an irony of the first order that America's greatest statesman, who lived with contradiction and complexity beyond what it seems any heart could bear, and in whose soul ambiguity was graven like an indelible brand, never went to college but learned what he knew of our broken nature from experience mostly, and from the books he read on his own, especially the Bible and the plays of Shakespeare, which read with care are enough to teach the rest of us what Lincoln knew.

V.

There is no law of renaming. There are only better and worse judgments about the treatment of historical memory in one setting or another. Yale is the only school in the country even to have attempted to formulate a set of general principles to deal with the issue. It did so in the context of an intensifying debate over the name of Calhoun College. The president of Yale characterized the effort as an act of national leadership. Some schools have indeed followed Yale's lead. But the most remarkable thing about the decision to rename Calhoun College is not that it was made in a principled fashion that other schools might imitate, following the logic of Yale's approach. It is the poor judgment the decision displayed and its failure to defend the most important educational value that was at stake in the dispute.

As a member of the Yale faculty, I found this especially disappointing. But the resolution of the Calhoun controversy reflected the same uneasiness with ambiguity—and the same tendency to misunderstand and undervalue the special excellence of an "enlarged mentality"—that characterize many of the renaming disputes on campuses across the country. In this sense, it was symptomatic of a larger problem. Examining it in detail will confirm how strong the presumption against renaming ought to be in an academic setting; how easily a school's leaders can persuade themselves that the presumption has been overcome; and illustrate what is lost when a school yields to a morally inspired egalitarianism that gives too little weight to the rarer virtue for whose sake, in part at least, its students are there.

In the fall of 2015, in an address to the freshman class, the president of Yale asked whether Calhoun College should be renamed. He briefly surveyed the pros and cons and then called for a longer "conversation" to consider the matter. The question had been simmering at Yale for years, but the president's speech raised the temperature considerably and strengthened the expectation, in many quarters, that the name of the college would finally be changed.

When he announced, the following April, that it would not be, the decision came as a shock to many. But Yale's president offered a thoughtful defense of his decision. He expressed a view not far off from the one I have been defending here. Now forgotten in the rush of later events, his words are worth quoting at length:

> After a careful review of student and alumni responses, scholarly views, and public commentary—which were exceptionally thoughtful, measured, and helpful on all aspects of the question—it became evident that renaming [Calhoun College] could have the opposite effect of the one intended. Removing Calhoun's name obscures the legacy of slavery rather than addressing it.
>
> Ours is a nation that continues to refuse to face its own history of slavery and racism. Yale is part of this history, as exemplified by the decision to recognize an ardent defender of slavery by naming a college for him. Erasing Cal-

houn's name from a much-beloved residential college risks masking this past, downplaying the lasting effects of slavery, and substituting a false and misleading narrative, albeit one that might allow us to feel complacent or, even, self-congratulatory. Retaining the name forces us to learn anew and to confront one of the most disturbing aspects of Yale's and our nation's past. I believe this is our obligation as an educational institution.

The president then went on, in a measured way, to describe a number of initiatives designed to "ensure that [the Yale] community acquires a deeper, more consistent, and more explicit understanding of our institution's past" by putting the name of John Calhoun in a richer historical context, in furtherance of Yale's "obligation" as a place of teaching and learning.

The president's words were greeted with howls of derision. The attack was so intense that it jeopardized his authority. A few months later he retreated from the decision, stating that he had acted precipitously and needed to give the matter further thought. To help him, he appointed a "Committee to Establish Principles on Renaming." He instructed the committee to develop a set of general rules to guide the university in deciding all matters of this kind, including but not limited to the renaming of Calhoun College.

The committee released its report on December 2, 2016. It is an ably written document with three principal parts. One reviews the history of renaming disputes on other campuses; a second examines in much greater detail the Calhoun controversy at Yale; and a third, while informed by the Calhoun debate, purports to lay down a series of "principles" for deciding future renaming disputes without stating how these apply to the Calhoun question itself.

Before I turn to the substance of the committee's report, a few preliminary observations are in order.

In "constituting the committee," the president said in an interview with the *Yale Alumni Magazine* not long after, "the most important guiding idea was bringing relevant expertise to the questions at hand." The previous "conversation" concerning the renaming of Calhoun College had been defective, he suggested, because it had failed to take full advantage of the "expertise" of various faculty members who had something special to contribute to the discussion.

What this "expertise" might be, or why it should be thought relevant to the work of the committee, the president never clearly explained. Presumably, he had in mind the kind of special knowledge that a professional historian who has written articles and books about John Calhoun might be expected to possess. But all the facts about Calhoun's life and career that are mentioned in the committee's report were well-known to those on both sides of the debate who had been paying even modest attention. The same is true of the history of the dispute at Yale. The report offers a few new anecdotal details but no previously unknown facts of real importance to the resolution of the Calhoun question or to the framing of a set of general principles to guide such decisions in the future.

Nor can it be argued with any real plausibility, as the president suggests in the same magazine interview, that the "legal training" of the chair of the committee was a help in "developing principles and arguing from principles." The committee was not, after all, being asked to draft a statute. Its assignment was within the competence of ordinarily intelligent men and women with no specialized knowledge of the law. This kind of expertise was as irrelevant to its work as the professional historian's.

The questions the committee had to address were moral and political ones calling for some subtlety of judgment but incapable of being answered on the basis of expert knowledge. The most important of these was the question of how best to understand the relation between memory and responsibility, and to define Yale's special role as an institution of higher learning (which, in fairness to the committee, it does discuss but without any pretense of offering an "expert" view on the matter). By invoking the idea of untapped faculty "expertise" as an explanation for his decision to revisit the question of the renaming of Calhoun College after it appeared to have been settled, the president sought to give the committee's deliberations an aura of authority they could never possess on these grounds, and to draw attention away from the embarrassing fact that he had been pressured into abandoning his earlier position by faculty and student protesters who simply refused to accept it.

The president's other announced reason for establishing the committee was even more disingenuous. He insisted that he wanted to find a principled approach to questions of renaming, rather than answering them in an ad hoc fashion. This sounds good. It draws on our devotion to "the rule of law." But the principles the committee outlines in its report are so broad, and the priority among them so vague, that they can be used to justify almost any decision to rename with the same plausibility as a decision not to rename, depending on whether this fact or that one is given special weight in a particular case. Worse, the principles give the appearance of having been tailored to ensure that certain names—most prominently, that of Yale itself—would not be changed. Although the president of Yale and the authors of the report denied it, anyone who was paying close attention could see that the effect of the report, if not indeed its purpose, was to provide a justification for changing the name of Calhoun College *while leaving every other name on campus in place*. That can hardly be called the "rule of law." To invoke the idea of principled decision-making as the basis for renaming Calhoun thus not only concealed the real political grounds for the decision; it also damaged the honor and prestige of the idea itself, which is always vulnerable to the charge that it is being manipulated for partisan purposes.

The way in which the committee's scheme of general principles was later brought to bear on the Calhoun matter specifically further compromised the integrity of the process.

At the beginning of its report, the Committee to Establish Principles on Renaming declared that it was not *its* responsibility to resolve the Calhoun question. It had only been asked to lay down some broad rules for doing so. The job of applying these rules to the Calhoun dispute fell to a *second* committee. But *that* committee's responsibility for making the decision was likewise diluted because the elastic concept it used to do so—that of a historical figure's "principal legacy," to which I shall return—had already been defined by the first committee in terms the second committee felt bound to accept. And of course *the president himself* was not responsible for the decision: he only appointed the two committees and then accepted the results of their work. So whose responsibility *was* it? No one's in particular, it seems. It just "happened" in the way that bureaucratic decisions often do without anyone being accountable for them.

The misleading idea that the question of whether to rename Calhoun College was one that ought to be informed, if not settled, on the basis of some ill-defined "expertise"; the disingenuous invocation of the rule of law as the justification for restarting a process that was driven from the beginning by the political need to rename Calhoun while insulating all other names on the Yale campus from attack; and the bureaucratic diffusion of responsibility for the decision itself—these together give one reason to question the soundness of the decision even before coming to the merits of the arguments for and against. But it is the latter that I want to examine more closely now—for, regardless of the defects in the process leading to the decision, the most disturbing thing about it is its intellectual shallowness and misjudgment of the educational values at stake.

Everywhere one looks on the Yale campus, one sees the names of men who said or did something that today we consider unjust or immoral. Eli Yale participated profitably in the slave trade. Samuel

Morse, after whom another of Yale's residential colleges is named, was an ardent anti-Catholic who defended the institution of slavery as a positive good in much the same terms that John Calhoun did. Unless all of their names are to be removed, some basis must be found for separating out the smaller group of those whose moral offenses were sufficiently great to warrant removal. The Committee to Establish Principles on Renaming found the needed criterion in the idea of a person's "principal legacy."

"Principal legacies, as we understand them, are typically the lasting effects that cause a namesake to be remembered. Even significant parts of a namesake's life or career may not constitute a principal legacy. Scholarly consensus about principal legacies is a powerful measure." When a person's "principal legacy" is "fundamentally at odds with the mission of the university," the strong presumption against renaming may be overcome. To determine whether this is so in any particular case, a twofold determination is required. First, one must define the "mission" of the university and, second, make a judgment regarding an individual's "principal" legacy, as opposed to all the other things for which he may be known or honored. The first (the "mission") functions as a kind of ruler. One lays it against the second (the "principal" legacy) and finds that the latter either "fundamentally" conflicts with the former or does not.

The university's "mission" presumably remains fixed from case to case. That is why it is able to function as a ruler. The variable (which gets measured) is the "principal" legacy that is laid against it. The Committee to Establish Principles on Renaming defines Yale's "mission" by invoking the 2016 version of the university's official "mission statement." (Before 1992, Yale had no statement of this kind). I quote it in full:

> Yale is committed to improving the world today and for future generations through outstanding research and schol-

arship, education, preservation, and practice. Yale educates
aspiring leaders worldwide who serve all sectors of society.
We carry out this mission through the free exchange of ideas
in an ethical, interdependent, and diverse community of faculty, staff, students, and alumni.

It is difficult to imagine an emptier formula. These words mean
nothing—or all things. They provide no guidance; offer no insight
into the nature of the work done at Yale; and merely blanket with
soothing platitudes all the real, interesting, and difficult questions
that one might ask about the aspirations and responsibilities of Yale
as an academic community with three hundred years of tradition.
Like many "mission statements," this one gives only the illusion of
saying something important. In truth, it is just a puff. Its words can
be bent to any purpose. It is incapable of serving as a measure or rule
in any meaningful sense. For the committee to have relied on it as a
standard of judgment, rather than attempting the more difficult task
of defining Yale's "mission" in fresh words of its own, was a glaring
intellectual failure.

Whatever definition of Yale's "mission" one employs, however,
the greater challenge in deciding whether to rename Calhoun College is that of making a judgment about Calhoun's "principal" legacy.
The Committee to Establish Principles on Renaming recites some
facts about his career and historical reputation but refrains from offering a judgment one way or the other. This was left to a second
committee, the Presidential Advisory Group on the Renaming of
Calhoun College, whose creation was announced the day the report
of the first committee was released. This second committee delivered
its report six weeks later.

In its covering letter, the advisory group announced that it found
"*no* . . . principles [laid down by the first committee on renaming] that
weigh heavily against renaming [Calhoun College] . . . *three* commit-

tee principles that weigh heavily toward renaming, and a fourth that suggests the need to rename," conveying the impression that its rec-ommendation had been reached on arithmetical grounds and could be justified by counting up the "principles" for and against. But the body of the report makes it clear that the advisory group's judgment was based on its qualitative assessment of Calhoun's legacy, which it considers first and at greatest length. The report concludes that Calhoun's "principal" legacy was one of "racism and bigotry," and thus "fundamentally at odds" with the "mission" of the university as defined in its mission statement. Had the advisory group thought otherwise, it is difficult to imagine that it would have recommended that Calhoun College be renamed. Its judgment regarding Calhoun's "principal" legacy is at least a necessary if not sufficient condition of that recommendation. It is the heart of the advisory group's report. On what is it based?

The report first mentions a few positive facts about Calhoun, reciting the offices he held and recalling his reputation as a "con-stitutional theorist." But of course that is only half the story. The report next quotes the *Encyclopædia Britannica* to remind its readers that Calhoun also "championed states' rights and slavery and was a symbol of the Old South." All of this is true and well-known. The question is, how are the various strands of Calhoun's life and ca-reer connected, and is there one among them that may be said to be dominant or decisive—to be his "principal" legacy, as opposed to the other, subordinate aspects of it?

This is the crucial issue. The advisory group begins to address it in the following paragraph. It starts by stating that "Calhoun's most recent academic biographer balances all of these legacies judi-ciously." The word "judiciously" implies a measure of approval, but in a footnote the report states that "a new biography is long overdue," suggesting a more critical view without explaining the grounds for it.

The biography to which the report refers is by Irving H. Bartlett.

It was published by Norton in 1993. As one historian notes in his review of the Bartlett biography in the *Journal of American History*, Bartlett "leans toward a favorable interpretation of Calhoun, though less so than Charles M. Wiltse's three-volume *John C. Calhoun* (1944–51) or Margaret Coit's similarly titled one-volume biography (1950). Yet Bartlett tempers his treatment by reminding us that Calhoun's defense of slavery bespeaks 'a flawed heritage.'"

The gist of Bartlett's "favorable interpretation" is the following. Calhoun was imbued in his youth with the spirit of republicanism and a Jeffersonian fear of centralized government. This remained the leitmotif of his career. But, from its start, Calhoun's republicanism was accompanied by a devotion to his native South and to the institution of slavery in particular. As a general matter, he feared the tyranny of majorities. His abstract philosophical writings are all directed at this problem and the search for structural solutions to it. This is the leading theme of his most famous work, *A Disquisition on Government*, which does not mention slavery once. At a more particular and personal level, however, Calhoun was preoccupied with the protection of the South—its economy, culture, and way of life—from the growing power of the North. The Southern slave-owning class was the minority he sought to protect. As the country became increasingly democratic, both socially and politically, in the Age of Jackson, Calhoun's fears about the dangers of majoritarianism intensified and his defense of the Southern slave owners grew shriller. It was in this context that he offered his infamous defense in 1837 of slavery as a "positive good."

Bartlett's overall judgment is that Calhoun's republicanism was his deepest and most enduring commitment; that his defense of slavery, though genuine and heartfelt, should be understood against the background of this commitment, rather than the other way around; and that it is possible to separate the one from the other in a way that gives the first continuing relevance and value today as an inspiration for the protection of minorities whose interests Calhoun himself fiercely denied in his speeches on the benefits of slavery—a historical irony, to put it mildly.

Irving Bartlett is the only writer to whom the advisory group refers in its attempt to define Calhoun's "principal legacy." Not everyone, of course, agrees with his assessment. Some of Bartlett's reviewers complain that he excuses Calhoun's defense of slavery too easily on the grounds of his Southern upbringing. But others, while acknowledging that "Calhoun's status as determined slaveholder in the Age of Emancipation blighted forever his desired historical reputation as a champion of liberty," agree that "his increasingly anachronistic republicanism left him well placed to articulate political ideas sharply critical of the rising political spirit of the age" and conclude, with Bartlett, that "[m]ore keenly than any other observer of nineteenth-century America, with the possible exception of Alexis de Tocqueville, Calhoun saw in unalloyed democracy the dangers of majoritarian tyranny"—a legacy that remains of value today.

This suggests that among those who know the most about Calhoun and his "legacy" the question of which of its elements is the "principal" one remains a matter of debate, some historians tending to want to salvage Calhoun's republicanism from its "blighted" association with slavery, others inclining to see the latter as so poisonous as to eclipse all the other facets of his thought and career. If there is a "scholarly consensus" about Calhoun, it is surely this: that identifying his "principal" legacy is and is likely to remain a controversial enterprise in which different historians express different views depending, among other things, on their political beliefs, which inevitably shape, to some degree, their interpretation of the historical record.

The Committee to Establish Principles on Renaming defines "principal legacies" as those that "are typically the lasting effects that cause a namesake to be remembered." It states that "scholarly consensus about principal legacies is a powerful measure." But by this "measure," the most accurate thing one can say about the name of John Calhoun is that its "lasting effect," the one that causes it "to be remembered," is its role as a prod to impassioned debate over questions not only of historical but of contemporary importance— those touching on constitutional government and personal liberty as well as racism and discrimination. It is an oversimplification to say, as the advisory group does, that the "principal" legacy of John Calhoun is one of "racism and bigotry."

That it *is* an oversimplification is confirmed by another fact that neither the advisory group nor the Committee to Establish Principles on Renaming mentions in its report.

Today, Yale has fourteen residential colleges. Twelve are named for men and two for women. Of these, only three wrote books that are regularly read in courses at Yale. One is Jonathan Edwards. Another is Benjamin Franklin. The third is Pauli Murray. Each is studied as a historical figure but also as an author whose works continue to deserve close and even sympathetic attention.

The same cannot be said of any of the other eleven individuals for whom Yale's residential colleges are named. They may have done great things for the world (invent the telegraph like Samuel Morse or contribute to the modern field of computing, like Grace Hopper). They may have done great things for Yale (like Abraham Pierson, who founded the Collegiate School in 1701 that became Yale College a few years later). But none is an author of remotely the same importance as the three that I have mentioned, and whatever their value as an inspiration for students today their *ideas* play little or no role in the intellectual life of Yale's undergraduates.

Calhoun's ideas still do. Some students find certain of his constitutional arguments attractive; others reject them, but are challenged to say why. In deciding whether the positive side of Calhoun's contribution to American thought is part of a larger and still contested complex of ideas or is obliterated by his "principal" legacy of "racism and bigotry," the two committees that addressed the issue ought to have given at least some weight to the fact that Calhoun's ideas are still studied and debated on their own terms and not dismissed as a mere "symbol of the Old South." Yale is first and foremost an institution devoted to the study of ideas. Unlike all but three of the individuals for whom Yale's fourteen colleges are now named, Calhoun remains a figure of intellectual substance. This should have been a factor in assessing his "principal" legacy, especially on the Yale campus. That it was not suggests that the question was never really an open one at all.

I have noted that the advisory group cites only Irving Bartlett in its discussion of Calhoun's life and reputation. It nevertheless rejects Bartlett's attempt to "judiciously" balance the various strands of Calhoun's legacy—to "cast" Calhoun in what one reviewer calls "an objective mode"—in favor of its own judgment that Calhoun's "principal" legacy is defined by a single strand alone. The advisory group gives two reasons for preferring its view of the matter. Neither is persuasive.

First, after mentioning Bartlett's 1993 biography of Calhoun—without discussing either it or any other scholarly writings in detail—the advisory group tells us that the issue of Calhoun's "principal" legacy is settled by "Calhoun himself," who, "when he knew he was dying, set his own balance." "He left no funeral instructions and prepared no will, but instead dictated a 42-page valedictory, read for him in the Senate by a colleague on March 4, 1850, while Calhoun sat slumped at his desk, wrapped in a black cloak, listening intently. He made this last public statement his most dramatic, and he meant it to convey, to the future, what *he* wanted it to remember." This is a dramatic and unflattering image. In the view of the advisory group, Calhoun wanted to be remembered, above all, as a champion of slavery and thus deliberately bequeathed to later generations a "principal" legacy of "racism and bigotry." In accepting this conclusion, we are therefore only following Calhoun's lead.

It is questionable, though, whether Calhoun's "last public statement" should be given the decisive weight the advisory group assigns it—one great enough to eclipse not only all his earlier statements on various subjects but the judgments of historians who have reviewed the entire record of his career from a more detached and better-informed point of view. Furthermore, even if the speech makes it clear what Calhoun "wanted" to be remembered for—which is far from clear since the speech does not read, in style or substance, like the "valedictory" the advisory group calls it—that is not the same as what he *was* remembered for at the time the speech was made, or *is* remembered for today. Clearly, the speech has some probative value but not the decisive kind the advisory group attributes to it and invokes as an excuse to avoid a more careful examination of the question.

More important, a close reading of the full speech leaves the question of where Calhoun himself placed the central emphasis in his system of ideas in greater doubt than the advisory group suggests. Was his primary concern, and hence his "principal" legacy, the protection of slavery, and his constitutional theory a mere means to this end? Or should we understand the first against the background of the second? That they were intimately connected, there can be no doubt. But where should the *emphasis* be placed? The search for a "principal" legacy seems to demand some answer to this question. The advisory group takes the position that Calhoun himself gives us a decisive answer in his "valedictory" address, which makes it clear, they say, that in his own mind he put the defense of slavery first. But the speech is more ambiguous.

Calhoun begins with the observation that "agitation of the subject of slavery," if "not prevented by some timely and effective measure," must "end in disunion." Several paragraphs later he states that "as things now are" the "people of the Southern states" cannot remain "consistently with honor and safety in the union." Calhoun acknowledges that "one of the causes" of their "discontent" is "undoubtedly to be traced to the long-continued agitation of the slave question on the part of the North and the many aggressions they have made on the rights of the South during [that] time."

But then he says that "there is another [cause] lying back of it [i.e., of the agitation over slavery], with which this is intimately connected, that may be regarded as the great and primary cause." In Calhoun's view, this is the disturbance of the constitutional "equilibrium" that existed at the time of ratification, which ensured that no one "section of the country" would have "the exclusive power of controlling the government." This introduces the main theme of his speech, which is devoted to a detailed examination of the various ways in which, in Calhoun's judgment, this original equilibrium has been upset.

The growing division between North and South over the question of slavery plays a leading role—*the* leading role—in Calhoun's account. But his discussion of the question is framed by the constitutional issue. That is the main one he wants to put before his colleagues in the Senate. And while it is possible to accuse Calhoun of bad faith, if we make his own words the basis for settling the question of his "principal" legacy, as the advisory group does, it is no clearer, judging by what he says in his last speech, whether Bartlett's estimate of the relative weight of the different strands in Calhoun's legacy is a "judicious" one or not, than if we try to make that judgment on the basis of everything Calhoun said and did over the course of his entire career.

Calhoun's valedictory is not a solution to that puzzle, as the advisory group suggests. It is a part of it. To claim that we need look no further than Calhoun's last words to settle the matter in a decisive way makes no sense if we read the words themselves. The truth of the matter lies where Bartlett and his critics leave it. Calhoun's "principal" legacy is the debate, which continues to this day, over how to balance and weigh the inseparable threads of his defense of a particular version of constitutional republicanism and of the indefensible practice of slavery. (I note in passing that while the advisory group faults Calhoun for constructing his "defense of the Constitution" without reference to the Declaration of Independence, the latter acquired its constitutional significance only with the Gettysburg Address and the Civil War amendments. To criticize Calhoun on these grounds is absurd.)

Second, the advisory group looks to what it calls the "trajectory" of Calhoun's thinking to determine his principal legacy. Many of Calhoun's contemporaries, including many opponents of slavery, also "believed strongly in white supremacy." But "few public figures of his era went as conspicuously as he did from a nationalist perspective ... to a regionally based insistence that the states had the right to 'nullify' federal legislation, to a personal characterization of slavery as a 'positive good,' ..." No one will deny this. But the question is how this "trajectory" should be interpreted.

In Bartlett's view, for example, Calhoun remained all his life a foe of democratic majoritarianism, even in his early "nationalist" phase. This was the unifying theme of his career, as Bartlett sees it. As the country moved more sharply toward the majoritarianism that Calhoun loathed, his opposition to it hardened. It became more brittle. His insistence on the right of Southerners to keep their slaves grew stronger and the grounds on which he justified it shifted. But Bartlett puts these shifts of opinion and expression in the context of what he takes to be Calhoun's most abiding convictions, which he locates in Calhoun's vision of limited government and fear of democratic tyranny, not in his commitment to white supremacy. One may of course reject this interpretation and put the emphasis at a different point. Some of Bartlett's reviewers do. But the fact that Calhoun's career followed a "trajectory" does not by itself answer the question of where to locate the beliefs whose gravitational pull determined its arc—whether in the doctrine of white supremacy or that of concurrent majorities or, what seems more realistic, in the fusion of the two. It therefore does not answer the question of how to define Calhoun's "principal" legacy. The development of Calhoun's thinking is a datum that those who disagree about what is "principal" in it and what is secondary or subordinate must all take into account. But it does not settle the disagreement among them. It is part of their quarrel, not a way of ending it, as the advisory group seems to suppose.

The advisory group's conclusion that Calhoun's "principal" legacy was one of "racism and bigotry" can therefore be justified on neither of the two grounds it suggests. It also conflicts with the more ambivalent and nuanced view of the one historian it cites in its report. What this judgment reflects is not, as the Committee to Establish Principles on Renaming puts it, a "scholarly consensus" about the matter but the view of John Calhoun's life and thought that most Yale faculty and students already held at the time its report was issued. In their eyes, Calhoun's "principal" legacy was just what the advisory group says it is. Its report merely confirms something they knew, or thought they knew beforehand. But then one can hardly describe it as an independent standard, informed by some nonexistent faculty expertise, against which to measure the propriety of their popular demand that Calhoun College be renamed. In any case, the advisory group's judgment regarding Calhoun's "principal" legacy is based on reasoning too flimsy to overcome what the Committee to Establish Principles on Renaming quite properly describes as the "strong presumption against renaming a building on the basis of the values associated with its namesake"—a course that "should be considered," the committee says, "only in exceptional circumstances."

Still, one might object that it is wrong to put too much emphasis on the advisory group's woefully inadequate discussion of Calhoun's "principal" legacy. No one questions that *part* of his legacy was the defense of slavery on particularly odious grounds. If the name of Calhoun College is meant to honor the man as a whole, for all he represents, without distinguishing between the good and bad parts of his life and thought, it is hard to avoid the conclusion that the name stands, in part at least, for ideas that everyone in the Yale community rejects and that some of its members experience as a special wound to their dignity and self-respect. Putting aside the question of Calhoun's "principal" legacy, shouldn't the fact that his name is a symbol of white supremacy, *among other things*, be enough of a reason to change it, at least where it is the name of a residential college in which some of Yale's undergraduates, including African-American and other minority students, are required to live?

This, I think, was the real gravamen of the demand that the name of Calhoun College be changed. In the eyes of those supporting the change, the subtleties involved in determining Calhoun's "principal" legacy were beside the point. The real issue was whether his white supremacy was a significant enough part of his legacy to justify the complaint of those who experienced a special hurt on account of the institutional honor done to a man who, whatever else he said or did, defended slavery as a "positive good." But this raises a series of questions that neither the Committee to Establish Principles on Renaming nor the Presidential Advisory Group discusses in its report. If naming a college for John Calhoun was an act of commemoration, *who or what* was commemorated by it? If a decision, years later, to keep the name of the college, after it had been called into question, was an act of commemoration too, *who or what* was commemorated by *that* act? And is the object of commemoration the *same* in both cases?

When the Yale Corporation decided, in 1930, to name one of its newly constructed residential colleges for John Calhoun, the decision was plainly meant to honor the man himself. Calhoun was Yale's "most eminent [graduate] in the field of Civil State." The histori-cal record is thin, but we can assume that the corporation believed there was much in Calhoun's legacy as a politician and political theo-rist that justified such an honor. Whether the corporation simply ignored the other, hateful part of his legacy or discounted it as of little significance, as it might well have done in an era in which Cal-houn's racism was widely shared among Northerners and Southern-ers alike, we do not know. It is implausible, though, to think that the corporation chose to honor Calhoun *on account of* his racist beliefs. Its decision to do so is perhaps best described as one of selective memory—or, better, of selective forgetting.

The fact that Calhoun was also Yale's most famous *Southern* graduate may also have played some role in the Yale Corporation's decision, though this too is speculation.

For the first century of its existence, Yale had a minuscule num-ber of Southern students. Then beginning in the early nineteenth century, as the result of efforts by Timothy Dwight (who visited the Carolinas in the late 1790s), the number grew until by 1850, at the time of Calhoun's death, it had reached 11 percent. It declined pre-cipitously during the Civil War and remained below 3 percent until the end of the nineteenth century. In the twentieth, it very slowly began to climb again. By 1929, it had reached 6 percent. It dipped in the period immediately after but then grew steadily until 1970, when it was near 9 percent.

During these years, Yale was competing for Southern students with Princeton in particular. Princeton had a strong Southern con-nection on account of its Scots-Irish Presbyterian ties. In 1930, the Yale Corporation may have thought that naming a residential col-lege for John Calhoun would boost its presence in the South and strengthen the university's claim to be an institution of national reach, drawing students from all sections of the country and sending them back to positions of leadership in their home cities and states.

There is no evidence that this was the case, but it does not seem implausible, and it would certainly have been consistent with Yale's ambition, which was already well established, to be what today we would call, in geographical terms at least, a community of "diversity and inclusion."

This is speculative, as I say. What is crystal clear is that beginning in the 1960s and 1970s, as the number of African-American students at Yale increased, the name of Calhoun College became a subject of controversy and debate. There were some, even at the time of the original naming, who expressed their opposition to it on the grounds that Calhoun had been the voice of the slaveholding South. But now the number of those objecting and the strength of their opposition increased.

What was happening in these years can be described in different ways. The best way, I think, is as a process of recollection. What had been forgotten—ignored, discounted, or not even seen—when Calhoun College was named in 1930, was remembered and brought back into view. The ugly part of Calhoun's legacy was rejoined to the parts that presumably had been the object of the Yale Corporation's decision to honor him in the first place. The name "Calhoun" came to stand for something more complex—a composite of good and bad: a legacy of hate as well as anti-majoritarian republicanism, of white supremacy along with the principle of states' rights, of high service to the United States and treasonous encouragement of nullification and disunion.

Then in recent years, with accelerating speed, the bad began to eclipse the good. Increasingly it seemed to many faculty and students that to keep the name of Calhoun College was, if not to honor, at least to tolerate a symbol of white supremacy on a campus committed to racial equality. The other sides of Calhoun's legacy were demoted in importance. Indeed, they were mostly forgotten. What was remembered now—for many, all that was remembered—was Calhoun's defense of slavery and his invention of fancy constitutional arguments to support it. In its report, the Presidential Advisory Group effectively confirmed that this most recent view is the correct one. It put a seal of approval on what had come to be the widespread and deeply felt conviction that to continue to honor John Calhoun, by allowing the name of the college to stand, was to commemorate a legacy of "racism and bigotry."

But there is another way of understanding this history—not the history of Calhoun himself, but of Yale's relationship to him.

Those who chose to name a college for Calhoun in 1930 had the man in mind. They were honoring *him*, or at least *a part* of him. In a similar way, those who demanded, nearly ninety years later, that the name of the college be changed also had the man in mind. They weighed the strands of his legacy differently but likewise sought to dishonor *him*. In the time between these two events, however, the name of Calhoun College had come to stand, in part at least, for something other than the man. It now also represented Yale's own fitful, incomplete, but honorable attempt to come to terms with its complicated past.

In the spring of 2016, Yale struggled to decide what the name of Calhoun College represents. One answer was "the memory of a great statesman, stained forever by his devotion to slavery." A second, more widely accepted, but also directed at the man was "the life of a racist and bigot who happened, incidentally, to make a contribution to public service and political thought." These are the only possibilities the Presidential Advisory Group appears to have considered. But there is a third and better answer it might have given.

It might have said, "The name of Calhoun College memorializes Yale's struggle to live in the full light of its own ambiguous history, to fight against the forces of forgetfulness that threaten, now as in the past, to simplify the truth and that encourage us to think too well of ourselves." It might have characterized the original naming of the college as an act of forgetfulness and pointed out that renaming it would be an act of forgetfulness too—the erasure of a painful reminder, like Clementis's hat, that the world once appeared in a different and now disturbing light.

It might have acknowledged that if Yale were writing on a blank wall today, no one would propose honoring John Calhoun, given all the other possible candidates, but pointed out that keeping the name is not the same as adopting it in the first place. It might have described a decision to keep it, surrounded by counter-memorials and commentaries on Yale's choice of the name in 1930 and on the growing controversy since, as an homage not to *any* aspect of *Calhoun's* career but to *Yale's* aspiration to be a place of light and truth. It might have used the occasion to remind everyone in the Yale community that its most cherished values today do not need to bought at the price of a simpler view of the past but are strengthened by the capacity to live with its ambiguous record of glory and shame. It might even have called this capacity the uncommon strength of morally mature men and women.

This seems to have been the spirit in which, in 1973, Charles T. Davis, onetime head of the African American Studies Department at Yale and the first black master of Calhoun College, told the president of Yale that this was the only mastership he would accept. Davis understood that the name of Calhoun College, unlike that of all the other residential colleges, means something of great importance, and that what it means is not "hats off to racism and bigotry," but "be strong enough to face the past and fight it, which those who forget, by chance or by will, lose the power to do."

What does it mean to be a student in Davenport College? Or Timothy Dwight? Pretty much nothing at all. But to be a student in Calhoun—that signifies. It is an expression of something worth honoring even—indeed especially—today. For some students living in Calhoun College, their identification with it might be a source of discomfort, even of pain. But the discomfort is not gratuitous. It is connected to an educational value of the first importance. Indeed, it is a part of it. Those who insist that students be protected against the pain confuse a residential college with a home. They conflate comfort with moral maturity. And if it is objected that the pain falls unfairly on minority students, who feel it more sharply than others, the best response is to convert the pain to a badge of pride, as Charles Davis did. What serious young person would not want to wear it?

When Yale changed the name of Calhoun College in order to promote a spirit of inclusion on campus, it threw away a uniquely precious asset and the opportunity to affirm the value of inclusion in a community more honorable, more demanding, and worthier of praise than anything having to do with the legacy of John Calhoun the man. It sacrificed a deeper form a solidarity for a more comfortable and superficial one. That is always a loss. But in an academic institution it is a particularly grievous one, for here, if anywhere in our diverse and democratic country, the harder, higher task of remembering ought always to take precedence over the political demands of the hour.

Those who made these demands deserved a thoughtful response—like those who insisted that the title "master" be changed, although in the case of Calhoun College the issues were far more serious. But in neither case should feelings have decided the matter. The students and faculty who felt that Calhoun's name was a sign they were unwelcome at Yale, and those who sympathized with them, ought to have been told that Yale is something more than an echo chamber of comforting ideas and symbolic goodwill: that it is a community with the courage to live with its past; that this is one of the most difficult but important things for individuals and communities to do; that amplifying and augmenting the record of Calhoun's legacy at Yale, rather than simplifying or removing it, would be an expression of such strength; and that *everyone* at Yale is welcomed with open arms into this exceptionally demanding adventure.

They should have been told that the original fault in naming a college after John Calhoun was one of forgetfulness and that it would repeat the fault, not repair it, to un-name the college now. They should have been told that the way forward ought to be one of *redou-bled remembering* and that changing the name of Calhoun College, however good it might make people feel, would be less likely to lead in this direction, toward an "enlarged mentality," than to underwrite a reduced tolerance for ambiguity and a heightened immodesty of belief—the enemies of liberal learning and of liberal politics too.

This would have been the responsible thing to tell them. It would have been consistent with the special obligation that Yale and schools like it have to educate their students—to educate *themselves*—instead of deferring to prevailing opinion. It was in fact what the president of Yale *did* tell the Yale community in the spring of 2016 when he explained why the name of Calhoun College would not be changed. How sad that he felt he had to rescind his educationally responsible decision in the face of "political realities." Whether they really were is anyone's guess.

Epilogue

I AM AN AMERICAN HUMANIST. I AM DEVOTED TO MY COUNTRY and to the tradition of humanist learning. The first is a local attachment. It is a loyalty to one country among many. The second is universal. It is a devotion to the timeless pursuit of the question that Socrates raised when he asked how it is best for a human being to live.

Neither is uncomplicated nor are its implications always clear. Each is more an open question than a settled fact. What does it mean to be loyal to America? The answer depends on what one understands America to be. That is a notoriously divisive subject. And what is the best way for a human being to live? That too is a topic on which there will always be disagreement. And yet in each case the indefiniteness of the loyalty does not make it pointless or vain. I have a good idea of what each means despite its vagueness. Indeed, were I to lose or abandon either, I would not know where to turn. I would not even know who I was. These two loyalties make me the person I am.

The first took shape before the second. I was born an American, although it was some time before I had even a basic idea of what this means. But it was only in college that I began to think of myself as a humanist; to develop some understanding of the people, books, and ideas to which humanists like me feel loyal; and to acquire some capacity for explaining what this loyalty entails.

As I did, I came to see that there is a tension between my two loyalties.

The first is a commitment to the democratic promise of American life. America is not a pure democracy. Its government is designed to moderate the vicissitudes of a pure democracy with a system of carefully constructed checks and balances. Still, the fundamental idea of America is that of democratic self-rule, along with its essential corollary: the belief, which Jefferson called a "self-evident truth," that "all men are created equal." The idea of equality lies at the heart of the American venture. One might even say that this venture has consisted, and consists still, in discovering what equality means and in living up to its demands.

The second loyalty is aristocratic in nature. It assumes that some ways of living are better than others—that they more fully enact and express the human powers we all share. If this assumption is abandoned, the humanist tradition of study loses its mooring. It is cut adrift. There is no longer anything for a humanist to be loyal to.

The tension between these two loyalties—the first to a democratic experiment, the second to an aristocratic ideal—might seem to make them mortal enemies. But I have not found this to be the case. Indeed, I have come to believe that the two are compatible and perhaps even harmonious.

The American experiment in democracy is as grand as any that human beings have ever devised. But it has its own pathologies. It levels the distinction between great men and women and ordinary ones; converts greatness into popularity; encourages conformism and group thinking; and denounces all aristocracies, including the natural one that John Adams thought essential to wise leadership in his newly founded country.

The humanist tradition, with its aristocratic respect for excellence in living, is a partial antidote to these pathologies. It softens and offsets them. It encourages a respect for standards and independence of mind. In this sense it helps our democracy rather than hurts it.

This tradition is principally in the custody of our colleges and universities. Because it is, they have a special duty to conserve it. They have an obligation to protect the aristocratic idea that some human beings get further than others in mastering the art of living—not just because it is true, but also because it provides some balance against the worst shortcomings of our glorious if imperfect democracy.

Those who feel, as I do, a double loyalty to America and to the humanist idea of excellence know how foolish it would be to try to extend the latter idea to the country at large. That would be undemocratic. It would be unwise and unjust. There is not, however, much danger of this happening.

But there is a real danger from the opposite direction: that some will try to remake our colleges and universities in the image of the principle of democratic equality. This danger has always existed. Today it is very great. The three movements I have discussed in this book are warning signs. The move to restrict campus speech in the name of respect and inclusion; the transformation of diversity from a political to a pedagogical value; and the demand that the past be renamed to fit our current understanding of equality, are all symptoms of the increasingly aggressive intrusion of democratic politics into academic life. They are the manifestations of a general and intensified assault on the aristocratic ideal that underlies the humanist tradition. This hurts our colleges and universities, which have a responsibility to shelter this tradition from the hurricane of democratic belief. But it hurts the country too, by damaging one of the few places that cultivate the habits that counteract the worst tendencies that even the best democracies produce.

Those faculty and students who disdain the privilege of their elite institutions therefore do both these institutions and the country a disservice. I see every day how much harm they do to the culture of liberal learning. And while I value this culture for its own sake, I value it as well for the sake of my beloved and beleaguered country, which at the present moment needs all the wisdom and open-mindedness it can get.

The leaders of our finest colleges and universities have a responsibility to their schools and to the country at large. They meet neither responsibility by capitulating to "the effervescence of democratic negation" that is such a powerful force on our campuses today. Instead of disowning their elitism, they ought to embrace it. They ought to keep faith with the idea that there is such a thing as greatness in the work of being human and that it is recognizably, teachably, lastingly different from mediocrity and failure. Against the levelers they ought to insist on the value of what is rare and fine: on the strength to persevere in the search for truth; the capacity to live with awful ambiguities; and the resolve to be an individual, not just the representative of a group. These qualities are good in themselves—supremely good. They are also indispensable in the leaders and citizens of a democracy that aspires to long life. Affirming their nobility serves the life of the mind and that of America too.

When I graduated from Williams College a half century ago, I gave a commencement speech attacking the Vietnam War. I thought the war a tragic mistake. I still do. I was a student radical then, and although my politics have mellowed since, I still endorse progressive positions on the whole. But when it comes to the academy, where I have made my career, my views have become steadily more conservative. If you have read this far, you know that. Yet one of my convictions has remained more or less the same over the past fifty years.

I still believe, as I did then, that our colleges and universities are not political institutions; that their work is not the pursuit of politics by other means; that they belong to a different order of values and expectations; and that their first responsibility is to themselves and their undemocratic way of life.

This belief has remained constant, as I say. But what I see more clearly now is that in meeting their responsibilities our colleges and universities make our democracy stronger, although this is not their principal aim. They make it stronger by respecting themselves and the humanistic habits they convey from teacher to student. The dual loyalties of American humanists like me are therefore not as contradictory as they seem. The real danger of the present hour is not the tension between them. It is the drive to eliminate the tension by making these loyalties one and the same—by democratizing the inner life of our colleges and universities so that the rule of equality that prevails outside them comes to be the norm in the now masterless world of teaching and learning as well. What a grievous loss that would be: for our students, their schools, the country at large. Enough is enough. It is time to rally round the ivory tower.

Acknowledgments

I wish to record my thanks to Nathaniel Zelinsky of the Yale Law School Class of 2018 and Will Kamin of the Class of 2020. Both provided invaluable assistance in preparing the book for publication. I also wish to thank my editor, Priscilla Painton, whose keen advice helped me see more clearly where I wanted to go and whose encouragement kept me moving forward. Finally, I want to express my gratitude to my students, both in the law school and Yale College. I have been their teacher and they mine. After forty years together in the classroom, what I owe to their wisdom, enthusiasm, and love of learning, can no longer be measured. It is to them that I dedicate the book.

Notes

Introduction

1 *by some more neutral term instead:* Emma Platoff and Vivian Wang, "Stephen Davis Asks Pierson Students Not to Call Him 'Master,'" *Yale Daily News*, August 14, 2015, https://yaledailynews.com/blog/2015/08/14/stephen -davis-asks-pierson-students-not-to-call-him-master/.

2 *in referring to the heads of any of its residential colleges:* Peter Salovey, email to the Yale Community, "Decisions on Residential College Names and 'Master' Title," *Yale University: Official Yale University Messages*, April 27, 2016, https://messages.yale.edu/messages/University/univmsgs/detail /137123.

3 *how the question would be answered, or when or by whom:* Peter Salovey, "The Freshman Address" (speech, August 29, 2015), reprinted as "Launching a Difficult Conversation," *Yale Alumni Magazine*, November– December 2015, https://yalealumnimagazine.com/articles/4201-launching -a-difficult-conversation.

4 *the one surrounding Calhoun College:* Peter Salovey, "Campus Update: Committee to Establish Principles on Renaming," *Yale University: Office of the President*, August 1, 2016, https://president.yale.edu/speeches-writings /statements/campus-update-committee-establish-principles-renaming.

5 *a video seen by millions:* Anemona Hartocollis, "Yale Lecturer Resigns After Email on Halloween Costumes," *New York Times*, December 7, 2015, https://www.nytimes.com/2015/12/08/us/yale-lecturer-resigns-after-email -on-halloween-costumes.html. Recently, Milo Yiannopoulos was scheduled

to give a talk at New York University on "issues raised by Halloween," such as "costumes, identity, identity politics and the left's censorious policing of what was once a holiday for 'misrule' and harmless play." The university "postponed" Yiannopoulos's appearance at the urging of New York City mayor Bill de Blasio, who cited "public safety reasons in light of the nearby Halloween parades and NYPD assessments of risk." Patrick Strickland, "Students Call for NYU to Cancel Milo Yiannopoulos Lecture," *Al Jazeera*, October 30, 2018, https://www.aljazeera.com/news/2018/10/students-call -nyu-cancel-milo-yiannopoulos-lecture-181030170250806.html.

5   *the ideal of free expression on the other:* Peter Salovey, "Yale Believes in Free Speech—and So Do I," *Wall Street Journal*, October 17, 2016, https://www .wsj.com/articles/yale-believes-in-free-speech-and-so-do-i-1476745961.

5   *At Evergreen State College:* Anemona Hartocollis, "A Campus Argument Goes Viral. Now the College Is Under Siege," *New York Times*, June 16, 2017, https://www.nytimes.com/2017/06/16/us/evergreen-state-protests.html.

5   *At the University of Southern California:* Nathan Fenno, "Traveler, USC's Mascot, Comes Under Scrutiny for Having a Name Similar to Robert E. Lee's Horse," *Los Angeles Times*, August 18, 2017, http://www.latimes.com /sports/la-sp-usc-traveler-20170818-story.html.

6   *At Claremont McKenna College:* Howard Blume, "Protesters Disrupt Talk by Pro-Police Author, Sparking Free-Speech Debate at Claremont McKenna College," *Los Angeles Times*, April 9, 2017, http://www.latimes.com/local /lanow/la-me-ln-macdonald-claremont-speech-disrupted-20170408-story .html.

6   *At the University of Pennsylvania:* Alex Rabin, "A Penn TA Said She Calls on Black Women First in the Classroom. Now, Some Want Her Suspended," *Daily Pennsylvanian*, October 20, 2017, http://www.thedp.com/article/2017 /10/a-penn-ta-said-she-calls-on-black-women-first-in-the-classroom-now -some-want-her-suspended.

6   *At Oberlin:* Jennifer Medina, "Warning: The Literary Canon Could Make Students Squirm," *New York Times*, May 18, 2014, https://www.nytimes.com /2014/05/18/us/warning-the-literary-canon-could-make-students-squirm .html.

6   *At Lebanon Valley College:* Colin Deppen, "'Not Good Enough': Some Lebanon Valley College Students Unsatisfied with New Equality Plan," PennLive.com, January 21, 2016, http://www.pennlive.com/news/2016/01 /not_good_enough_some_lebanon_v.html.

8   *"enjoy and abuse":* Edward Gibbon, *The History of the Decline and Fall of the Roman Empire*, ed. J. B. Bury (New York: Fred de Fau, 1906), 1:1.

8   *what he called the "tyranny of the majority":* Alexis de Tocqueville, *Democracy in America,* trans. Harvey Mansfield & Debra Winthrop (Chicago: University of Chicago Press, 2000), 243–46.

9   *he mentions our colleges and universities:* Ibid., 450–52.

10   *special emphasis on the role of a free press:* Ibid., 493–95.

11   *the "effervescence of democratic negation":* Oliver Wendell Holmes, "The Use of Law Schools: Oration Before the Harvard Law School Association, November 5, 1886," *Collected Legal Papers* (New York: Harcourt, Brace, 1920), 37.

11–12 *"I think we should all agree that . . . the democratic feeling which will submit neither to arrogance nor to servility":* Ibid., 37–38.

17   *since the Supreme Court's decision in* Regents of the University of California v. Bakke: *Regents of the University of California v. Bakke,* 438 U.S. 265 (1978).

19   *the "spirit of liberty":* See Learned Hand, "The Spirit of Liberty" (speech, May 21, 1944), reprinted in *The Spirit of Liberty: Papers and Addresses,* ed. Irving Dillard (New York: Alfred A. Knopf, 1960), 190. Judge Hand's use of the phrase "spirit of liberty" resonates with John Adams's frequent use of the phrase. See, for example, Letter from John Adams to Samuel Adams, October 18, 1790, *The Works of John Adams,* ed. Charles Francis Adams (Boston: Little Brown, 1851), 419.

Chapter One: Excellence

25   *a "procedural" form of government:* See Michael Sandel, "The Procedural Republic and the Unencumbered Self," *Political Theory* 12, no. 1 (1984): 81–96.

27   *similar standard of excellence by which to judge the performance of different human beings:* See Aristotle, *Nicomachean Ethics,* trans. Robert C. Bartlett & Susan D. Collins (Chicago: University of Chicago Press, 2011), 10–14 (Bk. I.7).

27   *obviously the one that is led and run by the best human beings:* Aristotle, *Politics,* trans. Carnes Lord (Chicago: University of Chicago Press, 2013), 77 (Bk III.10, 1281a4–8).

32   *published . . . as the* Discourses on Davila: John Adams, *Discourses on Davila: A Series of Papers on Political History,* in *The Works of John Adams,* ed. Charles Francis Adams (Boston: Little Brown, 1851), 6:223.

32   *"the passion for distinction":* Ibid., 232.

33   *"affection for the good of others . . . not a balance for the selfish affections":* Ibid., 234.

33   *To the passion for "benevolence":* Ibid.

33 *"has kindly added . . . to make us good members of society"*: Ibid.

33 *"self-preservation"*: Ibid.

33 *not to be "out of the sight of others, groping in the dark"*: Ibid., 239.

33 *the desire to be "seen"*: Ibid., 233.

33 *welded to genuine "merit"*: Ibid., 236.

33 *"beauty, elegance and grace"*: Ibid., 235.

33 *"intellectual and moral qualities"*: Ibid., 241.

33 *summarizes these qualities in the word "virtue"*: Ibid., 241–42.

33 *the goods of "health, strength and agility"*: Ibid., 242.

33 *those of "birth" and "riches"*: Ibid.

33 *"the only rational source and eternal foundation of honor"*: Ibid.

33–34 *"There is a voice within us . . . How shall the men of merit be discovered?"*: Ibid., 249.

34 *"real merit is confined to a very few"*: Ibid., 250.

34 *"numbers who thirst . . . seek it only by merit"*: Ibid.

34 *"intrigues and manœuvres . . . with scarce a possibility of preferring real merit"*: Ibid., 247.

34 *the most seductive "deception"*: Ibid., 249.

34 *the doctrine of "levelling"*: Adams to John Taylor, April 15, 1814, in *The Works of John Adams*, 6:459.

34 *"the self-styled philosophers of the French Revolution"*: Ibid., 454.

34 *"Every man and woman . . . equal rights"*: Ibid., 460.

34 *the "weight" or "power" they enjoy "ought not" to be*: Ibid.

35 *"a voice within"*: Adams, *Discourses on Davila*, 249.

35 *the best men ought to "govern the world"*: Ibid.

35 *"power," as distinct from "rights"*: Adams to Taylor, April 15, 1814, 460.

35 *"Is there a constitution . . . with balances than ours?"*: Ibid., 467.

36 *the leveling "democracy of France"*: Ibid., 485.

36 *They constitute a "natural" aristocracy*: Ibid., 460.

36 *"leisure for study must ever be the portion of the few"*: Adams, *Discourses on Davila*, 280.

36 *"the laboring part of the people can never be learned"*: Ibid.

37 *"knowledge will forever be monopolized by the aristocracy"*: Adams to Taylor, April 15, 1814, at 516.

37 *"the moment you give knowledge . . . you make him an aristocrat"*: Ibid.

37 *"no peculiar rights in society"*: Ibid., 495.

37 *giving their more learned views a special "weight"*: Ibid., 460.

37 *confers a "distinction" and "privilege" upon them*: Ibid., 495.

37 *"There is . . . between knowledge and virtue"*: Ibid., 520.

37   *"knowledge, upon the whole, promotes virtue and happiness":* Ibid., 519.

38   *"in the deepest democracy that ever was known or imagined":* Ibid., 453.

38   *human "thirst for respect":* Adams, *Discourses on Davila*, 250.

39   *the "tyranny of the majority":* Tocqueville, *Democracy in America*, 239–42.

39   *Its triumph makes the world more "just":* Ibid., 675.

39   *"finally reduces each nation . . . the government is the shepherd":* Ibid., 663.

39   *In "democratic societies . . . the social body becomes more tranquil and less lofty":* Ibid., 604.

39   *"The spectacle of this universal uniformity . . . regret the society that is no longer":* Ibid., 674.

40   *"scarcely believe themselves to be a part of the same humanity":* Ibid., 535. The kind of separation whose effacement Tocqueville notes resembles what Nietzsche calls the "pathos of distance" between different ranks of human beings in an aristocratic society. See Friedrich Nietzsche, *On the Genealogy of Morality*, ed. Keith Ansell-Pearson, trans. Carol Diethe (Cambridge, UK: Cambridge University Press, 2006), 12 (I.2), 91 (III.14).

40   *"the spirit of conservation against democratic instability":* Tocqueville, *Democracy in America*, 142.

41   *the education and practice of lawyers . . . are preserved amid the continual reforms of democratic life:* Ibid., 251–58.

41   *(though their independent beliefs tend to converge in a consolidated mass opinion):* Ibid., 403.

42   *the "opulent or well-to-do" . . . inclined "to engage in the works and pleasures of the intellect":* Ibid., 431.

42   *"rises toward the infinite, immaterial, and beautiful":* Ibid., 431.

42   *they have an aristocratic character . . . but are open to the outside world and founded on agreement:* Ibid.

42   *what Holmes calls "spiritual things":* Oliver Wendell Holmes, "The Use of Law Schools: Oration Before the Harvard Law School Association, November 5, 1886," *Collected Legal Papers* (New York: Harcourt, Brace, 1920), 38.

42   *a taste for "the infinite":* Tocqueville, *Democracy in America*, 431.

42–43   *"Give democratic peoples enlightenment and freedom . . . he will finally degrade himself":* Ibid., 518–19.

43   *"the most precious inheritance from aristocratic centuries":* Ibid., 519.

43   *"When any religion whatsoever has cast deep roots within a democracy, guard against shaking it":* Ibid., 519.

43   *"the search for ideal beauty constantly shows itself" . . . in these ancient languages:* Ibid., 451.

43   *"the ills that equality can produce"*: Ibid., 668.

43   *"that in democratic centuries . . . the greatest number be scientific, commercial and industrial rather than literary"*: Ibid., 451.

43   the study of *"belles-lettres"* and *"ancient literature"*: Ibid., 451–52.

44   *"it is important that . . . destines them to cultivate letters or predisposes them to that taste"*: Ibid., 452.

44   *"To attain this result . . . prevent necessary studies from being done well"*: Ibid.

45   the few who long to spend their time in the company of *"ideal beauty"*: Ibid., 451.

46   *from the arid criticism of "the decaying caste of literary Brahmins" at Harvard . . . to the experimental writers "of Greenwich Village" . . . ridiculing these standards themselves*: H. L. Mencken, "The National Letters," *Prejudices: First, Second, & Third Series*, ed. Marion Elizabeth Rogers (New York: Library of America, 2010), 160, 163.

46   *we have been promised (in Whitman's words) "a great original literature"*: Ibid., 154. Mencken quotes from Walt Whitman, *Democratic Vistas and Other Papers* (London: Walter Scott, 1888), 6.

46–47   *"a defect in the general culture . . . in all departments of thinking"*: Mencken, "The National Letters," 186.

47   *"the lack of a civilized aristocracy . . . delighting in the battle of ideas for its own sake"*: Ibid.

47   *"a civilized aristocracy"*: Ibid.

47   *"word . . . by no means intend[s] to convey"*: Ibid.

47   *"Any mention of an aristocracy . . . upon the daughters of breakfast-food and bathtub kings"*: Ibid., 186–87.

47   this is a *"bugaboo aristocracy"*: Ibid., 188.

47   the *"mob mind"* from which it springs: Ibid., 187.

47   *"What the inferior man and his wife see . . . humanity in every land under the cross"*: Ibid., 187–88.

47–48   *"Its first and most salient character is its interior security . . . it pays for its high prerogatives by standing in the forefront of the fray"*: Ibid., 189.

49   *"is badly educated . . . lacking in the most elemental independence and courage"*: Ibid., 190–91.

49   *"extraordinary men of the lower orders"*: Ibid., 189.

49   *"the vast mass of undifferentiated human blanks"*: Ibid., 190.

49   *"breathe . . . clear air"*: Ibid., 189.

49   *"the capacity for . . . what Nietzsche calls the joys of the labyrinth"*: Ibid., 194.

49   *"artificial immunities"* that shield the few who love *"the battle of ideas for its own sake"* from the *"society of half-wits"*: Ibid., 189, 186, 194.

49 an *"entrenched fold" whose protections allow for a playful experimentation with ideas:* Ibid., 189.

49 *"has left only a vacuum in its place":* Ibid., 194.

49 *"in a century and a half . . . its inherent stupidity and swinishness":* Ibid.

49–50 *"The whole drift of our law . . . into a capital crime against society":* Ibid.

50 institutions whose *"artificial immunities" do permit a "genuine aristocracy":* Ibid., 189.

50 *"this small brotherhood of the superior . . . a gigantic disappointment":* Ibid., 194.

50 *"all the marks of a caste of learned and sagacious men":* Ibid.

50 It lacks *"curiosity" and "courage":* Ibid., 194–95.

50 characterized by *"pretentiousness" and a ponderous sense of dignity:* Ibid., 195.

50 *"all the qualities of an aristocracy . . . about the fashionable aristocrats of the society columns":* Ibid.

50 life *"under the campus pump . . . veneration for mere schooling":* Ibid., 194–95.

50 *"the most prudent and skittish of all men":* Ibid., 196.

50 *"[H]e yields to the prevailing correctness . . . heresy is not only a mistake, but also a crime":* Ibid., 196–97.

50–51 *"the eager curiosity . . . of a true aristocracy":* Ibid., 199.

51 *"the loudest spokesmen of . . . the mob run wild":* Ibid., 197.

51 what Mencken calls *"correctness":* Ibid., 196–97.

51 *"the late lamentable war":* Ibid., 197.

51 *"What was the reaction . . . downright insanity?":* Ibid.

51 *"They fed it . . . bogus heroics,"* all in the name of *"correctness":* Ibid.

51 *"all my instincts . . . side of the professors":* Ibid., 196.

52 *"decaying caste of literary Brahmins":* Ibid., 160.

52 *"solemn, highly judicial, coroner's inquest . . . intellectual audacity . . . aesthetic passion":* Ibid., 159.

52 *"The thing is correctly done . . . for what remains is next to nothing":* Ibid.

52 the intrusion of *"the democratic spirit":* Irving Babbit, *Literature and the American College: Essays in Defense of the Humanities* (Boston: Houghton Mifflin, 1908), 72–87.

52 promoting a *"humanistic" culture:* Ibid., 31.

52 distinguished from *"humanitarianism":* Ibid., 5–9.

52 Its watchword is *"service":* Ibid., 44.

52 what Babbitt calls *"impressions":* Ibid., 26, 47, 83.

53 *"high and objective standards of human excellence":* Ibid., 74.

53   *"the principle of equality"*: Irving Babbitt, *Democracy and Leadership* (Boston: Houghton Mifflin, 1924), 238.

53   *"a truly human hierarchy and scale of values"*: Ibid.

53   to preserve *"the aristocratic principle"*: Ibid., 61.

53   *"We want no American equivalents . . . wealth, or power, or station"*: Ibid.

53–54 *"in a few of our Eastern colleges . . . not to a dangerous degree"*: Ibid.

54   *"should be democratic in the sense . . . distinctions of family and rank"*: Ibid.

54   *"the type of sentimental humanitarianism . . . judgment has been lost"*: Ibid., 78.

54   *"a means not so much for the thorough . . . uplift for the many"*: Ibid.

54   *"the democratic contention that everybody . . . live up to high standards"*: Babbitt, *Democracy and Leadership*, 312.

55   *"effervescence of democratic negation"*: Holmes, "The Use of Law Schools," 37.

58   *they reply that it is valuable because it is useful for* all sorts *of occupations*: See, for example, Kathrin Day Lassila, "Q & A: Peter Salovey—Why a Liberal Arts Education? The Value of Mental Agility in a Rapidly Changing World," *Yale Alumni Magazine*, May–June 2018, https:// yalealumnimagazine.com/articles/4676-why-a-liberal-arts-education (interview with Yale University President); Jill Tiefenthaler, "The Value of a Liberal-Arts Education," Hechinger Report, April 10, 2013, https:// hechingerreport.org/the-value-of-a-liberal-arts-education/ (opinion piece by Colorado College president); Edward J. Ray, "The Value of a Liberal Arts Education in Today's Global Marketplace," *Huffington Post*, July 24, 2013 (blog post by Oregon State University president).

59   *for a more meritocratic system*: See Daniel Markovits, *The Meritocracy Trap* (New York: Penguin), forthcoming.

63   *the "subtiler" joys*: Holmes, "The Use of Law Schools," 37.

63   *"high and objective standards of human excellence"*: Babbitt, *Literature and the American College*, 74.

63   *"autonomous, courageous, venturesome" and "curious"*: Mencken, "The National Letters," 189.

63   *"the tyranny of the majority"*: Tocqueville, *Democracy in America*, 239–42.

64   *touted for their vocational value*: See, for example, George Anders, "The Unexpected Value of the Liberal Arts: First-Generation Students Are Finding Personal and Professional Fulfillment in the Humanities and Social Sciences," *Atlantic*, August 1, 2017, https://www.theatlantic.com /education/archive/2017/08/the-unexpected-value-of-the-liberal-arts /535482/ (profiling a student who "has capitalized on a seldom-appreciated

liberal-arts discipline—sociology—to power her career forward"); Jose
Ferreira, "Don't Defund Humanities: They're Crucial to the Economy, Too,"
Knewton, September 17, 2013, https://web.archive.org/web/20150131212022
/http://www.knewton.com/blog/ceo-jose-ferreira/stem-vs-humanities/ ("A
liberal arts education provides excellent training in . . . communications
skills, critical thinking skills, and learning about other cultures and ideas. As
any nation's economy increasingly becomes a global knowledge economy,
these skills only grow more important. All knowledge economies—the USA
among them—want more high-skill workers, of any type.")

66   *otherwise expansive democracy is limited to the first:* Tocqueville, *Democracy
      in America*, 302–96.

68   *prejudice against them hardened:* Ibid., 329.

68   *"The slave went free . . . back again toward slavery":* W. E. B. Du Bois, *Black
      Reconstruction in America, 1860–1880* (New York: Free Press, 1998), 30.

68   *culminating in* Brown v. Board of Education: *Brown v. Board of Education of
      Topeka*, 347 U.S. 483 (1954).

68   *the Civil Rights and Voting Rights Acts:* Civil Rights Act of 1964, Pub. L.
      88–352, 78 Stat. 241 (July 2, 1964); Voting Rights Act of 1965, Pub. L.
      89–110, 79 Stat. 437 (August 6, 1965).

69   *what some call the principle of "anti-subordination":* For discussions of
      the principle in the context of Equal Protection Clause jurisprudence,
      see Ruth Colker, "Anti-Subordination Above All: Sex, Race, and Equal
      Protection," *New York University Law Review* 61, no. 6 (1986): 1003–66;
      Ruth Colker, "The Anti-Subordination Principle: Applications," *Wisconsin
      Women's Law Journal* 3 (1987): 59–80; Rebecca E. Zietlow, "Free at Last:
      Anti-Subordination and the Thirteenth Amendment," *Boston University
      Law Review* 90, no. 1 (2010): 255–312; Victor C. Romero, "Rethinking
      Minority Coalition Building: Valuing Self-Sacrifice, Stewardship and Anti-
      Subordination," *Villanova Law Review* 50, no. 4 (2005): 823–36.

69   *formal legal equality is not enough to uproot the system of caste:* See, for
      example, Owen M. Fiss, "The Fate of an Idea Whose Time Has Come:
      Antidiscrimination Law in the Second Decade after *Brown v. Board of
      Education*," *University of Chicago Law Review* 41, no. 4 (1974): 742–73; Owen
      M. Fiss, "Foreword: The Forms of Justice," *Harvard Law Review* 93, no. 1
      (1979): 1–58; Owen M. Fiss, "Racial Imbalance in the Public Schools: The
      Constitutional Concepts," *Harvard Law Review* 78, no. 3 (1965): 564–617.

73   *"of the true, the beautiful, and the good":* Thorstein Veblen, *The Theory of the
      Leisure Class: An Economic Study of Institutions* (New York: B. W. Huebsch,
      1899), 120.

73   *"salient feature" of which is "*otium cum dignitate *[leisure with honor]":*
     Ibid., 95–96.

74   *distinction between superior and inferior human beings:* Letter from Thomas
     Jefferson to John Adams, October 28, 1814, reprinted in *The Adams-*
     Jefferson Letters: The Complete Correspondence Between Thomas Jefferson
     and Abigail and John Adams, ed. Lester J. Cappon (Chapel Hill: University
     of North Carolina Press), 2:387–92.

Chapter Two: Speech

77   *Milo Yiannopoulos:* Benjamin Oreskes and Javier Panzar, "Milo
     Yiannopoulos Confronted by Dozens of Counter-protesters During Brief
     Appearance on UC Berkeley Campus," *Los Angeles Times,* September
     24, 2017, https://www.latimes.com/local/lanow/la-me-ln-berkeley-milo
     -20170924-story.html.

77   *Richard Spencer:* Ella Nilsen, "Richard Spencer Had Speeches Scheduled at
     2 Colleges, and They've Both Uninvited Him," *Vox,* August 16, 2017, https://
     www.vox.com/policy-and-politics/2017/8/16/16156130/richard-spencer
     -speeches-canceled.

77   *Charles Murray:* Eugene Volokh, "Protesters at Middlebury College Shout
     Down Speaker, Attack Him and a Professor," *Washington Post,* March 4,
     2017, https://www.washingtonpost.com/news/volokh-conspiracy/wp/2017
     /03/04/protesters-at-middlebury-college-shout-down-speaker-attack-him
     -and-a-professor/?utm_term=.b2e7904377b6. Note, however, that the
     students who disrupted Murray's appearance were met with sanctions
     "ranging from probation to official college discipline, which places a
     permanent record in the student's file." See Stephanie Saul, "Dozens of
     Middlebury Students are Disciplined for Charles Murray Protest," *New York*
     Times, May 24, 2017, https://www.nytimes.com/2017/05/24/us/middlebury
     -college-charles-murray-bell-curve.html.

77   *Heather Mac Donald:* Howard Blume, "Protesters Disrupt Talk by
     Pro-Police Author, Sparking Free-Speech Debate at Claremont McKenna
     College," *Los Angeles Times,* April 9, 2017, http://www.latimes.com/local
     /lanow/la-me-ln-macdonald-claremont-speech-disrupted-20170408-story
     .html.

77   *hate speech is legally protected: R.A.V. v. City of St. Paul,* 505 U.S. 377 (1992).

77   *have regularly been struck down as well: Dambrot v. Central Michigan*
     University, 55 F.3d 1177 (6th Cir. 1995); *UWM Post v. Board of Regents*

of the University of Wisconsin, 774 F. Supp. 1163 (E.D. Wis. 1991); *Doe v. University of Michigan*, 721 F. Supp. 852 (E.D. Mich. 1989).

77 *Some in fact have done so:* The Foundation for Individual Rights in Education's 2018 report on campus speech codes found that 53.9 percent of private universities have "at least one policy both clearly and substantially restricting freedom of speech, or [bar] public access to [their] speech-related policies . . ." Foundation for Individual Rights in Education, *Spotlight on Speech Codes 2018: The State of Free Speech on Our Nation's Campuses*, 5–7, https://d28htnjz2elwuj.cloudfront.net/wp-content/uploads/2017/12/20151222/FIRE-scr-2018-rev.pdf.

77 *or, have simply chosen to ignore it:* The 2018 FIRE report found that 26 percent of public universities have "at least one policy both clearly and substantially restricting freedom of speech, or [bar] public access to [their] speech-related policies." Ibid.

78 *Yale's official substitution of "first year" for "freshman":* Marvin Chun, "First-Year? Upper-Level? A Guide to Yale College's Usage," *Yale College: Messages from the Dean*, September 7, 2017, https://yalecollege.yale.edu/deans-office/messages/first-year-upper-level-guide-yale-colleges-usage.

78 *so-called micro-aggressions:* See, for example, "The College's Actions to Promote Diversity and Inclusion," *Amherst College: Diversity and Inclusion*, November 2016, https://www.amherst.edu/amherst-story/diversity/actions-to-promote-diversity-and-inclusion ("The Office of Diversity & Inclusion has initiated micro-aggression sensitivity training, as well as unconscious bias education workshops for staff."); Emelyn A. de la Peña, "Micro-aggressions & Micro-affirmations: Unconscious Actions & Implicit Bias," Office of Diversity and Inclusion: Harvard Resources, Offices, & Initiatives, August 2015, https://www.hsph.harvard.edu/diversity/harvardresources/; "Ally and Sensitivity Training," University of California at Irvine Office of Inclusive Excellence, https://inclusion.uci.edu/ally-sensitivity-training/.

82 *"willfully disturb[ing] or break[ing] up . . . not unlawful in its character":* California Penal Code § 403 (enacted January 1, 1995).

84 *get their ideas out into a "marketplace" where they can compete with other ideas and hopefully prevail:* The origins of the "marketplace of ideas" analogy are generally traced back to Milton, who in 1644 argued that truth was most apt to emerge from "a free and open encounter" between conflicting ideas. John Milton, *Areopagitica and Of Education* (Wheeling, IL: Harlan Davidson, 1951), 50. Justice Oliver Wendell Holmes Jr. imported the concept into American jurisprudence when he made reference to the "free trade in ideas" within "the competition of the market." *Abrams v.*

United States, 250 U.S. 616, 630 (1919) (Holmes, J., dissenting). The pithier phrasing of a "marketplace of ideas" is owed to Justice William O. Douglas. *United States v. Rumely*, 345 U.S. 41, 56 (1953) (Douglas, J., concurring). The analogy of the marketplace has been criticized in recent years, particularly within the context of campus speech debates. See, for example, Aaron R. Hanlon, "The Myth of the 'Marketplace of Ideas' on Campus: Conservative Speakers Like Milo Yiannopoulos and Charles Murray Are Rewarded for Provocation, Not Quality of Thought," *New Republic*, March 6, 2017, https://newrepublic.com/article/141150/myth-marketplace-ideas-campus -charles-murray-milo-yiannopoulos. For a more nuanced and rigorous critique of the "marketplace of ideas" metaphor, see Vincent Blasi, "Holmes and the Marketplace of Ideas," *Supreme Court Review* 2004: 1.

85 R.A.V. v. City of St. Paul *(1992) is illustrative: R.A.V. v. City of St. Paul*, 505 U.S. 377 (1992).

85 *"on public or private property . . . basis of race, color, creed, religion or gender"*: "St. Paul Bias-Motivated Crime Ordinance," St. Paul, Minnesota, Legislative Code § 292.02 (1990).

85 National Socialist Party of America v. Village of Skokie*: National Socialist Party of America v. Village of Skokie*, 432 U.S. 43 (1977).

85 *effectively frustrating their right of free expression:* Ibid., 44.

86 *most famous case is* Chaplinsky v. New Hampshire *(1942): Chaplinsky v. New Hampshire*, 315 U.S. 568 (1942).

86 *a "damned Fascist" and a "god-damned racketeer":* Ibid., 569.

86 *"insulting or 'fighting' words" that are of "slight social value as steps to truth" and whose "very utterance inflict injury or tend to incite an immediate breach of the peace":* Ibid., 572.

86 *In* Cohen v. California *(1971): Cohen v. California*, 403 U.S. 15 (1971).

87 *"prohibited maliciously . . . [by] offensive conduct":* Ibid., 16 (quoting California Penal Code § 415).

87 *(although this is sometimes controversial): New York Times Co. v. United States* ("The Pentagon Papers Case"), 403 U.S. 713 (1971).

88 *"the best test of truth is . . . competition of the market": Abrams v. United States*, 250 U.S. 616, 630 (1919) (Holmes, J., dissenting).

89 *what we more grandly call a habit of toleration:* Hume wrote that "the more these refined arts [of commerce] advance, the more sociable men become. . . . [I]t is impossible but they must feel an increase of humanity, from the very habit of conversing together." See David Hume, *Essays: Moral, Political, and Literary*, ed. Eugene F. Miller (Indianapolis: Liberty Press, 1987), 271.

91   *statements like the following:* A University of North Carolina–Greensboro
      faculty handbook encourages instructors to facilitate class discussions with
      comments such as: "As you can see from Dan's and Jean's comments, the
      words we use can offend people. Both of them have given us an example of
      how they feel excluded by gender-bound words." "Ten Tips When Facili-
      tating Discussion," *University of North Carolina Greensboro: The University
      Speaking Center,* https://speakingcenter.uncg.edu/wp-content/themes/sc/
      docs/facilitatingclassdiscussion/TenTipsWhenFacilitatingDiscussion.pdf.
      For other examples of this rhetorical genre, see Siraj Ahmed Sindhu, "Do
      Liberal Amherst Students Have a Responsibility to Pay Far-Right Conserva-
      tives to Speak on Campus?" *AC Voice,* November 14, 2014, https://acvoice
      .wordpress.com/2014/11/14/do-liberal-amherst-students-have-a-respon
      sibility-to-pay-conservatives-to-speak-on-campus/ ("Some argue college
      students should expose themselves to a variety of ideas and worldviews
      because acceptance of diversity is fundamental to a liberal education. This
      is ludicrous."); Ezinne Ukoha, "When I Talk About Black People, I Don't
      Expect White People to Understand," *Medium,* August 16, 2017, https://
      medium.com/@nilegirl/when-i-talk-about-black-people-i-dont-expect
      -white-people-to-understand-512c45bba4eb; Damian Alonso, "Here's
      Why Reverse Racism Isn't Real," *Everyday Feminism,* April 28, 2017, https://
      everydayfeminism.com/2017/04/reverse-racism-isnt-real/ ("White people
      can't understand racial oppression when they've never been in the context
      of experiencing racial oppression").

95   *is that the feelings in question should be treated as trumps:* See, for example,
      Ryan Wilson et al., "Open Letter to Associate Master Christakis," *DOWN
      Magazine,* October 31, 2014, http://downatyale.com/post.php?id=430 ("To
      ask marginalized students to throw away their enjoyment of a holiday, in
      order to expend emotional, mental, and physical energy to explain why
      something is offensive, is—offensive."); Association of Amherst Students,
      "Poll on Lord Jeff Results," *Amherst College,* November 20, 2015, https://
      www.amherst.edu/campuslife/aas/surveys/poll-on-lord-jeff ("There are
      students from different backgrounds who are offended by the mascot for
      fully legitimate reasons. I do not believe that anyone should be forced to
      call themselves the name of someone they find repulsive. For this reason
      alone, I support the removal of the Lord Jeffs as our unofficial mascot").

98   *by the commonplace that education sets one free:* See, for example, David D.
      Corey, "Liberal Education: Its Conditions and Ends," *The Future of Liberal
      Education,* ed. Timothy W. Burns & Peter Augustine Lawler (London:
      Routledge, 2015) ("The purpose of liberal education is, of course, to set

us free . . . by removing us from the confines of a particular place and time . . . by introducing us to paradigmatic lives and therewith to the many subtle ways that lives can described and evaluated . . . [by] expanding our moral imagination . . . but [also] by introducing us to other modes" of thought, beyond the moral.); William Johnson Cory, *Eton Reform* (London: Longman, Greene, Longman, and Roberts, 1861), 7 ("But you go to a great school, not for knowledge so much as for arts and habits; for the habit of attention, for the art of expression, for the art of assuming at a moment's notice a new intellectual posture, for the art of entering quickly into another person's thoughts, for the habit of submitting to censure and refutation, for the art of indicating assent or dissent in graduated terms, for the habit of regarding minute points of accuracy, for the habit of working out what is possible in a given time, for taste, for discrimination, for mental courage and mental soberness").

99   *what a community of this kind looks like in practice:* We see this most clearly in the early ('Socratic') dialogues as narrated by Plato. For a collection of famous examples, see Plato, *Five Dialogues: Euthyphro, Apology, Crito, Meno, Phaedo,* trans. G. M. A. Grube, ed. John M. Cooper (Indianapolis: Hackett, 2002). For examples of contemporary scholarship and commentary on Socratic conversation, see Alexander Nehamas, *The Art of Living: Socratic Reflections from Plato to Foucault* (Berkeley: University of California Press, 1998); Jonathan Lear, "Irony and Identity: The Tanner Lectures of Human Values at Harvard University," November 4–6, 2009, http://philosophy.uchicago.edu/faculty/files/lear/Tanner%20I.February%2022,%202010.pdf.

100   *can "know himself," as he explained at his trial:* Plato, "The Apology," *The Dialogues of Plato, Vol. 1: Euthyphro, Apology, Crito, Meno, Gorgias, Menexenus,* trans. R.E. Allen (New Haven, CT: Yale University Press, 1984), 59–104 (38a–38e).

100   *new aristocracy based upon a different principle of rank or distinction:* See Friedrich Nietzsche, "The Problem of Socrates," *Twilight of the Idols,* trans. Anthony M. Ludovici, ed. Oscar Levy (Edinburgh: T. N. Fouls, 1911), 33–45.

101   *that of Plato's philosopher-king:* See Plato, *The Republic,* trans. Allan Bloom (New York: Basic Books, 1968), 153 (473 c-d). ("Unless . . . the philosophers rule as kings . . . there is no rest from ills for the cities.")

110   *physically assaulted as he and his faculty host left the building:* Volokh, "Protesters at Middlebury College Shout Down Speaker, Attack Him and a Professor."

110   *the grounds that many of his opinions constituted "hate speech":* Adam Falk,

"John Derbyshire's Scheduled Appearance at Williams," *Williams College: Office of the President*, February 18, 2016, https://president.williams.edu/letters -from-the-president/john-derbyshires-scheduled-appearance-at-williams/.

111 *challenge the wisdom of affirmative action:* Compare Charles A. Murray, "Narrowing the New Class Divide," *New York Times*, March 7, 2012, https:// www.nytimes.com/2012/03/08/opinion/reforms-for-the-new-upper-class .html; with Volokh, "Protesters at Middlebury College Shout Down Speaker."

111 *question the factual and moral basis of the Black Lives Matter movement:* Compare Heather Mac Donald, "Hard Data, Hollow Protests," *City Journal*, September 25, 2017, https://www.city-journal.org/html/hard-data-hollow -protests-15458.html; with Blume, "Protesters Disrupt Talk by Pro-Police Author."

111 *attack gay marriage:* Compare Hadley Arkes, "Marriage in the Court," *National Review*, March 26, 2013, https://www.nationalreview.com/bench -memos/marriage-court-hadley-arkes/; with Liya Rechtman, "Do Not Take That Arkes Class," *AC Voice*, September 12, 2013, https://acvoice.wordpress .com/2013/09/12/do-not-take-that-arkes-class/; and "A Conversation with President Martin" (at 52:50), *Amherst College*, May 31, 2014, https://www .amherst.edu/alumni/events/reunion/media/2014/president-martin ("They wanted us to censure or even remove one of our faculty members because of his writings on gay marriage . . .").

111 *brought into line with the requirements of the criminal justice system:* Compare Jed Rubenfeld, "Privatization and State Action: Do Campus Sexual Assault Hearings Violate Due Process?" *Texas Law Review* 96, no. 1 (2017): 15; and Jed Rubenfeld, "Mishandling Rape," *New York Times*, November 14, 2015, https://www.nytimes.com/2014/11/16/opinion /sunday/mishandling-rape.html; with Lauren Barbato, "Yale Professor Jed Rubenfield's *[sic]* Students Passionately Reject His 'Reductive, Paternalist' Op-Ed On Sex Assault," *Bustle*, November 18, 2014, https://www.bustle .com/articles/49810-yale-professor-jed-rubenfields-students-passionately -reject-his-reductive-paternalist-op-ed-on-sex-assault.

111 *former president of Harvard did not too long ago:* Lawrence H. Summers, "Remarks at NBER Conference on Diversifying the Science & Engineering Workforce," *Harvard University: Office of the President*, January 14, 2005, https://www.harvard.edu/president/speeches/summers_2005/nber.php.

112 *those who condemn every drop of Richard Spencer's poisonous brew:* Simon D. Schuster & Susan Svrluga, " 'Nazis Go Home!' Fights Break Out at Michigan State as Protesters, White Supremacists Converge for Richard

Spencer Speech," *Washington Post*, March 5, 2018, https://www
.washingtonpost.com/news/grade-point/wp/2018/03/05/michigan-state
-braces-for-white-nationalist-speech-as-protesters-converge/?utm
_term=.740483e09a9c; Matt Pearce, "White Nationalist Shot at Protesters
After Richard Spencer Speech in Florida, Police Say," *Los Angeles Times*,
October 20, 2017, http://www.latimes.com/nation/la-na-richard-spencer
-speech-20171020-story.html.

114 *the overriding importance of creating a culture of inclusion on campus:* See,
for example, Wallace D. Loh, "Making Our Campus More Inclusive and
Respectful for All," *University of Maryland: Office of the President*, May 3,
2018, https://president.umd.edu/communications/statements/making
-our-campus-more-inclusive-and-respectful-all; Presidential Task Force
on Inclusion and Belonging, "Pursuing Excellence on a Foundation of
Inclusion," *Harvard University*, March 27, 2018, https://inclusionandbe
longingtaskforce.harvard.edu/files/inclusion/files/harvard_inclusion
_belonging_task_force_final_report_full_web_180327.pdf; John A. Fry, "A
Welcoming Culture of Inclusion," *Drexel University: Office of the President*,
November 18, 2015, http://drexel.edu/president/messages
/message/2015/November/inclusion/; President's Task Force on Civility and
Campus Culture, "Toward a Culture of Inclusion: Striving for Acceptance,"
University of Connecticut, December 15, 2013, https://president.uconn.edu
/wp-content/uploads/sites/1800/2016/06/Final-Civility-Task-Force-Report
-Dec-24-2013-2.pdf.

115 *threw rocks at the police and set fire to a campus building:* Thomas Fuller
and Christopher Mele, "Berkeley Cancels Milo Yiannopoulos Speech, and
Donald Trump Tweets Outrage," *New York Times*, February 1, 2017, https://
www.nytimes.com/2017/02/01/us/uc-berkeley-milo-yiannopoulos-protest
.html.

115 *sparked a riot in which a man was shot:* Katherine Long, Lynn Thompson,
and Jessica Lee, "Man Shot During Protests of Breitbart Editor Milo
Yiannopoulos' Speech at UW; Suspect Arrested," *Seattle Times*, January
21, 2017, https://www.seattletimes.com/seattle-news/education/violence
-punctuates-uw-talk-by-breitbart-editor-milo-yiannopoulos/.

Chapter Three: Diversity

119 *"offer all students . . . cultural differences, values systems, etc.":* "Advertising
For and Actively Recruiting an Excellent and Diverse Pool of Candidates,"

Boston University: Office of the Provost, http://www.bu.edu/apfd
/recruitment/fsm/advertising_and_recruiting/.

120　*Yale's President announced a $50 million initiative:* Office of Diversity and
Inclusion," *Yale University: It's Your Yale*, https://your.yale.edu/community
/diversity-inclusion/office-diversity-and-inclusion; "Lofton Named First
FAS Deputy Dean for Diversity and Faculty Development," *Yale News*, April
14, 2016, https://news.yale.edu/2016/04/14/lofton-named-first-fas-deputy
-dean-diversity-and-faculty-development; "Office of Gender and Campus
Culture," *Yale University: Yale College*, http://gcc.yalecollege.yale.edu/; "Office
of LGBTQ Resources," *Yale University*, http://lgbtq.yale.edu/; "Cultural Affairs
& Centers," *Yale University: Yale College*, http://yalecollege.yale.edu/campus
-life/cultural-affairs-centers; "Initiative for Faculty Excellence and Diversity,"
Yale University: Faculty Development & Diversity, https://faculty.yale.edu/
diversity/initiative-faculty-excellence-and-diversity; "President's Procedure
for Addressing Students' Complaints of Racial or Ethnic Harassment," *Yale
University: Office for Equal Opportunity Programs*, http://equalopportunity.yale
.edu/presidents-procedure-addressing-students-complaints-racial-or-ethnic
-harassment; "Women Faculty Forum," *Yale University*, http://wff.yale.edu/.

120　*Columbia recently announced that it would commit $100 million:* Leslie
Brody and Melissa Korn, "Columbia University Commits $100 Million
to Faculty Diversity," *Wall Street Journal*, October 5, 2017, https://www
.wsj.com/articles/columbia-university-commits-100-million-to-faculty
-diversity-1507243179.

120　*Brown has pledged $165 million:* "Brown Releases Final Action Plan
to Create a Diverse and Inclusive Campus," *News from Brown, Brown
University*, February 1, 2016, https://news.brown.edu/articles/2016/02/diap.

120　*Hamilton College now requires that "each concentration" include at
least "one course . . . to the relevant discipline," to "help students gain . . .
sexuality, age, and abilities/disabilities":* Hamilton College, *Periodic
Review Report* (Clinton, NY: Hamilton College, 2016), 19, https://www
.hamilton.edu/documents/2016%20Periodic%20Review%20Report%20
-%20Hamilton%20College.pdf.

120　*At UCLA, all students must "earn at least . . . other types of diversity":* Scott
Jaschik, "UCLA Faculty Approves Diversity Requirement," *Inside Higher
Ed*, April 13, 2015, https://www.insidehighered.com/news/2015/04/13/ucla
-faculty-approves-diversity-requirement.

120　*Georgetown:* "Engaging Diversity," *Georgetown College, Georgetown
University*, https://college.georgetown.edu/academics/core-requirements
/engaging-diversity.

120   *Cornell:* Miguel Soto & Anne Snabes, "New 'Social Difference' Requirement One of Changes in Newly Passed A&S Curriculum Proposal," *Cornell Daily Sun*, November 1, 2018, https://cornellsun.com/2018/11/01/new-social -difference-requirement-one-of-changes-in-newly-passed-as-curriculum -proposal/.

120   *the University of Pennsylvania:* "College Curriculum: Structure and Requirements," *College of Arts and Sciences, University of Pennsylvania*, https://www.college.upenn.edu/curriculum-structure.

120   *Hunter College:* "The Hunter Core Requirement," *Hunter College*, http:// www.hunter.cuny.edu/academics/hunter-core-requirement.

120   *a building intended principally for those with a specific racial, ethnic, or other identity, including sexual orientation:* At the University of Colorado at Boulder, for instance, students can live in a dorm for LBGTQ students; one for "community and programming for black-identified students and their allies, and anyone with a passion for equal rights for all students"; and one for "students interested in social justice and diversity issues and anyone with a desire to further their education of identities and cultural intersec- tionality." "Housing & Dining," *University of Colorado, Boulder*, https:// www.colorado.edu/campus-life/housing-dining. At California State Univer- sity's Los Angeles campus, students can live in a dorm "designed to enhance the residential experience for students who are a part of or interested in issues regarding the Black community." "Themed Living Communities," *California State University, Los Angeles: Housing and Residence Life*, http:// www.calstatela.edu/housing/themed-living-communities.

120   *some form of mandatory diversity training for faculty and students:* For example, in April 2016, Clemson University's president announced that "all employees will participate in diversity education and training that promotes cultural competencies and awareness." Jim Clements, "Dear Campus Community," *Clemson University: Clemson Blogs*, April 21, 2016, http://blogs.clemson.edu/president/2016/04/21/dear-campus-community -2/. Students at the University of Oklahoma must complete a mandatory three-part "Freshman Diversity Experience" program, either during their summer orientation or in their first semester. "Freshman Diversity Experience," *University of Oklahoma: University Community*, http://www .ou.edu/community/experience.html.

121   *professional guides to help them frame a convincing reply:* See, for example, Tanya Golash-Boza, "The Effective Diversity Statement," *Inside Higher Ed*, June 10, 2016, https://www.insidehighered.com/advice/2016/06/10/how -write-effective-diversity-statement-essay.

121 *career administrators whose job is to promote the cause of diversity, not to ask why it is a value:* See, for example, Samuel J. Abrams, "Opinion: Think Professors Are Liberal? Try School Administrators," *New York Times,* October 16, 2018, https://www.nytimes.com/2018/10/16/opinion/liberal -college-administrators.html.

124 Regents of the University of California v. Bakke: 438 U.S. 265 (1978).

124 *voted to invalidate the school's special admissions program on the grounds that it violated the 1964 Civil Rights Act:* Ibid., 408–21. (Stevens, J., joined by Burger, CJ., and Stewart and Rehnquist, JJ., concurring in the result in part and dissenting in part.)

124 *concluded that the Davis admissions program was constitutionally permissible:* Ibid., 324–79 (Brennan, White, Marshall, and Blackmun, JJ., concurring in part and dissenting from the result).

124 *"only those racial classifications":* Ibid., 287 (Powell, J.).

125 *"on the basis of [their] race and ethnic status":* Ibid., 289.

125 *"of integrating the medical profession and increasing the number of physicians willing to serve members of minority groups":* Ibid., 279.

125 *discrimination by "society at large":* Ibid., 301.

125 *must be guilty of past discrimination of an individualized sort:* Ibid., 307–10.

125 *equally specific system of preferences as a means to cure them:* Ibid.

126 *"the effects of 'societal discrimination,' an amorphous concept of injury that may be ageless in its reach into the past":* Ibid., 307.

126 *"amorphous" group, than to . . . an "innocent" individual . . . made to "bear the burdens of redressing grievances not of [his own] making":* Ibid., 298, 307.

127 *Justice Marshall makes this point with special force in his separate opinion in* Bakke: Ibid., 387–402 (Marshall, J., separately concurring in part and dissenting from the result).

127 *Those who are impressed by these two facts:* Owen M. Fiss, "Groups and the Equal Protection Clause," *Philosophy and Public Affairs* 5, no. 2 (1976): 107–77.

128 *for the sake of what he calls various "educational benefits":* Bakke, 438 U.S. at 306 (Powell, J.).

128 *"ideas and mores":* Ibid., 313.

128 *"that robust exchange of ideas . . . notion of academic freedom":* Ibid., 312–13.

128 *"a special concern of the First Amendment":* Ibid., 312.

128 *"countervailing constitutional interest":* Ibid., 313.

128 *"speculation, experiment and creation":* Ibid., 312.

129 *"only one element in a range of factors":* Ibid., 314.

129   *"a 'plus' in a particular applicant's file"*: Ibid., 317.

129   *appends to his opinion Harvard's then-current description:* Ibid., 321–24.

129   *"properly devised . . . genuine diversity"*: Compare ibid., 315, 320 (Powell, J.) with ibid., 326 n.1 (Brennan, White, Marshall, and Blackmun, JJ., concurring in part and dissenting from the result: "We also agree with Mr. Justice POWELL that a plan like the 'Harvard' plan . . . is constitutional under our approach, at least so long as the use of race to achieve an integrated student body is necessitated by the lingering effects of past discrimination").

129   *Powell's discussion of diversity became a road map:* Powell's opinion rested on constitutional grounds and applied to the University of California, a public institution. However, because Powell and four other Justices held that Title VI imposes requirements identical to the Equal Protection Clause, *Bakke*'s diversity rationale also governs private schools that accept federal money and are consequently covered by Title VI. On this point, see *Bakke*, 438 U.S. at 287 (Powell, J.); ibid., 328 (Brennan, White, Marshall, and Blackmun, JJ., concurring in part and dissenting from the result).

129   *insulate their affirmative action programs from legal attack:* For example, in the *Grutter* litigation, twenty-eight small private schools filed an amicus brief claiming that, after *Bakke*, the schools had all adopted an admissions policy modeled on Powell's opinion. Brief of Amherst, Barnard, Bates, Bowdoin, Bryn Mawr, Carleton, Colby, Connecticut, Davidson, Franklin & Marshall, Hamilton, Hampshire, Haverford, Macalester, Middlebury, Mount Holyoke, Oberlin, Pomona, Sarah Lawrence, Smith, Swarthmore, Trinity, Vassar, Wellesley, and Williams Colleges, and Colgate, Wesleyan and Tufts Universities, Amici Curiae, Supporting Respondents at 26, *Grutter v. Bollinger*, 539 U.S. 306 (2003) (No. 02-241).

130   *growing impatience with Powell's position . . . affirmed the basic premises of Powell's analysis:* In a matched pair of cases decided on the same day in 2003—*Grutter v. Bollinger*, 539 U.S. 306 (2003), and *Gratz v. Bollinger*, 539 U.S. 244 (2003)—the Supreme Court reaffirmed Justice Powell's *Bakke* opinion, simultaneously upholding a holistic affirmative action admissions policy at the University of Michigan's law school but striking down a policy in which applicants to the university's undergraduate program received a fixed number of "points" based on their race. The decisions were more than mere formalities: Prior to *Grutter*, some circuit courts had begun to disregard *Bakke* and briefly outlawed the use of affirmative action policies. *Hopwood v. Texas*, 78 F.3d 932 (5th Cir. 1996); *Johnson v. Board of Regents of University System of Georgia*, 263 F.3d 1234 (11th Cir. 2001). While *Grutter*

endorsed Justice Powell's diversity rationale, the case also seemed to expand the justification for affirmative action beyond a university achieving a purely educational goal. For instance, the Court noted that, because law schools serve as a breeding ground for future American leaders, "in order to cultivate a set of leaders with legitimacy in the eyes of the citizenry, it is necessary that the path to leadership be visibly open to talented and qualified individuals of every race and ethnicity." *Grutter*, 539 U.S. at 332. A decade later, in 2013, the Supreme Court signaled that it might rethink its affirmative action jurisprudence, reversing a lower court that had largely deferred to a school, the University of Texas at Austin, regarding the necessity of a race-based admissions program. *Fisher v. University of Texas at Austin*, 133 S. Ct. 2411 (2013). But in a second decision in the same case three years later, the Court once again upheld affirmative action and permitted the University of Texas to consider an applicant's race alongside his or her academic record. *Fisher v. University of Texas at Austin*, 136 S. Ct. 2198 (2016).

130　*only a few pages in the* United States Reports: *Bakke*, 438 U.S. at 311–19 (Powell, J.).

131　*Jefferson's "empire of liberty":* Letter from Thomas Jefferson to George Rogers Clark, December 25, 1780, *The Papers of Thomas Jefferson, Vol. 4: 1 October 1780–24 February 1781*, ed. Julian P. Boyd (Princeton, NJ: Princeton University Press, 1951), 233–38.

132　*past discrimination might become, as he says, "ageless":* Bakke, 438 U.S. at 306 (Powell, J.).

132　*perhaps some time limit ought to be placed on the use of such distinctions even for diversity purposes:* In *Grutter*, the majority expressed its hope "that 25 years from now, the use of racial preferences will no longer be necessary . . ." *Grutter*, 539 U.S. at 343.

134　*a diverse student body offers a telling example:* In amicus briefs filed in both *Grutter* and *Fisher*, Harvard characterized its admissions policy in similar ways. In *Grutter*, the school touted an "individualized admissions process" in which admissions officers "give special attention to, among others, applicants from economically and/or culturally disadvantaged backgrounds, those with unusual athletic ability, those with special artistic talents, those who would be the first in their families to attend any college, those whose parents are alumni or alumnae, and those who have overcome various identifiable hardships." According to the school, "[n]o one factor, including race, is dispositive . . ." Brief of Harvard University, Brown University, The University of Chicago, Dartmouth College, Duke University, The University of Pennsylvania, Princeton University, and Yale University as Amici Curiae Supporting Respondents at 19-21, *Grutter v. Bollinger*, 539 U.S. 306 (2003) (No. 02-241). In the *Fisher* litigation, Harvard argued that "an individual's race or ethnicity, if self-identified, is but a piece of a larger mosaic, and is considered only to understand the applicant as a complete and distinct individual." Brief for Amicus Curiae Harvard University in Support of Respondents at 16-17, *Fisher v. University of Texas*, 136 S. Ct. 2198 (2016) (No. 14-981). For another analysis of these briefs and Harvard's admissions policy over time, see Complaint at 32-33, *Students for Fair Admissions v. President and Fellows of Harvard College*, No. 14-cv-14176-ADB (D. Mass. filed Nov. 17, 2014).

134 *"small numbers might also . . . to develop and achieve their potential":* Bakke, 438 U.S. at 323 (Powell, J.) (quoting Appendix to the Brief for Columbia University, Harvard University, Stanford University, and the University of Pennsylvania, as Amici Curiae).

134 *strongly suggests that something like a quota system is still at work:* A recent lawsuit alleging that Harvard illegally discriminates against Asian-American applicants highlights that institution's consistent racial makeup. From 2003 to 2013, the percentage of white undergraduates enrolled at Harvard always ranged between 49 percent and 44 percent of the student body. African-American students hovered between 6 percent and 8 percent. Asians made up 15 percent to 18 percent. And Hispanics never strayed beyond 7 percent to 9 percent. Complaint at 69, *Students for Fair Admissions v. President and Fellows of Harvard College*, No. 14-cv-14176-ADB (D. Mass. filed Nov. 17, 2014). To pick another example, at Princeton, the percentage of African-American students was 8 percent in 2001, 7 percent in 2011, and 10 percent in 2016—although the percentage of white students did decline significantly in that period and the relative number of Asian students rose. Princeton's demographic data can be found at "University Enrollment Statistics," *Princeton University: Office of the Registrar*, https://registrar .princeton.edu/university_enrollment_sta/. Similarly, at the Yale Law School (where I teach), racial demographics remained relatively constant from 2005 to 2016. *Yale University Race/Ethnicity and International Student Enrollment by School 2005–06 to 2016–17* (2016), https://oir.yale.edu/sites /default/files/w010_enroll_mininternl.pdf.

136 *what has come to be called a "cultural appropriation":* The term "cultural appropriation" first emerged among academics in the 1970s of the so-called post-colonial school and has since trickled into common parlance. Margaret Drabble, Jenny Stringer, and Daniel Hahn, eds., *The*

Concise Oxford Companion to English Literature, third ed. (New York: Oxford University Press, online version, 2013), s.v. "cultural appropriation." On campuses across the country, student newspaper op-eds routinely denounce everyday facets of life for appropriating a foreign culture. Witness the Louisiana State University freshman who claimed that American women desiring "thick" eyebrows "shows a prime example of the cultural appropriation in the country" because ethnic women typically possess "bushy, harder-to-maintain eyebrows." Lynne Bunch, "Eyebrow Standards Makes Women Feel Ostracized, Ridiculed," *Daily Reveille* (Louisiana State University), January 25, 2017, http://www.lsunow.com/daily/opinion-eyebrow-standards-makes-women-feel-ostracized-ridiculed/article_180863ea-e2ad-11e6-afa8-335d23e10243.html. Or consider the University of Washington student who denounced drinking beer on Oktoberfest and wearing traditional Swiss/German clothing because it insensitively appropriated those two European cultures. Joy Geerkens, "My Experience with Cultural Appropriation, *Daily* (University of Washington), March 1, 2017, http://www.dailyuw.com/opinion/article_008a1a66-fe27-11e6-ab4c-4b6e4ab90120.html. And note the Southern student from Francis Marion University who objected to non-Southerners using the term "y'all," because "you can't pick and choose what to take from a culture." Leah Power, "Leah's Life Lessons: The Appropriation of Y'all," *Patriot* (Francis Marion University), October 30, 2016, https://patriotnewsonline.com/opinion/2016/10/30/leahs-life-lessons-the-appropriation-of-yall/.

137–138 *by insisting that* all *lives do is likely to provoke such a reaction:* See, for example, Ibram X. Kendi, "The Heartbeat of Racism Is Denial," *New York Times*, January 13, 2018, https://www.nytimes.com/2018/01/13/opinion/sunday/heartbeat-of-racism-denial.html. Kendi identifies the phrase "All Lives Matter" as part of the "vocabulary" which "all those racists who refused to believe they were racist in 1968" designed to "avoid admitting to [themselves] that [they were] attracted [to the] racist appeal." Rounding out his list of concepts and phrases understood to be used only by bigots are: "[L]aw and order. War on drugs. Model minority. Reverse discrimination. Race-neutral. Welfare queen. Handout. Tough on crime. Personal responsibility. Black-on-black crime. Achievement gap. No excuses. Race card. Colorblind. Post-racial. Illegal immigrant. Obamacare. War on Cops. Blue Lives Matter. . . . Entitlements. Voter fraud. Economic anxiety."

138 *means to an "educational benefit" instead: Bakke*, 438 U.S. at 306 (Powell, J.).

139 *recognized the distinction between politics and intellectual inquiry:* So-called "teach-ins"—the most iconic expression of the 1960s' student antiwar

movement—were continuous with the educational mission of the university itself. Teach-ins were held on 120 campuses in the spring of 1965. They provided students and faculty with an outlet to express their moral opposition to the Vietnam War though "lectures, debates, and discussion groups." Rather than disrupting the conversational ideal, these actively ratified it instead. See Michael Levitas, "Vietnam Comes to Oregon U.," *New York Times Magazine*, May 9, 1965, at 92; see also Charles DeBenedetti and Charles Chatfield, *An American Ordeal: The Antiwar Movement of the Vietnam Era* (Syracuse, NY: Syracuse University Press, 1990), 107–9, 114–16.

Alternative views were allowed and often even sought out. Lines of rigorous dialogue were opened between members of university communities who would otherwise have little interaction with one another. At the University of Oregon, "raw freshmen argued fearlessly with senior professors. Platoons of 'Greeks'—fraternity men—debated with intellectuals they ordinarily ignore as 'smokies.'" Levitas, "Vietnam Comes to Oregon U.," 25. Their conversations "blend[ed] the politics of protest with the decorum of academia." Ibid.

Indeed, the very concept of the teach-in was born of a commitment to the principle that protest must not undermine the fundamental work of the academy. When faculty at the University of Michigan were threatening to strike in protest of the war, their colleague, anthropologist Marshall Sahlins, conceived of the teach-in as a way to respect that commitment. "They say we're neglecting our responsibilities as teachers," said Sahlins. "Let's show them how responsible we feel. Instead of teaching out, we'll teach in—all night." Ibid., 92.

The teach-ins reflected the broader values of the movement that spawned them. The Marxist intellectuals of the 1960s insisted on the need to know the Western canon and engage deeply with it even as they criticized what they saw as the reactionary political ideology undergirding the Western tradition. See Bridget Fowler, "The 'Canon' and Marxist Theories of Literature," *Cultural Studies* 1, no. 2 (1987): 162–78. For scholars like Noam Chomsky, there was no inherent contradiction between being a free-speech libertarian *and* a committed Marxist. See Noam Chomsky, "The Responsibility of Intellectuals," *New York Review of Books*, February 23, 1967, https://www.nybooks.com/articles/1967/02/23/a-special-supplement -the-responsibility-of-intelle/.

To be sure, as the fateful year of 1968 approached, the student movement became angrier, louder, and more disruptive. With this evolution in the movement's tone came an erosion of the imagined wall separating the space of political protest from that of academic life. On one exceptional night in May 1968, as protests reached their peak at Columbia University, students occupied the office of history professor Orest Ranum, ransacked his papers, and burned ten years' worth of research. John Castelluci, a student of Professor Ranum, recalled the incident as "a sobering reminder that not all student radicals were starry-eyed idealists," and that "[i]n more than a couple of cases, they were power-hungry extremists jostling for control of the student-protest movement." John Castellucci, *The Night They Burned Ranum's Papers*, February 14, 2010, https://www.chronicle.com/article/The-Night-They-Burned-Ranums /64115. It is worth noting that even Castellucci's account, though decidedly unsympathetic to the student protest movement on the whole, recognizes that the arsonists in Ranum's office did not represent the core of the movement but only a fringe element of it.

Most students who insisted on carrying their movement into the once-sacrosanct space of academic inquiry did so in a decidedly less aggressive fashion, by demanding curricular as well as political reform. At Columbia, for example, the University's renowned Core Curriculum came under attack when "students, obsessed with the military draft and the bombing of Cambodia, [voiced doubts about] the value of Aristotle, St. Thomas, and Kant." See Timothy P. Cross, *An Oasis of Order: The Core Curriculum at Columbia College* (New York: Columbia College, Office of the Dean, 1995), https://www.college.columbia.edu/core/oasis/history5 .php, Chapter 5, text accompanying nn. 37–39. Yet even then, students criticized the academy more or less on its own terms. They complained that they had "'looked to the university to help them discover what life was about' but were not satisfied with the answers they received." Ibid., text accompanying n. 36 (quoting *Crisis at Columbia: Report of the Fact-Finding Commission Appointed to Investigate the Disturbances at Columbia University in April and May 1968* [New York: Vintage Books, 1968], 23.). They criticized the university for falling short of its responsibility to provide an intellectual space in which inquiry could shed light on the most pressing questions of justice and human flourishing. In doing so, they implicitly affirmed the worthiness of this endeavor itself. That stands in stark contrast to the ethic of today's identarian student protests neatly captured in the 2015 statement of a Yale College student who shouted down her college master, saying, "It is not about creating an intellectual space! It is not! Do you understand that? It's about creating a home here!" Liam Stack, "Yale's Halloween Advice Stokes a Racially Charged Debate," *New York Times*, November 8, 2015, https://www.nytimes.com/2015/11/09/nyregion/yale-culturally-insensitive-halloween-costumes-free-speech.html.

141 *"a type but not a will" and produced an "autobiographical blank . . . a watermark had been stamped"*: Henry Adams, *The Education of Henry Adams: An Autobiography* (New York: Houghton Mifflin Company, 1918), 55.

141 *PhD as a requirement for college or university teaching were signposts along the way:* For Eliot's discussion of his own views on American higher education, see Charles W. Eliot, "The New Education," *Atlantic*, February 1869, https://www.theatlantic.com/magazine/archive/1869/02/the-new-education/309049/. For a scholarly analysis of the educational revolution Eliot set in motion during his presidency at Harvard, see, for example, Hugh Hawkins, *Between Harvard and America: The Educational Leadership of Charles W. Eliot* (New York: Oxford University Press, 1972); Henry James, *Charles W. Eliot: President of Harvard University, 1969–1909*, two vols. (Boston: Houghton Mifflin, 1930).

142 *best expresses their* individual *judgments about what is important and why:* Anthony T. Kronman, *Education's End: Why Our Colleges and Universities Have Given Up on the Meaning of Life* (New Haven, CT: Yale University Press, 2007).

142 *Hartz associated this tradition with the political philosophy of John Locke:* Louis Hartz, *The Liberal Tradition in America* (New York: Harcourt, 1955; reprint, New York: Harcourt, 1991), 11.

142 *Franklin with his strategies of self-discipline:* For Benjamin Franklin's discussion of his "bold and arduous project of arriving at moral perfection," see *The Autobiography of Benjamin Franklin*, ed. Charles W. Eliot (New York: P. F. Collier & Son, 1909), 173–95.

142 *Douglass with his exhortation to "Work! Work! Work!":* Frederick Douglass, "Self-Made Men: An Address Delivered in Carlisle, in March of 1893," *The Frederick Douglass Papers: Series One: Speeches, Debates, and Interviews: Vol. 5: 1881–95*, eds. John W. Blassingame and John R. McKivigan (New Haven, CT: Yale University Press, 1992), 556.

142 *Lincoln with his ethic of free labor:* See, for example, Abraham Lincoln, "Speech at Kalamazoo, Michigan, August 27, 1856," *Collected Works of Abraham Lincoln*, ed. Roy P. Basler (New Brunswick, NJ: Rutgers University Press, 1953), 2:364.

142 *Carnegie with his gospel of wealth:* Andrew Carnegie, "Wealth," *North American Review* 148, no. 391 (June 1889): 653.

143 *Emerson's essay on "Self-Reliance" is a famous example:* Ralph Waldo Emerson, "Self Reliance," *Essays,* ed. Edna H. L. Turpin (New York: Charles E. Merrill, 1907), 79–116.

143 *cultivation of an "idiocrasy" . . . his or her "special nativity," "soaring its own flight, following out itself" . . . spirit of "perfect individualism" that "deepest tinges . . . the idea of the Aggregate":* Walt Whitman, *Democratic Vistas: The Original Edition in Facsimile,* ed. Ed Folsom (Iowa City: University of Iowa Press, 2010), 17, 38, 57.

143 *no two are "alike" and every one is "good":* Walt Whitman, *Leaves of Grass, 1860: The 150th Anniversary Facsimile Edition,* ed. Jason Stacy (Iowa City: University of Iowa Press, 2009), 31.

145 *"robust" exchange that Justice Powell exalts: Bakke,* 438 U.S. at 312–13 (Powell, J.).

145 *who won't want to have one of his or her own?:* See, for example, Conor Friedersdorf, "The Rise of Victimhood Culture," *Atlantic,* September 11, 2015, https://www.theatlantic.com/politics/archive/2015/09/the-rise -of-victimhood-culture/404794/; Bradley Campbell & Jason Manning, "Microaggression and Moral Cultures," *Comparative Sociology* 13, no. 6 (2014): 692–726.

147 *a representative is often required to exercise independent judgment:* Edmund Burke, "Speech to the Electors of Bristol," in *The Political Tracts and Speeches of Edmund Burke, Esq. Member of Parliament for the city of Bristol* (Dublin: Wm. Wilson, 1777; Eighteenth Century Collections Online edition), 346–55.

151 *It is here that the orthodoxy of diversity is officially proclaimed:* See, for example, Rachel Treisman, "Faculty Vote to Diversify English Major Curriculum," *Yale Daily News,* March 30, 2017, https://yaledailynews.com /blog/2017/03/30/faculty-vote-to-diversify-english-major-curriculum/; Franklin Crawford, "Faculty Institute for Diversity Members Take on Task of Diversifying Curricula," *Cornell University: Cornell Chronicle,* June 10, 2008, http://news.cornell.edu/stories/2008/06/faculty-diversity-institute -looks-ways-diversify-curriculum. See also Emma Buzbee, "Protesters Storm Butler Demanding 'Decolonization' of Curriculum, Campus Monuments," *Columbia Daily Spectator,* April 29, 2018, https://www .columbiaspectator.com/news/2018/04/25/protesters-storm-butler -demanding-decolonization-of-curriculum-campus-monuments/.

152 *failure to do so amounts to a kind of "erasure":* For examples of this kind of argument, see Sara Carrigan Wooten, "Revealing a Hidden Curriculum of Black Women's Erasure in Sexual Violence Prevention Policy," *Gender*

and Education 29, no. 3 (2017): 405–17; Alicia Wong, "History Class and the Fictions About Race in America: High-School Textbooks Too Often Gloss Over the American Government's Oppression of Racial Minorities," *Atlantic*, October 21, 2015, https://www.theatlantic.com/education/archive /2015/10/the-history-class-dilemma/411601/; Renee Martin, "Black History Month and the Continued Erasure of African-Canadian History in Schools," *XOJane*, February 15, 2015, https://www.xojane.com/issues/black -history-month-and-the-continued-erasure-of-african-canadian-history-in -schools.

152　*fiercely opposed to every form of "privileging":* For one of the original examples of this usage of "privilege" and "privileging," see Peggy McIntosh, "White Privilege and Male Privilege: A Personal Account of Coming to See Correspondences Through Work in Women's Studies," *Wellesley College Center for Research on Women: Working Paper Series* 189 (1986). For a striking example of the argument against the culture of "privilege-checking," see Tal Fortgang, "Checking My Privilege: Character as the Basis of Privilege," *Princeton Tory*, April 2, 2014, http://theprincetontory.com /checking-my-privilege-character-as-the-basis-of-privilege/.

152–153　*autonomous member of what Kant calls "the kingdom of ends," as well as a "natural" being with all sorts of characteristics that God does not possess:* Immanuel Kant, *Groundwork for the Metaphysics of Morals*, trans. and ed. Allen W. Wood (New Haven, CT: Yale University Press, 2002), 68–69 (AkIV:452); Immanuel Kant, *Critique of Practical Reason*, trans. and ed. Mary Gregor (Cambridge, UK: Cambridge University Press, 1997), 37–39 (AkV:42–43); Immanuel Kant, *Religion within the Boundaries of Mere Reason*, trans. and ed. Allen Wood and George di Giovanni (Cambridge, UK: Cambridge University, 2018), 64–65 (AkVI:31–32).

153　*John Rawls's* Theory of Justice *is a striking example:* John Rawls, *A Theory of Justice* (Cambridge, MA: Harvard University Press, 1971, rev. ed. 1999).

153　*Rawls's famous "veil of ignorance":* Ibid., 118–23.

153　*just persons with the power to plan our lives:* Ibid., 358–65.

153　*None of our other characteristics possess any inherent moral worth:* Ibid., 441–49.

153　*think of ourselves and everyone else as standing above all our other, more limited identities and freely assigning them whatever value they possess:* Ibid., 81–86.

157　*Aristotle offers one:* Aristotle explicates his theory of *megalopsuchia* (generally translated as "greatness of soul" or "magnanimity") in Book IV, Chapter 3, of his *Nicomachean Ethics*. See Aristotle, *Nicomachean Ethics*,

75–80 (1123a35–1125a35). He identifies fulfillment with the realization of political as well as intellectual virtues. See ibid., 223–29 (Bk. X.7–8) (1177a13–1179a32).

157   *Spinoza another:* See Baruch Spinoza, *The Essential Spinoza: Ethics and Related Writings,* trans. Samuel Shirley, ed. Michael L. Morgan (Indianapolis: Hackett, 2006), 138–42 (Part IV, Appendix), 143–61 (Part V).

157   *Walt Whitman a third:* See Walt Whitman, *Leaves of Grass,* 1855 ed. (New York: Penguin, 2005), 10, 13. For further analysis of the aristocratic element in Whitman, see Anthony T. Kronman, *Confessions of a Born-Again Pagan* (New Haven, CT: Yale University Press, 2016), 1039–61.

159   *that we are free to choose among the various versions of it in whatever way we please:* For examples and a critique of this "anticulture" of unrestrained choice between different visions of human flourishing, see Patrick J. Deneen, *Why Liberalism Failed* (New Haven, CT: Yale University Press, 2018), 64–90.

159   *Aristotle, for example, believed that a state of complete fulfillment is attainable despite our limitations:* See Aristotle, *Nicomachean Ethics,* 229–35 (Bk. X.9) (1179a33–1181b23).

161   *"effervescence of democratic negation":* Holmes, "The Use of Law Schools," 37.

162   *"all the children are above average":* Garrison Keillor, *Leaving Home* (New York: Viking, 1987), xvii.

Chapter Four: Memory

163   *At Princeton:* See, for example, Gabriel Fisher, "Princeton and the Fight over Woodrow Wilson's Legacy," *New Yorker,* November 25, 2015, https://www.newyorker.com/news/news-desk/princeton-and-the-fight-over-woodrow-wilsons-legacy.

163   *A Harvard committee recommended:* Harvard Law School Shield Committee, "Recommendation to the President and Fellows of Harvard College on the Shield Approved for the Law School," *Harvard Law School,* March 3, 2016, https://today.law.harvard.edu/wp-content/uploads/2016/03/Shield-Committee-Report.pdf. Note, however, that two members of the Committee (a student and a professor) dissented from the committee's recommendation that the Harvard Corporation retire the Royall shield. See Annette Gordon-Reed and Annie Rittgers, "A Different View," *Harvard Law School,* March 2016, https://today.law.harvard.edu/wp-content/uploads/2016/03/Shield_Committee-Different_View.pdf.

Notes

164 *Amhersi students protested:* Anemona Hartocollis, "With Diversity Comes Intensity in Amherst Free Speech Debate," *New York Times*, November 28, 2015, https://www.nytimes.com/2015/11/29/us/with-diversity -comes-intensity-in-amherst-free-speech-debate.html; "Our Immediate Demands," *Amherst Uprising*, November 12, 2015, http://amherstuprising .com/demands.html.

164 *At Yale:* "Calhoun College: A Timeline," *Yale Alumni Magazine*, March/April 2017, https://yalealumnimagazine.com/articles/4434-calhoun-college-a -timeline.

164 *At USC:* Nathan Fenno, "Traveler, USC's Mascot, Comes Under Scrutiny for Having a Name Similar to Robert E. Lee's Horse," *Los Angeles Times*, August 18, 2017, http://www.latimes.com/sports/la-sp-usc-traveler-20170818 -story.html.

164 *Middle Tennessee State University agreed to rename:* Note, however, that while the university agreed to rename the building, the Tennessee Historical Commission denied its request to do so. Adam Tamburin, "Commission Denies MTSU's Request to Change the Name of Forrest Hall," *Tennesseean* (Nashville), February 16, 2018, https://www.tennessean.com/story /news/2018/02/16/commission-denies-mtsus-request-change-name -forrest-hall/346998002/. The university has waived its right to appeal the historical commission's decision, so Forrest's name will remain on the building. Mariah Timms, "MTSU President: Forrest Hall Will Retain Name, University Will Not Appeal Ruling," *Daily News Journal* (Murfreesboro, TN), June 6, 2018, https://www.dnj.com/story/news/2018/06/06/mtsus-forrest -hall-retain-name-university-not-appeal-ruling-mcphee/677982002/.

164 *Student protesters at the University of North Carolina toppled a statue:* Amir Vera, "UNC Protesters Knock Down Silent Sam Confederate Statue," *CNN*, August 21, 2018, https://www.cnn.com/2018/08/20/us/unc-silent-sam -confederate-statue/index.html.

164 *he expressed the hope that it might produce a set of general rules:* Peter Salovey, "Campus Update: Committee to Establish Principles on Renaming," *Yale University: Office of the President*, August 1, 2016, https://president.yale.edu/speeches-writings/statements/campus-update -committee-establish-principles-renaming.

164 *the "rules" contained in the committee's report:* Letter from the Committee to Establish Principles on Renaming to Peter Salovey (hereinafter "CEPR Letter"), November 21, 2016, https://president.yale.edu/sites/default/files /files/CEPR_FINAL_12-2-16.pdf; Committee to Establish Principles on Renaming, *Report of the Committee to Establish Principles on Renaming*

(hereinafter "CEPR Report"), November 21, 2016, https://president.yale
.edu/sites/default/files/files/CEPR_FINAL_12-2-16.pdf.

166   *"In February 1948 . . . the fur hat on Gottwald's head":* Milan Kundera, *The
Book of Laughter and Forgetting,* trans. Aaron Asher (New York: Harper
Collins, 1999), 3–4.

167   *"Memory says, 'I did that.' . . . Eventually—memory yields":* Friedrich
Nietzsche, *Beyond Good and Evil: Prelude to a Philosophy of the Future,*
trans. Helen Zimmern (New York: Macmillan, 1907), 86.

167   *know more about this age-old habit than we once did:* The concept of
"repressed memory" is generally traced to Sigmund Freud, "Zur Ätiologie
der Hysterie," *Wiener Klinische Rundschau* (May–June 1896), reprinted as
"The Aetiology of Hysteria," *The Standard Edition of the Complete Psychological Work of Sigmund Freud* (London: Hogarth Press, 1966), 3: 191–221.
In recent decades, Freud has been gradually disappearing from university
curricula—even more pronouncedly so from the curricula of university
psychology departments. See, for example, Russell Jaco, "Why Are the Great
Masters of Western Thought Being Expelled from Their Disciplines?" *UCLA
Today,* August 12, 2008, http://newsroom.ucla.edu/stories/080812_jacoby_
great-masters; Patricia Cohen, "Freud Is Widely Taught at Universities,
Except in the Psychology Department," *New York Times,* November 25,
2007, https://www.nytimes.com/2007/11/25/weekinreview/25cohen.html.

168   *He wants "to efface her from the photograph . . . where we can retouch photos
and rewrite biographies and history":* Kundera, *Laughter and Forgetting,*
30–31.

168   *"the ghosts of monuments torn down":* Ibid., 256.

168   *"President of Forgetting":* Ibid.

168   *"applauding and shouting his name . . . 'Children, never look back!' ":* Ibid.,
256–57.

168   *"that we must never allow the future . . . magical innocence of their smiles":*
Ibid., 257.

168–169 *" 'You begin to liquidate. . . . The world at large forgets it still faster' ":*
Ibid., 218.

169   *"The struggle of man against power . . . memory against forgetting":* Ibid., 4.

169   *"organized forgetting":* Ibid., 218.

170   *Machiavelli's classic advice to princes accepts this as a given:* See Niccolò
Machiavelli, *The Prince,* trans. Angelo M. Codevilla (New Haven, CT: Yale
University Press, 1997), 18, 65.

170   *as George Orwell had thirty years before:* See George Orwell, *1984* (New
York: Signet Classics, 1961).

Notes

170   *key text is Arendt's 1967 essay:* Hannah Arendt, "Truth and Politics," *New Yorker*, February 25, 1967, https://www.newyorker.com/magazine/1967/02/25/truth-and-politics.

170   *between rational truth and political judgment:* Ibid.

171   *what the philosopher Thomas Nagel calls the "view from nowhere":* See Thomas Nagel, *The View from Nowhere* (Oxford, UK: Oxford University Press, 1989).

171   *what Arendt calls an "enlarged mentality":* See Hannah Arendt, *Lectures on Kant's Political Philosophy*, ed. Ronald Beiner (Chicago: University of Chicago Press, 1992), 43, 71–74.

172   *confusing the distinction between factual truths and rational ones or of attempting to erase it altogether:* Hannah Arendt, *Between Past and Future: Eight Exercises in Political Thought* (New York: Viking, 1968), 238–41.

173   *Scientists strive to transcend history, politicians to honor it:* See Paul W. Kahn, *Legitimacy and History: Self-Government in American Constitutional Theory* (New Haven, CT: Yale University Press, 1992).

174   *to cultivate an "enlarged mentality":* Arendt, *Lectures on Kant's Political Philosophy*, 43, 71–74.

174   *as the condition of "plurality" . . . without collapsing the "space" that sets them apart:* For examples of Arendt's discussions of these concepts and their relationship to each other, see Hannah Arendt, *The Origins of Totalitarianism* (San Diego: Harcourt/Harvest Books, 1985), 465–66; Hannah Arendt, *The Human Condition* (Chicago: University of Chicago Press, 1998), 76–77.

175   *must always look upon the Chinese with an "unconquerable repulsion":* John H. Boalt, "The Chinese Question" (speech before the Berkeley Club, August 1877), reprinted in *The Chinese Question: Report of the Special Committee on Assembly Bill No. 13* (Sacramento, CA: D. W. Gelwicks, State Printer, 1870), 257.

184   *retention plus contextualization is preferable in every case to destruction:* A number of municipalities and universities have taken this approach in dealing with their Confederate monuments. See, for example, Deborah Strange, "UF to Keep St. Augustine Confederate Monument: UF Plans to Keep a Monument Honoring a Confederate General on the Property It Manages," *Gainesville Sun*, July 12, 2018, https://www.gainesville.com/news/20180712/uf-to-keep-st-augustine-confederate-monument; Katie Garwood, "City to Create Contextualization Plan for Confederate Monuments," *Flagler College Gargoyle*, October 24, 2017, http://gargoyle.flagler.edu/2017/10/city-to-create-contextualization-plan-for-confederate

-monuments/; Stephanie Saul, "Ole Miss Edges out of Its Confederate Shadow, Gingerly," *New York Times*, August 9, 2017, https://www.nytimes.com/2017/08/09/us/ole-miss-confederacy.html.

184   *we are all, as the psalmist says, "broken vessel[s]":* Ps. 31:12 (King James Version).

188   *"statesmen will not always be at the helm":* James Madison, "Federalist No. 10" (November 22, 1787), reprinted in Alexander Hamilton, James Madison, John Jay, *The Federalist*, ed. J. R. Pole (Indianapolis: Hackett, 2005), 51.

189   *Yale characterized the effort as an act of national leadership:* Kathrin Lassila, "A Deeper Look at Renaming" (interview with Peter Salovey), *Yale Alumni Magazine*, September–October 2016, https://yalealumnimagazine.com/articles/4362-a-deeper-look-at-renaming.

189   *Some schools have indeed followed Yale's lead:* The CEPR Report has been consulted in deliberations over renaming buildings and removing monuments on campuses including Stanford University, the University of Mississippi, and the University of Michigan. See Hailey Fuchs, "Renaming Principles Reach Other Universities," *Yale Daily News*, October 13, 2017, https://yaledailynews.com/blog/2017/10/13/renaming-principles-reach-other-universities/.

190   *the president of Yale asked whether Calhoun College should be renamed:* Peter Salovey, "The Freshman Address" (speech, August 29, 2015), reprinted as "Launching a Difficult Conversation," *Yale Alumni Magazine*, November–December 2015, https://yalealumnimagazine.com/articles/4201-launching-a-difficult-conversation.

190–191   *"After a careful review of student and alumni responses . . . this is our obligation as an educational institution":* Email from Peter Salovey to the Yale Community, "Decisions on Residential College Names and 'Master' Title," *Yale University: Official Yale University Messages*, April 27, 2016, https://messages.yale.edu/messages/University/univmsgs/detail/137123.

191   *"ensure that [the Yale] community . . . understanding of our institution's past":* Ibid.

191   *greeted with howls of derision:* See, for example, Victor Wang and David Yaffe-Bellany, "Students Confront Salovey at Town Hall," *Yale Daily News*, April 29, 2016, https://yaledailynews.com/blog/2016/04/29/students-confront-salovey-at-town-hall/; Sarah Brown, "Students Vent Frustrations as Yale Leaves a Slave Champion's Name Intact," *Chronicle of Higher Education*, April 29, 2016, https://www.chronicle.com/article/Students-Vent-Frustrations-as/236300.

191   *he retreated from the decision:* Salovey, "Campus Update: Committee to Establish Principles on Renaming."

191   *The committee released its report on December 2, 2016:* Email from Peter
       Salovey to the Yale Community, "Report of the Committee to Establish
       Principles on Renaming," December 2, 2016, https://messages.yale.edu
       /messages/University/univmsgs/detail/145800.

192   *In "constituting the committee," the president said . . . "the most important
       guiding . . . expertise to the questions at hand":* Lassila, "A Deeper Look at
       Renaming."

192   *previous "conversation" . . . failed to take full advantage of the "expertise":* Ibid.

192   *the "legal training" of the chair of the committee was a help in "developing
       principles and arguing from principles":* Ibid.

194   *the Committee to Establish Principles on Renaming declared that it was not its
       responsibility to resolve the Calhoun question:* CEPR Letter, 1.

194   *a historical figure's "principal legacy":* CEPR Report, 19–22.

194   *he only appointed the two committees and then accepted the results of their
       work:* See Salovey, "Campus Update: Committee to Establish Principles
       on Renaming" (appointing the first committee); Salovey, "Report of the
       Committee to Establish Principles on Renaming" (appointing a second
       committee to apply the principles articulated by the first committee).

195   *"Principal legacies, as we understand them. . . . Scholarly consensus about
       principal legacies is a powerful measure":* CEPR Report, 20.

195   *"fundamentally at odds with the mission of the university":* Ibid., 19–22.

195   *the university's official "mission statement":* Ibid., 17.

195–196 *Yale is committed. . . . diverse community of faculty, staff, students, and
       alumni:* Ibid.

196   *This second committee delivered its report six weeks later:* Letter from the
       Advisory Group on the Renaming of Calhoun College to Peter Salovey
       (hereinafter "Advisory Group Letter"), January 13, 2017, https://president
       .yale.edu/sites/default/files/files/Presidential%20Advisory%20Group%20
       -%20Calhoun%2001_13_17.pdf; Advisory Group on the Renaming of
       Calhoun College, Report of the Advisory Group on the Renaming of
       Calhoun College (hereinafter "Advisory Group Report"), January 13,
       2017, https://president.yale.edu/sites/default/files/files/Presidential%20
       Advisory%20Group%20-%20Calhoun%2001_13_17.pdf.

196–197 *"no principles . . . suggests the need to rename":* Advisory Group Letter, 1.

197   *that Calhoun's "principal" legacy was one of "racism and bigotry":* Advisory
       Group Report, 4.

197   *"constitutional theorist." . . . "championed states' rights and slavery and
       was a symbol of the Old South":* Ibid., 3 (quoting *The New Encyclopædia
       Britannica,* 15th ed., 1:741–42).

197   *"Calhoun's most recent academic biographer balances all of these legacies judiciously . . . a new biography is long overdue":* Ibid., 3 n. 4 and accompanying text.

197   *The biography to which the report refers:* Irving H. Bartlett, *John C. Calhoun: A Biography* (New York: W. W. Norton, 1993).

198   *"leans toward a favorable interpretation . . . bespeaks 'a flawed heritage'":* John Niven, review of *John C. Calhoun: A Biography*, by Irving H. Bartlett, *Journal of American History* 82, no. 1 (June 1995): 220. As Niven notes [ibid.], some of Calhoun's other biographers have portrayed him more favorably than did Bartlett. See Charles M. Wiltse, *John C. Calhoun: Nationalist, 1782–1828* (Indianapolis: Bobbs-Merrill, 1944); Charles M. Wiltse, *John C. Calhoun: Nullifier, 1829–1839* (Indianapolis: Bobbs-Merrill, 1949); Charles M. Wiltse, *John C. Calhoun: Sectionalist, 1840–1850* (Indianapolis: Bobbs-Merrill, 1951); Margaret L. Coit, *John C. Calhoun: American Portrait* (Boston: Houghton Mifflin, 1950). The central thesis of Wiltse's three volumes is that throughout Calhoun's evolution from "nationalist" to "nullifier" to "sectionalist," he remained first and foremost "a lover of the Union, always working to preserve it." Roy F. Nichols, review of *John C. Calhoun: Sectionalist, 1840–1850* by Charles M. Wiltse, *American Historical Review* 57, no. 3 (April 1952): 694. Coit's treatment similarly contemplates Calhoun as a universalist, rather than parochial figure, insisting that his goals as a statesman and political philosopher were to protect the rights of "*all* the shifting minorities in the complex Union of the future" and not only those of the slaveholding South. Coit, *Calhoun: American Portrait*, 190.

199   *too easily on the grounds of his Southern upbringing:* See, for example, Melba Porter Hay, review of *John C. Calhoun: A Biography*, by Irving H. Bartlett, *Georgia Historical Quarterly* 78, no. 4 (1994): 850–51 ("Yet, Bartlett gives Calhoun full credit for consistency and dedication to principle—perhaps too much so."); William W. Freehling, review of *John C. Calhoun: A Biography* by Irving H. Bartlett, *Journal of the Early Republic* 13, no. 4 (1993): 574–76 ("In one unfortunate way, Bartlett escapes Wiltse's shadow. . . . By defending minority rights, Bartlett claims, Calhoun made himself . . . useful . . . in our multicultural struggles. But as Irving Bartlett . . . well know[s], Calhoun's theory of minority rights deployed the Constitution to preserve one minority's power over another. . . . Calhoun is not exactly a prophet for our times.").

199   *"Calhoun's status as determined . . . desired historical reputation as a champion of liberty":* Lacy K. Ford, review of *John C. Calhoun: A Biography* by Irving H. Bartlett, *Journal of Southern History* 61, no. 3 (1995): 597.

199 *"his increasingly anachronistic republicanism . . . rising political spirit of the age"*: Ibid.

199 *"[m]ore keenly than any other observer . . . the dangers of majoritarian tyranny"*: Ibid.

199 *"are typically the lasting effects that cause a namesake to be remembered"*: CEPR Report, 20.

199–200 *"scholarly consensus about principal legacies is a powerful measure"*: Ibid.

201 *"Calhoun himself . . . set his own balance"*: Advisory Group Report, 3.

201 *"He left no funeral instructions . . . what he wanted it to remember"*: Ibid.

202 *"agitation of the subject of slavery . . . not prevented by . . . effective measure . . . end in disunion"*: John C. Calhoun, "On the Admission of California—And the General State of the Union" (speech, March 4, 1850), reprinted in *Union and Liberty: The Political Philosophy of John C. Calhoun*, ed. Ross M. Lence (Indianapolis: Liberty Fund, 1992), 573.

203 *"as things now are . . . people of the Southern states . . . consistently with honor and safety in the union"*: Ibid., 575 (quoted in Advisory Group Report, 3).

203 *"one of the causes . . . discontent . . . undoubtedly to be traced . . . the rights of the South during [that] time"*: Ibid.

203 that *"there is another . . . regarded as the great and primary cause"*: Ibid.

203 *"equilibrium . . . section of the country . . . the exclusive power of controlling the government"*: Ibid.

204 *acquired its constitutional significance only with the Gettysburg Address and the Civil War Amendments*: See, for example, Garry Wills, "The Words That Remade America: The Significance of the Gettysburg Address," *Atlantic*, February 2012, https://www.theatlantic.com/magazine/archive/2012/02/the -words-that-remade-america/308801/ ("[Lincoln] not only presented the Declaration of Independence in a new light, as a matter of founding law, but put its central proposition, equality, in a newly favored position as a principle of the Constitution. . . . What had been mere theory in the writings of James Wilson, Joseph Story, and Daniel Webster—that the nation preceded the states, in time and importance—now became a lived reality of the American tradition."); Jonah Goldberg, "Like Lincoln, Martin Luther King Jr. Belongs to the Ages," *National Review*, April 6, 2018, https://www.nationalreview.com /2018/04/martin-luther-king-jr-like-abraham-lincoln/ ("It was not until Lincoln delivered the Gettysburg Address that the ideal embedded in the Declaration fully became both the plot and theme of the American story").

204 *"believed strongly in white supremacy"*: Advisory Group Report, 4.

204 *"few public figures of his era . . . characterization of slavery as a 'positive good'"*: Ibid., 4–5.

205   *"strong presumption . . . associated with its namesake . . . should be considered . . . only in exceptional circumstances":* CEPR Report, 18. Note that the committee announced only a presumption against *renaming of buildings* but omitted to articulate a parallel presumption against the *removal of symbols.* And yet, throughout its report, the committee repeatedly referred to "nomenclature and symbolism" together (ibid., 17), seeming to suggest that symbols may *also* be subject to removal if they offend the "principal legacy" test. Indeed, less than a year later, Yale cited the principles of the CEPR Report in announcing its decision to remove from the exterior walls of Sterling Memorial Library a stone carving of a Puritan and a Native American aiming at each other, respectively, with a gun and a bow and arrow. See "Yale to Move Stone Carving That Will Remain Available for Viewing and Study," *Yale News,* August 22, 2017, https://news.yale.edu/2017/08/22/yale-move-stone-carving-will-remain-available-viewing-and-study.

207   *"most eminent [graduate] in the field of Civil State":* George W. Pierson, *Yale: The University College, 1921–37* (New Haven, CT: Yale University Press, 1955), 408 (quoting a statement of university secretary Carl A. Lohmann).

207   *played some role in the Yale Corporation's decision, though this too is specu-lation:* The Committee to Establish Principles on Renaming gives credence to this speculation. See CEPR Report, 13 ("Ironically, the Calhoun name was attractive for some precisely because in the 1930s he seemed unlikely to engender controversy among the University's students, faculty, and alumni. To the extent the name would be able to help draw students from the South, it seemed to hold out the prospect of a certain kind of diversi-fication of the student body."). For a general discussion of Yale's historical relationship with the South, and Calhoun's place within that history, see Gary Lacy Reeder, "Elms and Magnolias: Yale and the American South," exhibition at Sterling Memorial Library (1996), *Yale University Library,* https://www.library.yale.edu/mssa/exhibits/elms/index.html.

207   *minuscule number of Southern students:* George W. Pierson, *A Yale Book of Numbers: Historical Statistics of the College and University, 1701–1976* (New Haven, CT: Yale University, 1983), 67.

207   *Timothy Dwight (who visited the Carolinas in the late 1790s):* Ibid., 66.

207   *it had reached 11 percent:* Ibid., 69.

207   *declined precipitously during the Civil War:* Ibid., 69–70.

207   *below 3 percent until the end of the nineteenth century:* Ibid., 70.

207   *very slowly began to climb again:* Ibid., 70–71.

207   *By 1929, it had reached 6 percent:* Ibid., 71.

207   *dipped in the period immediately after:* Ibid.

207   *grew steadily until 1970:* Ibid.

207   *when it was near 9 percent:* Ibid.

208   *Calhoun College became a subject of controversy and debate:* CEPR Report, 15.

210   *told the president of Yale that this was the only mastership he would accept:* Ibid. Henry Louis Gates Jr.—a protégé of Davis's, a 1973 alumnus of Calhoun College, and current Director of Harvard's Hutchins Center for African and African American Research—also notably supported retaining the name. See Christina Z. Peppard, "What's in a Name? Alumni and Students React to Decisions About the New Residential Colleges, Calhoun College, and the Title 'Master,'" *Yale Alumni Magazine*, May–June 2016, https://yalealumnimagazine.com/articles/4301-whats-in-a-name?page=1.

Index

Index

Index

Index

Index

About the Author

ANTHONY KRONMAN is Sterling Professor of Law at Yale, where he has been a member of the law school faculty for forty years. From 1994 to 2004, he served as dean of the law school. Since 2005, he has taught philosophy, literature, and history in the Directed Studies program in Yale College. His most recent book, *Confessions of a Born-Again Pagan*, was published by Yale University Press in 2016.